# THE VAMPIRE ECONOMY

# THE VAMPIRE ECONOMY
## Doing Business Under Fascism

GÜNTER REIMANN

MISES INSTITUTE 2014

ISBN: 978-1-61016-038-4

# WHAT A GERMAN AUTO MANUFACTURER HAS TO DO TO GET 5,000 TIRES FOR HIS CARS

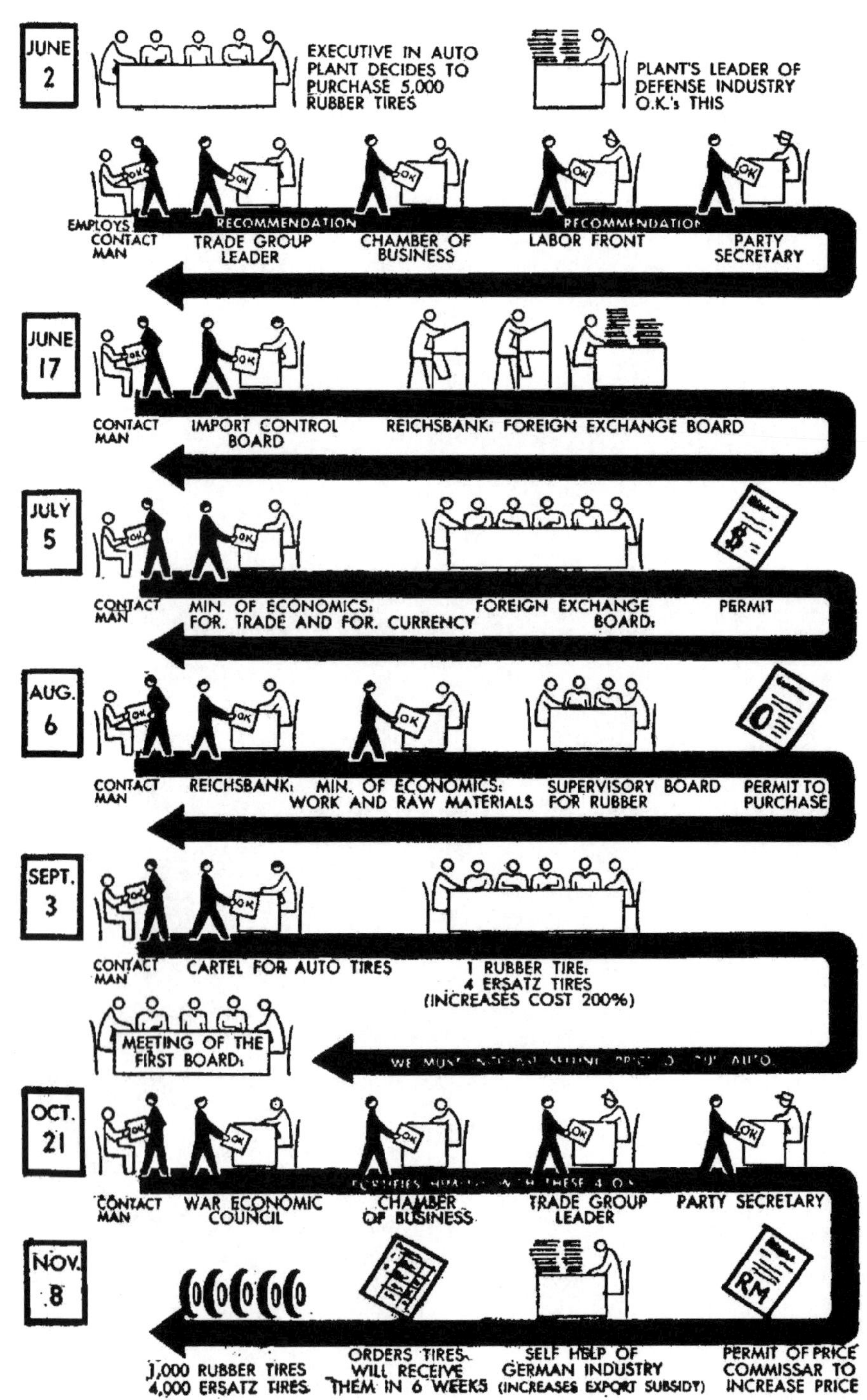

## *INTRODUCTORY NOTE*

THIS book could never have been written without the help of numerous friends and acquaintances in Europe who gave generously of their knowledge and experience and helped me to clarify manifold new trends and phenomena. During my stay in Europe I met many people of all social classes who lived or traveled in fascist countries—bankers, industrialists, importers and exporters, fascist or Nazi journalists, and radical opponents of the totalitarian states. Many of these people frankly discussed all the questions I raised. They helped me solely with the object of making the truth known; they had no private axes to grind. These collaborators must remain anonymous; the confidence and trust they reposed in me have placed upon me the grave responsibility of concealing their identity so that no evil will come to them or to their friends in Germany or Italy.

A number of American friends were very helpful in revising and improving this work. I am especially obligated to Miss Dorothy Davis, to Dr. Henri David, to Mrs. Edna Mann, to Dr. Ruben Gotesky, to Mr. Liston M. Oak, and to Dr. Sterling Spero. Needless to say, I am solely responsible for any statements made in this book.

I also wish to thank the editors of "Harper's Magazine" and of "The New Republic" for permitting me to use material from articles of mine published by them.

GUENTER REIMANN

# *PREFACE*

THIS book may be helpful as an answer to these burning questions: Why did Hitler start another war? How did it become possible that the "Fuehrer" could lead millions of intelligent and cultured people, who hate senseless slaughter, into a war which must have devastating effects upon Germany as well as upon the whole of mankind?

We cannot be satisfied with the answer that Hitler is a madman and that the German people are fools and slaves willing to go to war to satisfy a madman's dreams. Most people in Germany are like people in other countries, hard working and decent, with human qualities as good and as bad as those of other people throughout the world. But a system has been built up which has enabled one man to decide about war or peace; a system which held and still holds a whole nation in its iron grip and does not allow any individual German to escape the inherent fatalities of this regime.

The fatalism which was typical of the spirit of the German businessman before Europe was plunged into this war was not due to economic difficulties alone, but far more to a feeling that he had become part of a machine inexorably leading him to disaster. German businessmen once believed that the Fuehrer would lead them into a world of happiness and prosperity. They were willing to accept the first measures of regimentation as necessary but temporary emergency acts. They thought of the raids against the Jews and the sadistic brutalities of the Brownshirts as the excesses of "uncontrollable elements" which would soon disappear. These hopes had vanished before the start of the war. Those who hated bureaucracy and regimentation had been compelled to participate in the construction of a system which could end only in war and destruction. They had been made part of a monster-machine steered by a Fuehrer who was responsible to nobody.

This totalitarian Frankenstein could not exist peacefully. It could not transform armaments production into production of consumption goods, thus ending the war scare and creating another era of prosperity. Nor could it wait for the peaceful exploitation of new conquests which, as a matter of fact, were not sufficient to correct the shortage of basic raw materials. Any attempt to create a new era of peace would have precipitated a major crisis, economically and politically, for the totalitarian regime, and this would have meant the end of all far-reaching imperialist plans. Sacrifices and investments made in preparation for imperialist expansion and for world rule would have been in vain. The gradual decay of the totalitarian regime would have been inevitable had the Fuehrer chosen peace instead of war.

History is revengeful. Dictators are also dictated to by the necessities of their own regime. "The logic of the machine crushes the constructor and turns him into its slave," says Emil Ludwig.

We do not know what Adolf Hitler thought about Germany's capacity for waging totalitarian warfare when he decided to march into Poland and thus begin a new world war. It may be that he was convinced he would get another Munich without a large-scale war, or that he could conclude a "peace with honor," i. e., with Poland as a Nazi protectorate, a few weeks after the outbreak of a war with the Western Powers. Yet he must have realized that this war might become a major conflict, lasting many months, perhaps even years. How long can the Nazi economy stand the strain of such a war?

During the last pre-war years tremendous economic preparations were made for this conflict. German Army experts had worked out two schemes, one in preparation for a short "Blitzkrieg" or "lightning war," the second for a longer totalitarian war of attrition. The first plan was completed during the first Four-Year Plan. Then preparations for the longer totalitarian war were pushed through.

In accordance with these plans of the German General Staff, the Third Reich was getting ready for a two-year totalitarian war. But what such a war meant in practice depended on who was to be the enemy and who the ally. It is impossible to have on hand sufficient stocks of all essential materials needed for a totalitarian war of even a single year's duration. According to all estimates, Nazi Germany's fuel reserves during the Munich crisis would have been sufficient for a totalitarian war of not more than four months. But these same reserves might be quite sufficient if Rumanian and Russian oil is available in large quantities. Furthermore, the consumption of materials in a totalitarian war depends also on whether an aggressive or a defensive war is being contemplated. If, for instance, the war becomes purely defensive on all fronts and no large-scale offensives are carried out, consumption of war materials will be considerably less than in an offensive war, and the economic reserves of German militarism will last longer. But a defensive war cannot last forever and Germany's economic reserves will be exhausted earlier than those of the Western Powers if the latter are able to import materials from overseas.

The whole aspect of Germany's wartime economy seems to have changed as a result of the Stalin-Hitler pact. This pact assures the Third Reich that the Soviet Union will not stop exports to Germany even in wartime. Russian oil, manganese, foodstuffs and necessary materials will be available during the war, according to the terms of the Treaty signed on the eve of the war's outbreak. This pact is helpful to Hitler in overcoming economic deficiencies and in enabling him to avoid an early collapse of the military machine. Yet the economic significance of this pact may be overestimated. Stalin and Hitler did not decide to pool their economic and military forces. They are unlikely to do that because they do not sufficiently trust each other. Stalin will, however, sell Russia's products to the German militarists if he gets cash or other goods he needs in exchange. The size of this wartime trade will depend on the capacity of the Third Reich to pay for imports. Reserves of foreign currency or gold are negligible. Exports of German manufactured goods are restricted by the urgent demands of the army for arms and ammunition. The financial plight of the Third Reich makes it impossible to finance imports in unlimited quantities. Therefore, the pact with Stalin may enable Hitler to put up a more stubborn and longer fight, but will not necessarily solve his raw material difficulties.

Germany's military strategists would have preferred a "lightning war." For only a quick victory would be a real victory. A long-drawn out war, threatening economic collapse, would inevitably spell defeat whatever the military result. Hitler could not have expected a quick victory against the Western Powers when he decided to march into Poland, with Great Britain and France fully mobilized. The armaments race had put a much heavier strain upon the economy of the Third Reich than upon other countries. In no other industrial country were raw materials so scarce and the replacement of vital parts of the industrial machine so neglected as in Germany. The extent of the economic decay which preceded this war will be indicated in this book. True, the German War Economic Council has kept in store vast quantities of raw materials and other products essential for a wartime economy. But even if all storage possibilities were fully used, such preparations would have been sufficient at best only for a "lightning war" lasting no longer than a couple of months.

The deficiencies of a wartime economy are important and eventually decisive in a totalitarian war. Yet it is impossible to foretell when a military system will collapse as a result of a deficiency in foodstuffs, raw materials or other economic factors. As long as the state machine is in order, it has the power to cut down the consumption of the general public and to reduce—almost to eliminate—expenditures for the renewal of the industrial machine. The proportion of the national income or of industrial production spent for armaments is elastic. It is possible to increase production of arms and ammunition even with reduced supplies of raw materials. This can be done by drastically limiting production of consumption goods, by putting the population on starvation rations, and by letting vast sectors of the economy decay. How far this can be done is not merely an economic question, but also a question of morale and of the effectiveness of the totalitarian police forces.

Therefore, especially in a totalitarian war, the factor of morale is as important as the supply of war materials.

This becomes clear as we examine the manifold experiences of businessmen under fascism as well as the peculiar developments of business practices in a totalitarian state.

We might and must assume that Hitler is well aware of the dangers to which he has exposed himself and his system by beginning this war. His economic and political experts will have carefully considered any conceivable crisis. They will have organized the State power in such a way that they may hope to keep it intact even during the most perilous times. They are prepared to crush all internal opposition even in the case of the severest wartime difficulties. They will suppress all but a few "friendly" private interests, compelling all other individuals to sacrifice everything for their monstrous system. The "conservative" forces—all those who still own private property and who are not closely related to the supreme Leadership—will be expropriated and their property rights will be wiped out. The businessman who is an isolated individual in the gigantic and reckless totalitarian state is the helpless prey of his fascist masters.

The totalitarian dictatorship will become more ruthless in its attitude toward businessmen as well as toward the workers and middle classes. The so-called radicals among the Party bureaucrats will claim that their program has been fulfilled after the expropriation of most private property holders, while simultaneously the ruin of the middle classes will be completed and the workers will be exploited on an unprecedented scale.

This development is not unwelcome to Nazi Party

leaders. These leaders were extremely unpopular before the war broke out. Germans were beginning to place upon them the responsibility for the growth of a corrupt bureaucracy. The Party Leaders would have had to endure a "purge" had peace been preserved. They had reason to fear that during a peacetime depression the Fuehrer might, while renouncing his world imperialist dreams, throw them overboard to increase his own prestige. Instead of such a development, it is the turn of the Party Leaders and Nazi Storm Troopers to dictate. The author is reminded of a discussion, at the beginning of Mussolini's Abyssinian campaign, with an Italian friend who held an important post in the fascist State despite his secret anti-fascist sympathies. The author asked: "Why is Mussolini so mad as to start this Abyssinian adventure when he must realize that his gains will never equal what he must spend for the conquest? From the military point of view the war in Abyssinia will weaken rather than strengthen him." "The so-called radicals in the fascist Party bureaucracy," the Italian friend replied, "are jubilant about this war. They expect the economic difficulties in wartime to strengthen their authoritarian control of the so-called conservative forces. These will be weakened by further measures of expropriation. Those who still have privileges and property rights will live in fear that they may lose everything and that they will perish too if the dictatorship should break down."

Similarly, Nazi leaders in Germany do not fear possible national economic ruin in wartime. They feel that, whatever happens, they will remain on top, that the worse matters become, the more dependent on them will be the propertied classes. And if the worst comes to the worst, they are prepared to sacrifice all other interests to maintain their hold on the State. If they themselves must go, they are ready to pull the temple down with them. G. R.

*New York,*
*September 8, 1939.*

## *CONTENTS*

# THE VAMPIRE ECONOMY

*Chapter I*

# WHAT HAPPENED TO THE BUSINESSMAN

"The role of the individual businessman has been completely altered in the totalitarian States, and his position cannot be judged by American standards."

BUSINESSMEN all over the world are dissatisfied and apprehensive. The depression has proved to be not only the most drastic and widespread in modern times, but also the most lasting. It can no longer be dismissed as a mere trough between waves of good times, as just an unpleasant but passing phase of a business cycle. Economists and businessmen alike disagree as to what it portends and what measures should be taken to meet it—or whether, indeed, any governmental measures are helpful in the situation which faces us. While one school of thought demands increased activity from the State, another calls for a complete cessation of State economic activities and insists that private economy be permitted to work out a solution.

With the world still at the crossroads, one may well conclude that there is something to be learned from the experiences of businessmen in the two countries which, without abolishing private property, have gone farthest in State interference to insure national prosperity. In both Germany and Italy the problem of unemployment seemingly has been solved. The industries of both countries are running at full speed, demand apparently outstrips supply, labor unions have been abolished, and manufacturers have become authoritarian "leaders" of their employees. It is inevitable that American businessmen, harassed by what they regard as unreasonable government interference, finding a large part of their profits siphoned off by taxes, direct and indirect, confronted with what is apparently a shrinking market, worried by increasing competition, should examine critically, objectively, and even sympathetically, the situation in the totalitarian States.

What has been the result for the individual businessman in the two countries governed by administrations put in power by business interests and devoted to restoring economic prosperity?

What has the businessman gained in Germany? A great deal, if we may credit the headlines in the *Voelkischer Beobachter,* official newspaper of the Nazi party. There we read:

NO UNEMPLOYMENT—TREMENDOUS SUCCESS OF THE FOUR-YEAR PLAN—WORKERS WILLING TO WORK HARDER—CELEBRATING THE NEW WORK COMMUNITY—RISING SALES AND DIVIDENDS.

Beneath these headlines the reader will find many facts and figures designed to prove their truth, figures relating to the scarcity of workers, the increase in production, the rise in building activity, the rise in profits. These figures, upon analysis, prove to be largely correct so far as they go, but it is apparent that they tell merely part of the story. They do not reveal how Germany's new prosperity is distributed—whether it is shared by all industries or by only a few, and whether it is confined to a comparatively few large units. The figures do not show what happens to the profits, how large a proportion of them are absorbed by taxes, nor what the businessman is permitted to do with the portion that is left to him. They give little hint of the extent to which the government intervenes in every business transaction. They do not reveal whether the individual businessman is permitted to raise his prices if his costs advance nor whether he is allowed to shut down a department or even an entire factory, the operation of which is proving unprofitable.

We cannot be satisfied merely with official statistics and reports, nor with fragmentary comments. We must penetrate the mystery arising out of contradictory facts—an industrial boom coupled with increasing bureaucratic intervention, a mounting accumulation of State debts in order that the State may maintain its position as the consumer of the largest part of the nation's production.

The answer to this problem cannot be a simple one; it will be found in the pages of this book. It must be understood, however, that the role of the individual businessman has been completely altered in the totalitarian states, and his position cannot be judged by American standards. The reader must try to put himself in the place of the German or Italian businessman in order to understand the latter's problems and his new position. As a general introduction to the subject and as a means of approaching it from a sympathetic point of view, we cannot do better than read a letter written by a responsible German businessman during a visit to a neighboring country where he was free from censorship. The communication might be almost as appropriate if it came from an Italian industrialist, for there is little difference, so far as the individual is concerned, between conditions in the two totalitarian countries.

This man's letter expresses worries and fears unknown to the businessman in America. He writes:

Dear Mr. X. Y.:

This letter will probably be a disappointment to you, but I must confess that I think as most German businessmen do who today fear National Socialism as much as they did Communism in 1932. But there is a distinction. In 1932, the fear of Communism was a phantom; today National Socialism is a terrible reality. Business friends of mine are convinced that it will be the turn of the "white Jews" (which means us, Aryan businessmen) after the Jews have been expropriated. Just when this will happen and the extent to which "Aryan" businessmen will be pillaged depends on the internal struggle within the Nazi party . . .

When we consider that Hitler himself came not from the ranks of organized labor, but from the ruined middle class or the fifth estate, what guarantee have we that he will not make common cause with the bandits whom he has put into uniforms? The difference between this and the Russian system is much less than you think, despite the fact that officially we are still independent businessmen.

You have no idea how far State control goes and how much power the Nazi representatives have over our work. The worst of it is that they are so ignorant. In this respect they certainly differ from the former Social-Democratic officials. These Nazi radicals think of nothing except "distributing the wealth."

Some businessmen have even started studying Marxist theories, so that they will have a better understanding of the present economic system.

How can we possibly manage a firm according to business principles if it is impossible to make any predictions as to the prices at which goods are to be bought and sold? We are completely dependent on arbitrary Government decisions concerning quantity, quality and prices for foreign raw materials. There are so many different economic agreements with foreign countries, not to mention methods of payment, that no one can possibly understand them all. Nevertheless Government representatives are permanently at work in our offices, examining costs of production, profits, tax bills, etc. . . .

There is no elasticity of prices, sorely needed though it be by businessmen. While State representatives are busily engaged in investigating and interfering, our agents and salesmen are handicapped, because they never know whether or not a sale at a higher price will mean denunciation as a "profiteer" or "saboteur," followed by a prison sentence.

You cannot imagine how taxation has increased. Yet everyone is afraid to complain about it. The new State loans are nothing but confiscation of private property, because no one believes that the Government will ever make repayment, nor even pay interest after the first few years. Compared with these new State loans, the bonds issued during the World War were gilt-edged investments.

We businessmen still make sufficient profit, sometimes even large profits, but we never know how much we are going to be able to keep . . .

Workers also make a fair living, particularly where the hourly rate has not been changed. A workingman who worked six hours a day before must now work eleven and twelve hours daily. Often his wife and children are also employed so that the family income has considerably increased. . . .

You will find it hard to understand that, although from the financial point of view we ought not to complain, no one enjoys life any more. Everywhere there is a growing undercurrent of bitterness. This feeling is worse now than it has ever been. Everyone has his doubts about the system, unless he is very young, very stupid or is bound to it by the privileges he enjoys. Therefore the real enthusiasm we experienced after the occupation of the Saar is no more and it cannot be revived. Even great historical events, such as the Anschluss of Austria and the Sudetenland, did nothing to lift this bitter spirit. Everywhere I hear businessmen declare that Anschluss with bankrupt concerns makes a bankrupt enterprise still more bankrupt.

All of us—even convinced Nazis—are hungry for news from abroad. Somehow British broadcasts seem better than the French, but perhaps that is only our imagination, because we know England's attitude is decisive to us. An alliance with Italy is quite unimportant as compared to our relations with England. Most Germans feel that another war would be lost before it started if England as well as America were against us.

If a war should start, we should probably have a revolution in Germany very soon. The French Revolution will seem like nothing in comparison. A tremendous reservoir of hatred exists and it has no outlet at present. As in 1918, the workers will not start the revolution. It will begin with the army; young officers are as unpopular as they were in the old Prussian army. Personally I predict that there will be mass desertions. A good many people feel that the soldiers will start the revolution by massacring all the Nazis. In any case, our government is certainly not going to feel safe, and it is sure to introduce a reign of terror of Draconic proportions. Hatred and bitterness will increase just that much more.

There are terrible times coming. You can imagine how I feel when I think that I am going to have to go through this terrible debacle. If only I had succeeded in smuggling out $10,000 or even $5,000, I would leave Germany with my family . . .

The totalitarian state has fundamentally changed conditions of business life. In this book an attempt has been made to describe the experiences and to explain the anxieties of a businessman in a totalitarian State. We shall accompany him to various Party and State institutions. We shall try not merely to show how a private enterprise must be conducted in a State-regimented economy, but also how the fascist businessman is affected as a human being. We shall deal with the complexity of trends resulting from the existence of private economy side by side with State economy. In conclusion, we shall endeavor to arrive at an understanding of the new social position of the private capitalist in a totalitarian State and to give an evaluation of the historical role of the authoritarian bureaucracy.

The old type of capitalist who adheres to the traditional concepts of property rights is doomed to failure under fascism. The *Voelkischer Beobachter* predicts that "a new type of individual will arise in the economic field who will enjoy living dangerously and who by his individual efficiency will create freedom of economic action for himself." We shall have to find out what this "new type" of capitalist is like.

*Chapter II*

# *DESTRUCTION OF THE SANCTITY OF PRIVATE PROPERTY*

"The government of a totalitarian State would not be 'authoritarian' if the courts still functioned independently."

HERR V. is one of the largest landowners in Eastern Prussia. He is a conservative old landowner who was once proud of being the free and independent master of a huge domain and who boasted of his patriarchal relations with his employees. As an ardent German nationalist he felt certain, when Hitler came to power, that the country had been "saved from the Bolshevists and the Jews." He never dreamed that the new regime would dare interfere with his God-given rights far more than had the Social-Democratic government he had hated. Unable to grasp quickly enough the changes that were occurring, he did not conform to the ever-mounting requirements of the ruling Party. Soon he was on bad terms with the provincial Party secretary, whom he despised as an upstart. The Party leader tried to break his stubborn spirit by all manner of petty decrees and regulations, as, for instance, by ordering him to give lodging to S.A. men (Brownshirts) and members of the Hitler Youth League, who annoyed him endlessly.

There was no longer a Hindenburg, who as President of the Reich and Supreme Commander of the Army, would listen to the complaints of his agrarian friends and intervene with the government on their behalf. Herr V. learned only through bitter experience that there was no longer any court or official to protect him, and he began to fear that his estates might be expropriated. He visited his former banker, Herr Z., to whom he confessed:

> I want to invest my liquid funds in a way which is safe, where they can't be touched by the State or the Party. In the old days I always refused to speculate, to buy stocks. Now I would not mind. However, I would like best to buy a farm in South-West Africa. Perhaps my next crop will be a failure and I will be blamed, accused of "sabotage," and replaced in the management of my estates by a Party administrator. I want to be prepared for such a contingency and have a place to go should the Party decide to take away my property.

The banker was compelled to inform his landowner friend that there was no such way out. The State would not allow him to leave Germany with more than ten marks. South-West Africa was closed to him; he would have to stay where he was.

Formerly numbered among the most independent and largest landed proprietors in Germany, with estates that had been in his family for generations, Herr V. today shares the despair of numerous German capitalists, none of whom can be sure that their property rights will be regarded as sacred by the State.

Manufacturers in Germany were panic-stricken when they heard of the experiences of some industrialists who were more or less expropriated by the State. These industrialists were visited by State auditors who had strict orders to "examine" the balance sheets and all bookkeeping entries of the company (or individual businessman) for the preceding two, three, or more years until some error or false entry was found. The slightest formal mistake was punished with tremendous penalties. A fine of millions of marks was imposed for a single bookkeeping error. Obviously, the examination of the books was simply a pretext for partial expropriation of the private capitalist with a view to complete expropriation and seizure of the desired property later. The owner of the property was helpless, since under fascism there is no longer an independent judiciary that protects the property rights of private citizens against the State. The authoritarian State has made it a principle that private property is no longer sacred.

> The decree of February 28, 1933, nullified article 153 of the Weimar Constitution which guaranteed private property and restricted interference with private property in accordance with certain legally defined conditions . . . The conception of property has experienced a fundamental change. The individualistic conception of the State—a result of the liberal spirit—must give way to the concept that communal welfare precedes individual welfare. *(Gemeinnutz geht vor Eigennutz).*[1]

The government of a totalitarian State would not be "authoritarian" if the courts still functioned independently, as they do under liberal capitalism.

The division of power between the executive or legislative branch on the one hand and the judicial branch on the other was formerly a guarantee to the owner of private property that his property rights would be protected even against his own government. The totalitarian State, in abolishing this separation of power, abolishes the sanctity of private property, which thereupon ceases to be a basic principle of society fundamental to State morality.

Constitutionally the businessman still enjoys guarantees of property rights. But what is the value of such constitutional guarantees without courts that dare to defy the omnipotent bureaucracy or to enforce laws that are "out of date"? The judge who had the temerity to attempt this would land not in a concentration camp but in a lunatic asylum. A totalitarian State does not tolerate any "second government," any challenge to the power of the all-wise dictator.

"Within the constitution of the Third Reich any position independent of the will of the Fuehrer no longer exisits. The principle of separation of power is a thing of the past. Only the Party has a privileged position." [2]

Fritz Nonnenbruch, the financial editor of the *Voelkischer Beobachter,* states: "There exists no law which binds the State. The State can do what it regards as necessary, because it has the authority." [3]

"The next stage of National-Socialist economic policy consists of replacing capitalist laws by policy." [4]

This Nazi doctrine has nothing to do with Communism or Socialism. It is offered as a new justification for the State's use of private capital and it is a means of placing drastic limitations upon private property rights in the "national interest."

"National interests" are not determined by laws, courts, or any legislative body. The decision is made mainly by the Nazi party, or, rather, by its leaders, that is, by the State bureaucracy. It is a principle that only Party members shall occupy key positions in the government and in all organizations where the State influences the distribution of jobs. They must be engaged whenever there is a choice between a Party member and non-Party member. The carrying out of this essential part of the unwritten constitution is assured by the fact that Party members, devoted to the leader and to the maintenance of the Party's authority, occupy all key positions and appoint all new officials.

In the early days of the Nazi regime, some of the conservatives holding economic key posts, such as Dr. Hjalmar Schacht, former president of the Reichsbank and former Minister of Economics, and Dr. Kurt Schmitt, director of the largest German insurance company and Dr. Schacht's predecessor as Minister of Economics, sought to restrain the growth of bureaucracy. These men upheld the traditional position of conservative capitalists—economy in administration and efficiency in civil service—and they sought to win the leading Nazis to this point of view. In a speech to young bank clerks and students Schacht openly attacked Party careerists who sought a place in the new ruling caste and hoped to become a part of the privileged aristocracy, with nothing to recommend them except their record as loyal Party men. He declared:

> The aim of National Socialism is an economic and social order where everybody, whoever he is and whatever he did before, can obtain the highest posts in the economy and in the State if he has the strength, the will and the ability to do his job. This principle has been fully applied by the Reichsbank. At the Reichsbank, in contrast to conditions in the State offices, any employee can rise from a low to a high position. He is not evaluated according to recommendations or good friends, nor according to other similar things which

have nothing to do with his abilities, but he is judged merely by his fitness, his personal value, his knowledge and his performance.[5]

At the same time, however, the Party leaders asserted their right to continue in control of patronage, of the distribution of State jobs and special privileges to trusted old Party members personally devoted to the Fuehrer. Ministerialdirektor Sommer, as spokesman for Rudolph Hess, Hitler's official representative, wrote in the *Deutsche Juristenzeitung* of May 21, 1936:

> The influence of the Party cannot be seen in laws, but in practice, and personalities are the important factor. A large number of the ministers [at present all ministers] are Party members. Some of them are also Reich leaders of the Party, all *Reichstatthaelter* are Party members, and most are also provincial leaders of the Party. All Prussian *Oberpraesidenten* are district leaders in their area. Other personal connections exist through the office of *landrat* [governmental chief of a district administrative office] and the corresponding Party leader of the district, and finally, in general all jobs of political importance are held by old reliable Party members.* [6]

This does not mean that there are only Party members in the government. Even important branches have many non-Party members. But they are technical experts without freedom of decision rather than independent admin-

* The general meaning of this paragraph will be clear to the reader despite the obscurity of the manner in which the thought is phrased. The original German is written in the Nazi idioms that have become characteristic of German official documents; in their eagerness to demonstrate that there has been a complete break with the past, the present rulers of Germany have almost invented a new tongue.

Similar difficulty has been encountered in rendering into English other Nazi documents.

istrators. They must be particularly careful not to hurt the prestige of the Fuehrer in the application of any law or instruction. Because they are not subject to the rigid discipline of the Party, they are always suspected of being "unreliable." Consequently they are inclined to be stricter than Party members in adhering to the letter of the law or in refusing personal favors to a businessman. They have no "Party friends" in other key positions of the administration who can do anything for them or for their friends.

To a great extent a person's status depends upon the personal opinions and impressions of the Party secretary. It is exceedingly difficult to appeal from his authority; he can oust any person from his job and deprive him of his rights by simply declaring him "unreliable." Hence it is very important to remain on friendly terms with the Party secretary, for his one word "reliable" has greater value than the highest honors any king may bestow on his favorites.

In the administrative apparatus and the State police force all key positions are occupied by individuals whose devotion has met the acid test.

The Party is the whip with which the leaders control the administration as well as the behavior of the citizen, be he the manager of the steel trust, a small shopkeeper or a worker. The Party has its own courts and judiciary because Party members are not bound by official laws in their activities; they are permitted and indeed required to violate the laws in order to defend the prestige and authority of the Party leaders.

The official Union of German Civil Servants has a membership of 1,200,000, of whom one-sixth—206,000—are Party members,[7] but 81 per cent of the higher State officials in Prussia are members of the Nazi party—Nationalsozialistische Deutsche Arbeiter Partei, to give it its full name. In the national government, all leaders are in the Party and subject to its rigid discipline. Few exceptions are made to the rule that all important positions in the administrative apparatus must be held by Nazis. The majority of those holding State jobs are also leaders of the Nationalsozialistische Deutsche Arbeiter Partei (N.S.D.A.P.) in their districts or communities.

"No one is to be appointed unless in addition to the qualifications which fit him for his post he gives a guarantee that he will always defend the National Socialist State without reservation." [8] The equivalent of this German rule is common to all totalitarian countries.

In a totalitarian land where the "will of the Party" is in effect the unwritten constitution, the membership rolls are well guarded. Not everyone who declares himself a loyal supporter of Hitler can join. It is no ordinary party. Nor is it a party wherein members can help to formulate policy and criticize the leader, or choose the leader. The authoritarian Nazi party makes the will of the leader the supreme law.

"The Elite Guards [S.S. men] and the Brownshirts [S.A. men] do no productive work. They do not work for the State. They work solely and exclusively for the leader." [9]

The existence of the Party machine and its control of the government render hopeless any attempt of an industrialist or banker—though he may be the most important financial figure in the country—to get control of the executive power and to supersede the authority of the Party leaders.

The Party secretaries and those in leading positions

jealously guard their authority, so that no businessman, large or small, can gain in influence at their expense. The Party machine, as the vehicle of absolute power, was and is too valuable an asset to let slip into other hands. At all costs, the vested power of the leadership must be preserved.

The existence of a state within the State—the Party and the bureaucracy—is a phenomenon of the post-War world.

The Party and the government bureaucracy are above the law, but it must be pointed out that this special status of being above the law is reserved chiefly for the leadership. To create stability on which the leadership relies, there are strict laws regulating relationships among private businessmen. It is even conceivable that a businessman or concern might be successful in an appeal to the courts against some regulation of an over-zealous Nazi official, provided such a regulation were a gratuitous interference with private property and had no bearing on the defense of the Nazi regime. However, court action has been very rare because most business-men fear arousing the anger of Nazi officials who on some later occasion might have opportunity to take revenge.

As a rule, the relations between businessmen are still regulated by laws and customs. But customs have changed and modified law, and law has, in turn, been largely replaced by a vague conception of "honor." It is easier for a businessman to win a case in the German courts by appealing to "National-Socialist honor" than by referring to the exact text of the law.

This would lead to complete anarchy in business affairs unless a businessman knew when the "honor" of a National Socialist required payment of a debt or the execution of a commercial transaction. Consequently chambers of commerce and group or "estate" organizations in the various trades have instituted "Courts of Honor." A businessman who objects to another firm's conception of "honor" can apply to these "Courts" which settle commercial disputes. Officially they are only maintaining "national" or "group discipline." In reality, however, "Courts of Honor" are a kind of self-help organization for businessmen. The Party-controlled official courts are replaced by courts made up of businessmen. No businessman is officially compelled to submit his case to the "Court of Honor" or to accept its judgment, but the official trade organization urges its members to stick to certain rules which the group organization has established, except in cases where members have close relations with influential Party functionaries who show little respect for the businessmen's courts. On the whole, there is a definite trend toward substituting for the centralized State jurisdiction courts composed of businessmen representing different trades.

Businessmen feel the need of maintaining certain business rules and respect for property rights. Their self-help organizations are similar to the guild organizations of medieval times, which had their own courts for disciplining members. But at that time the State power was weak, while today the authoritarian State is strong in its maintenance of a gigantic bureaucratic and military machine. The "Courts of Honor," therefore, will always have to consider Party interests so as not to arouse the anger of important figures in the Party.

Employers have been badly shocked by their new legal

status, especially the "conservatives" who have held their property for generations and to whom the sanctity of private property has been a part of their religion. They might have excused previous violations of property rights as exceptional emergency measures, but they hoped that the buttressing of the State power through fascism would also bring about a strengthening of the sanctity of private property. They were independent and individualistic businessmen, not only economically, but politically and psychologically. For this very reason they are the most disappointed and unhappy over the new state of affairs and are likely to get into trouble with a Party secretary or the Gestapo (the Secret State Police) for having grumbled incautiously or for not having shown enough devotion to the Fuehrer.

The capitalist under fascism has to be not merely a law-abiding citizen, he must be servile to the representatives of the State. He must not insist on "rights" and must not behave as if his private property rights were still sacred. He should be grateful to the Fuehrer that he still has private property.

This state of affairs must lead to the final collapse of business morale, and sound the death knell of the self-respect and self-reliance which marked the independent businessman under liberal capitalism.

*Chapter III*

# CORRUPTION: MONEY POWER AGAINST ABSOLUTE POWER

"Under such conditions, corruption is not merely a vice but an economic necessity."

A GERMAN manufacturer, executive manager ("Factory leader") of an enterprise which employs 4,000 workers and a relatively large staff of office workers obtained a privileged position largely because he got along well with a prominent Party leader. This does not mean that the industrialist in question is necessarily an ardent Nazi. As a matter of fact, he is a man who makes friends easily both among Nazis and anti-Nazis. He sent a confidential report to a foreign friend about his experiences in Germany today.

Amsterdam, May 15, 1939.

My dear Mr. ——

I am here—in Amsterdam—for a couple of days and take this opportunity to write unrestrictedly to various friends abroad. I know you will be interested in hearing what is happening within Germany.

As for myself, my knowledge as a technical expert would not have been sufficient to enable me to struggle along during the past five years, were it not for the fact that our firm has the backing of a prominent Party man who comes to our assistance when we need certificates for foreign currency, raw materials, and so on. No firm in our trade can exist without such a "collaborator." As it is, we have to spend considerable money for "juridical advice."

It is not a question of simple bribery. The process is more complicated. I knew pre-War Russia. In general, bribery under Czarism was a simple affair. You could figure out how much you had to pay a State official by counting the number of stars on his uniform. The higher the rank, the more stars he wore, and the more you had to pay. It's different in Germany today. Party members who control the distribution of raw materials and similar matters do not accept money directly. You do not offer money to a Party leader. You ask him whether he knows a good "lawyer" who might be of help in proving to the authorities the urgency of your demand for foreign exchange or raw material. He refers you to a "lawyer," who gives you the necessary "juridical" advice—for which you pay—and eventually your request is granted. But the fees for this advice are extremely high, much higher than you would have had to pay in direct bribery or than you would have paid formerly to a first-rate lawyer on a retainer basis.

There are many cases, of course, where your "juridical adviser," despite the high fees, cannot assist you. For instance, until a short time ago it was possible by skillful—and expensive—"interpretation" of the law to circumvent the law prohibiting branch offices from opening new distributing agencies. A few months ago, however, it became absolutely impossible to circumvent that law, and even the best contact man or "lawyer" could no longer assist you in a case of this kind.

Nevertheless, it is virtually impossible to function at all without maintaining close relations with one of these "lawyers." He can tell you whether or not you have a chance to obtain what you are seeking. You come to depend upon him completely. A good "juridical adviser" knows exactly how far you can circumvent the law in any given case, or whether or not a recent change in Party leadership makes it possible to re-interpret a given decree.

I cite one of my own experiences: I needed foreign currency for my current trip to Amsterdam, and duly made a request for what I needed to the Administration for Foreign Currency. In reply, I received the following answer: "Absolutely impossible." I thereupon went to my adviser and inquired of him how I might prove the "special urgency" of my business trip. He told me something I had not known before. A new ruling had been issued to the effect that factory leaders in my particular line of business could no longer obtain foreign currency for a business trip abroad. "Well," I said, "what about a personal trip—in order that I might inspect some new types of machines for my personal information." "This might be possible," he said, "but it will cost you 300 Marks." I paid the 300 marks and got the foreign currency without further difficulty.

Everywhere you will find new bonds of "friendship" between businessmen, "contact men" and "Party men" who are tied to each other by complicity in violations of laws and decrees. It is a kind of community of interest based on common risks . . .

I shall have to return to Berlin tomorrow.

All the best,

Yours,

. . . . . . . . . . . . . . . . . . . . .

It is not unusual for businessmen to get together and discuss in a businesslike way how much has to be paid to a State or Party official in order to obtain some favor.

Two businessmen from western Germany, Herr Schmidt and Herr Mueller, met each other in a train on their way to Berlin.

Said Herr S.: "I must get in touch with the Raw

Material Distribution Board. How much is it going to cost me to approach a Party member in that office?"

Herr M. answered: "Well, it all depends on what kind of a Party member you have to deal with. If he no longer believes in National Socialism, it will cost you a hundred marks. If he still does, five hundred marks. But if he is a fanatic, you will have to pay a thousand marks."

An Italian economist and editor who is familiar with present conditions in Italy was asked by the author: "What are the relations between businessmen and the State bureaucrats in Italy?"

"I can answer in one word—corruption," he declared. "The businessman in Italy has as much influence as he has money to bribe the bureaucrats. Without cash you are a helpless subject of the State."

The word "corruption" is not to be taken in the sense in which we normally use it in democratic countries. Under fascism, it is not primarily the power of money which corrupts, but rather does corruption spring from the power of the State.

Whereas in democratic countries the businessman may use his money to influence legislation and public opinion and thus operate as a source of power and corruption, in fascist countries he can exist only as the subject upon whom State power operates. The corruption in fascist countries arises inevitably from the reversal of the roles of the capitalist and the State as wielders of economic power.

Viewed in this light, the statement of the Italian economist is more comprehensible and is well illustrated by several cases which he cited. Unfortunately, the names and data which he gave to prove his point cannot be revealed, for to disclose them would endanger the lives of those involved. But these cases are so typical that names do not matter. For example, an Italian manufacturer, owner of an enterprise in which his family had worked for generations, produced a certain kind of light machine of chrome steel. Knowing that he would have to replenish his supply of steel shortly, he wrote to the proper State official in plenty of time to avoid any interruption of work in his plant. Two months passed without a reply. He wrote again and again, stressing his urgent need of materials. Finally the order permitting him to buy the necessary chrome steel arrived—but there was none obtainable. Only a few days' supply remained and he was faced with the necessity of closing down his factory. Then suddenly an "angel" appeared, a gentleman unknown to the firm, who said he had heard about the firm's plight through a friend in the State Office for the Distribution of Steel. He just "happened" to know that he would be unable to obtain immediately the required steel, unless a satisfactory private arrangement could be made, in which case, of course, he and his friend would use their influence to see that immediate delivery was effected. "By chance" he had at his disposal exactly the quantity of steel needed by the firm, but, unfortunately, the price was double the official rate—because steel, especially of the required quality, was scarce.

Such a transaction was, of course, illegal, but the Italian industrialist knew perfectly well that refusal to accept the proposition would not only result in the closing of his plant, but might mean his denunciation by fascist officials. His business would be ruined. He paid the price demanded. Having become a party to an illegal transaction, in which the fascist officials protected themselves through good friends among those higher up, he was, thereafter, even more at the mercy of the bureaucrats. Ultimately the fascist State official became a silent "partner" in the firm, and the manufacturer had no further trouble in obtaining steel and other materials.

Similar stories could be told about German manufacturers. Rome and Berlin have become the headquarters of many agencies specializing in providing "good connections" (that is, acting as glorified public relations counsels) for their clients. The "connections" are with State and Party officials holding key positions in offices which make decisions regarding the distribution of raw materials and the issuance of certificates for foreign exchange, subsidies for exports, permits for new construction, and the like.

Large German and Italian firms maintain branch offices in Berlin and Rome respectively with staffs of "reliables" whose sole job it is to visit the proper State officials and Party leaders, entertain them, establish good connections and friendly relations, and otherwise protect the interests of their concerns. Smaller firms which cannot afford such a staff are served by independent agencies. There are hundreds of such agencies, sometimes fraudulent in the sense that they have no genuine influence, more often with real friends in high places, from whom, unofficially and illegally, it is possible to get concessions and privileges.

New elements—not adequately covered by the term "graft"—exist in the relations between businessmen and State officials in Germany and Italy. It is not true that any capitalist with plenty of money can buy the influence of State bureaucrats. The businessman's influence depends on more than merely the amount of cash he spends for graft.

A businessman who is an old Party member may get many favors for which another would have to bribe some Nazi official. A businessman who has criticized the regime at some time or another may find it advisable to protect himself by improving his relations with a local Party leader. For this he will have to pay, while those who had always made regular contributions without grumbling would not feel it necessary to make an extra contribution to the Party. Consequently, many companies have found it too expensive to keep an executive who does not get along sufficiently well with Party authorities or whose political record makes him suspect in the eyes of a Party secretary. It is economical to replace such a man by a "reliable Party member" even though the latter may know nothing of the business. But he must have friends in power, or at least contact through intermediaries with the State officials upon whose goodwill the concern is dependent. The friends and intermediaries must, of course, be reliable Party people who have survived all purges and are still trusted by the government. The very nature of the Nazi party makes these "old Party members" realists who are apt to exploit their positions for personal gain within the safe limits dictated by national interest. They rarely, however, become active businessmen themselves, regardless of how much wealth they accumulate, as they find it far safer to remain in the bureaucracy and levy tribute for the distribution of patronage.

This tribute is paid in actual cash, for money has not lost its role under fascism. Even the Party badge does not entitle the wearer to appropriate whatever he sees or needs. He must have money to pay for it. There are exceptions, of course, such as the raiding of Jewish homes, but homage is paid to the general rule by terming such raids "spontaneous."

A superficial observer might easily claim that such a regime does not differ fundamentally from liberal capitalism; some governmental forms have changed perhaps, but the role and position of the capitalist or businessman have remained what they were before. Money still rules the world—democratic or fascist.

Such a conclusion would be just as false or incomplete as the opposite one, suggested in recent literature, that fascism is a new brand of feudalism in which the private capitalist has become merely a tool of the State—where absolute power has entirely taken the place of money power. This estimate overlooks new features in Nazi society and the unique position of the capitalist under fascism.

Fascist society still relies on a money economy, and is driven by money spending and the passion to earn more money. But there is a novel feature which does violence to the essence of liberal capitalism under which money must be earned through work or the use of capital.

Sources of money in the fascist State are open to those who have power, simply by virtue of their power. Nazi officials, though they cannot take what they want without paying for it, are in a position to obtain money for themselves by merely taking it from capitalists who have funds available with which to purchase influence and protection.

This power is not illegal but grows naturally out of

the system and is organized and made legitimate by the State. It is exercised by State organizations representing naked power—the S.S. (Elite Guard), the regular police forces under the command of Party leaders, the fanatics of the Hitler Youth organization, the Gestapo—all led by Party members who are personally tied up with one leader or another.

The leaders of these groups operate without the restriction of a constitution or of courts, and they wield a tremendous influence upon the economic and business life of the nation.

In this set-up, private capitalists who have funds at their disposal naturally still exert great influence. The social background of the Nazi official renders him particularly responsive to the lure of money and private property. As a former member of the ruined middle class, he lost his savings and economic security in the struggle for existence. His low salary as a State official would seem to bar him from wealth. But in his hands he now holds naked power—and the capitalist must share his funds with very many State officials if he wishes to share their political power, to win their favor and, thereby, provide for his own necessities.

Despite the great centralization of power in the hands of the highest leaders of the Party, there is wide variety in the role played by the provincial or municipal bureaucrats in their relations with private capital. Certain capitalists are so situated that they share in the power which a Party leader has at his disposal. A big industrialist, for example, who is in close contact with one of the important leaders of the Party, himself becomes an authority to the minor Party leader in his district. He reflects the authority of the national leader by whom he is befriended. He might even become a Party leader himself, at least of the provincial or district bureaucracy. Herr Thyssen and Herr Krupp need not court their district Party leaders. They themselves are greater authorities than the minor leaders, although neither Herr Thyssen nor Herr Krupp could defy the will of Hitler. Manufacturers who are of importance only on a provincial scale will endeavor to gain influence inside the district Party leadership—a low rung of the Party ladder—while the small businessman will be glad if he succeeds in being on good terms with his local leader.

Behind the scenes, different business interests compete with each other, influencing the "leaders" and trying to get their representatives appointed to key positions. The greater financial strength of the big concerns and trusts facilitates their getting into close contact with the chief political leaders.

Herr Kurt Weigelt is a leading member of the Kolonialpolitisches Amt of the N.S.D.A.P. He is also a managing director of the Deutsche Bank! Furthermore, Herr Weigelt is a member of the Supervisory Board of the Deutsch-Ostafrikanische Gesellschaft, Deutsch-Asiatische Bank, Dette Publique Ottomane, Straits and Sunda Syndicate (Batavia) and of other colonial enterprises. The Bureau for Foreign Affairs of the N.S.D.A.P. is under the leadership of an old Party member, but one of its National Office leaders is Herr Werner Daitz, a director of the Possehl concern, and a member of the Supervisory Board of two very powerful industrial concerns—Kloeckner and Flick. Obviously, big industrialists have been more successful than other groups in penetrating the decisive committees of the

Party, while the Party permeates the whole governmental bureaucracy.

There is a general correlation between the size of a business and the rank of the Nazi officials with whom personal contact is established. This correlation is weakest just where the need is greatest. There are too many small businessmen seeking the favors of the local Party leader, and they do not have enough money to make the granting of such favors interesting to him.

Of all businessmen the small shopkeeper is the one most under control and most at the mercy of the Party. The Party man, whose good will he must have, does not live in faraway Berlin; he lives right next door or just around the corner. This local Hitler gets a report every day on what is discussed in Herr Schultz's bakery and Herr Schmidt's butcher shop. He would regard these men as "enemies of the State" if they complained too much. That would mean, at the very least, the cutting of their quota of scarce and hence highly desirable goods, and it might mean the loss of their business licenses.

Small shopkeepers and artisans are not to grumble or to reveal any kind of dissatisfaction. But how can Herr A., a shoemaker in Augsburg, South Germany, avoid grumbling if he has to pay about 28 per cent of his small income—less than the wage of an industrial worker —for taxes. His case is quite typical.

In 1937-1938, Herr A. had a total income of 2,400 marks. He paid 1,012 marks for materials, tools, and costs for the maintenance of his workshop. His net income was 1,012 marks. But he must pay about 28 per cent of his small net income (88 marks monthly) for taxes and compulsory contributions, as follows:

| | | |
|---|---|---|
| 2 per cent Turnover Tax | 48 | marks |
| Income Tax | 85 | " |
| Trade Tax | 10 | " |
| Municipality Tax | 15 | " |
| Citizen Tax (Head Tax) | 36 | " |
| Church Tax | 3 | " |
| Guild Contribution | 24 | " |
| Winter Help | 3 | " |
| Contribution for Chamber of Artisans | 4 | " |
| Health Insurance | 60 | " |
| | 288 | |

The following story illustrates the plight of the independent artisan under the new regime. A Berlin locksmith, whom we shall call Herr Z., had a small but long-established shop. His father had owned it before him, and his grandfather before that. He had a modest but very steady trade in the neighborhood, consisting mostly of contracts to keep the locks of apartment houses in order. He had never engaged in politics.

About two years ago another locksmith, Herr Y., came into the district and opened a shop directly opposite Z.'s. Y. was an old Party member and also belonged to the S.S. He was a regular attendant at Party functions, and many of the neighbors suspected him of being connected with the Gestapo, the dreaded Secret State Police. It was remarkable how suddenly any neighborly gathering would break up when Y. joined it.

Owing to his being an outsider and to the aversion he aroused in the neighborhood, Y.'s business did not prosper particularly at first. Then, gradually, a change set in, which was brought about in the following way. Each of the apartment houses with which Z. enjoyed a repair contract had a Nazi housewatcher or *Blockwalter.* These are reliable Party members whose job it is to keep an eye on everyone in their apartment house, or their city block, and to report any person suspected of being a "dangerous element." Y. knew the local Party secretary well and, in due time, denounced Z. as a "dangerous element," constantly criticizing the system and stirring up his customers against it. As a result, the local Party secretary found it necessary "in the interest of the State" to influence the Nazi superintendents to transfer all their repair business to his friend Y.

Another report tells of the vain fight of the owner of a newspaper stand against a monopoly protected by the Nazi-dominated court.

At a Hamburg railway station, Herr P. used to sell his newspapers and magazines. He had a good stand which had been installed by his father many years before. Travelers who pass that station today can no longer meet Herr P., for after four years of National Socialism he had to leave his stand, having been put out of business by a large distributing concern, the Norddeutsche Zeitschriftenzentrale. This concern has close relations with influential Party leaders in Hamburg and dictates its terms to independent newspaper dealers. Those who do not accept the terms get no newspapers. Herr P., determined to defend his economic independence, appealed to the law. Believing Hitler's promises to the small businessman, he thought the courts would surely decide in his favor. But the decision of the court fully upheld the Norddeutsche Zeitschriftenzentrale, declaring:

> In the economic struggle the right of anybody to pursue his own interests even at the expense of somebody else can-

not be denied. . . . This applies also to monopolist articles. . . . The proprietor of a monopoly has the right to exploit his monopolist position. . . . The monopolist power has not been misused if it supplies one businessman with and excludes another businessman from the supply of monopolist articles.[1]

The authoritarian position of the provincial and local bureaucrats—and the degree to which the local Party bureaucracy is independent of industrialists and businessmen—varies with the social structure in different sections of the country. In districts where big industrial magnates have direct relations with the top flight of Party leaders, the local bureaucracy is largely dependent on—in some cases, a tool of—the big concern or trust. In districts where only small and medium-sized firms exist, however, the Party bureaucracy is much more authoritarian and independent.

A dual power exists under fascism: the indirect power of money and the direct power of the Party leader.

The minor Party leader of the district is dominated by the power of big money, but he is able to exercise his power over the smaller businessman and to extort from him contributions to funds under his control. However, in certain situations, this minor Party official might also become a threat to the big businessman by virtue of his position as a functionary in the State apparatus who takes his orders directly from the Fuehrer.

When the industrialist pays money to a Party official to obtain privileges, that is indirect power—corruption as we know it. But when the Party official extorts tribute as a result of the capitalist's outright fear, without guaranteeing the latter an equivalent in return, that is an example of direct power and is the distinct contribution of fascism to corruption as such.

If we are to seek an historic parallel, we must go back to feudal times. The small landed proprietor, who was a helpless victim of attacks and pillaging by war lords and knights, preferred to put himself under the "protection" of one feudal lord to whom he paid a regular tribute and from whom he expected a certain measure of protection against the attacks of other feudal barons.

Most businessmen in a totalitarian economy feel safer if they have a protector in the State or Party bureaucracy. They pay for their protection as did the helpless peasants of feudal days. It is inherent in the present line-up of forces, however, that the official is often sufficiently independent to take the money but fails to provide the protection.

The preceding chapter described the decline and ruin of the genuinely independent businessman, who was the master of his enterprise, and exercised his property rights. This type of capitalist is disappearing but another type is prospering. He enriches himself through his Party ties; he himself is a Party member devoted to the Fuehrer, favored by the bureaucracy, entrenched because of family connections and political affiliations. In a number of cases, the wealth of these Party capitalists has been created through the Party's exercise of naked power. It is to the advantage of these capitalists to strengthen the Party which has strengthened them. Incidentally, it sometimes happens that they become so strong that they constitute a danger to the system, upon which they are liquidated or "purged."

A few pointed examples of Nazi "get-rich-quick" success stories follow:

In Munich, Party Comrade Christian Weber's rise to wealth was meteoric. In 1932 he was employed as a janitor at the Blauer Ochsen restaurant where he devoted all his spare time to Nazi activity. As an old Party fighter he is now one of the wealthiest and most powerful of Munich's citizens. This former janitor now sports a string of race horses, is the proprietor of several transportation companies and owns the largest tract of land in Daglfing. He owns the big Hotel Wagner in Munich and the brewery connected with the hotel. He practically controls all the gas stations in Munich, and the suburban bus traffic, a source of great income in itself. Somehow, he learned in advance of the plan to construct an airdrome at Erding, bought land there cheap from the peasants, and sold it to the State at a handsome profit. A similar transaction in Reim, near Munich, where the largest airdrome in Europe is to be erected, added 500,000 marks to Weber's fortune. The land was purchased with State bonds.

Comrade Weber feels quite safe, for he is a personal friend of the Fuehrer himself. Weber once heard that the Gestapo was keeping a file in which the facts as to his graft occupied a prominent place. He went to Gestapo headquarters, was given the file, and destroyed it.

A minor State official in Bremen was charged with embezzlement of State funds. In defense he said: "The President of our Senate, Party Comrade Heidrich, has embezzled over 1,500,000 marks from a foundation established as a legacy by citizen Wolter. Our S.S. and S.A. leaders got a share of the spoils. One cannot take amiss what the big leaders do and should not be condemned for following their example." Detailed proof of the fraud perpetrated by the Bremen leaders was given to the court. The only result of these revelations was that Heidrich no longer appears quite so prominently at meetings and in the newspapers. He still keeps his job, and no one dares mention the facts exposed at the trial. The minor official is, of course, in prison, not so much for his crime as for his indiscretion.

Rudolph Hess, prominent member of the Reich Government as personal representative of the Fuehrer, was an undistinguished, unknown middle-class citizen when he entered the Nazi ranks. Recently he had built, for his own use, one of the finest and most luxurious homes in Germany. German industrialists have difficulty obtaining building materials and labor. Hess did not.

Propaganda Minister Goebbels was an impoverished intellectual in the days when the menace of fascism seemed remote to the German people. Until 1933 he lived on the meager salary which he received as a Party functionary. His rise illustrates the operation of direct power—getting without giving. He simply let it be known to his Party friends in the Municipal Council of Berlin that a large gift would be acceptable to him. He is now the owner of extensive estates near Berlin, formerly the property of the municipality, recently given to him as a "present" by the Berlin Chamber of Commerce in recognition of his "services to the nation."

Hitler, too, receives liberal presents. On Obersalzberg, near his domicile, Wachenfeld, a new estate has been created. The State bought up all the peasant holdings and demolished the farm buildings. In a short time there will be a model farm, under a management appointed by Hitler, with the most modern technical equipment—a gift from Hitler to Hitler.

This is only the latest of Hitler's acquisitions. He is a "partner" in the Franz Eher Publishing Company in Munich—the most prosperous in Germany. It controls more newspapers than did even Hugenberg when he was leader of the Deutsch-Nationale Volkspartei (Conservative Nationalists). The author of *Mein Kampf* has received royalties of several million marks; over 5,000,000 copies of the book have been printed. It is sold under State compulsion. Hitler's castle was bought with State funds, not with his private funds. It must be added that Hitler is a vegetarian, a "mystic" and a "romantic" who disapproves of drinking parties and other extravagant behavior, and who is extolled as a model of modesty and heroic simplicity—extolled as such by Party bureaucrats anxious to counterbalance widespread whispers about orgies and extravagances of Party leaders.

These cases feature outstanding "leaders." However, the same process is producing countless nouveaux riches in almost every town and district throughout Germany.

In an atmosphere of general distrust and corruption, "friends" help "friends" among the Nazis, but who can be sure of continued friendship and loyalty in an emergency, in a land where honor is a lost virtue? New jealousies constantly flare up among intriguing careerists who are apt to stab their best friends in the back. Family ties have acquired special and considerable importance—blood is thicker than water. A relative to whom one is attached is likely to be "reliable." Fortunate indeed is one who has a member of his family in the upper bureaucracy. Businessmen who possess relatives in the Party apparatus are relatively well protected from abuse by Party officials and can usually win special privileges which give them advantages over competitors less fortunately connected. These privileged capitalists are in turn willing to make larger contributions to the Party than others do. This business aristocracy is very restricted; it is almost impossible for outsiders to enter this inner circle.

The life of the German businessman is full of contradictions. He cordially dislikes the gigantic, top-heavy, bureaucratic State machine which is strangling his economic independence. Yet he needs the aid of these despised bureaucrats more and more, and is forced to run after them, begging for concessions, privileges, grants, in fear that his competitor will gain the advantage.

The press represents another unique feature of Nazi corruption. Under a parliamentary democracy, such as in France, political influence can be secured by using money to create favorable or unfavorable public opinion. Political corruption of this type cannot exist under totalitarian rule.

It is impossible in the totalitarian countries for a capitalist or political group to buy a newspaper, or to influence a newspaper's editorial policy through advertising or other financial means, in order to support a candidate in an election campaign or to oppose some proposed legislation. There are no parties or candidates to support or oppose and legislation is not proposed but decreed. The sole contribution to an "election" campaign would be a "gift," to the ruling party, for fascist propaganda. The logical outcome of a fascist system is that all newspapers, news services, and magazines become more or less direct organs of the fascist party and State. They are governmental institutions over which individual capitalists have no control and very little influence except as they are loyal supporters or members of the all-powerful party.

This does not mean that there are no connections between newspapers and private groups. The *Frankfurter Zeitung* is still under the influence of the chemical trust, I. G. Farbenindustrie A.G.; the *Deutsche Bergwerks Zeitung* and the *Deutsche Allgemeine Zeitung* are closely connected with the iron and steel trust, while the *Voelkischer Beobachter* is directly the property of the Nazi party—*i.e.,* the personal property of the Fuehrer and his business manager. These distinctions in newspaper ownership still find expression in the treatment given certain economic questions in the various papers. While these differences are sometimes illuminating they are relatively slight and never lead to open disagreements. Any differences of opinion are found solely in indirect allusions recognizable only by experts; 99 per cent of the contents of all newspapers are practically identical.

This absence of opportunity to buy editorial opinion does not mean that the editors of the newspapers in totalitarian countries are more honest than their brothers in the democracies. In countries where freedom of the press exists, editors may often be corrupt, but they are under no compulsion to be dishonest. If an English or American newspaper lies or distorts the facts for the benefit of certain business interests, if privately owned public utilities buy newspaper space for propaganda against public ownership, they risk exposure by rival independent newspapers, or investigation by governmental committees.

Under fascism or any totalitarian regime an editor no longer can act independently. Opinions are dangerous.

He must be willing to print any "news" issued by State propaganda agencies, even when he knows it to be completely at variance with the facts, and he must suppress real news which reflects upon the wisdom of the leader. His editorials can differ from another newspaper's only in so far as he expresses the same idea in different language. He has no choice between truth and falsehood, for he is merely a State official for whom "truth" and "honesty" do not exist as a moral problem but are identical with the interests of the Party.

The fascist dictator cannot be defeated in elections. He tolerates no criticism or opposition, inside or outside his party. The civil liberties which make it possible for a political opposition to get rid of unpopular rulers have been destroyed. Hence the fascist politicians can be far more independent of the financial oligarchy than is ever possible under the most autocratic of parliamentary systems. And it follows that fascist capitalists who pay graft do not necessarily get their *quid pro quo.*

Such a system also changes the psychology of businessmen. Their experiences teach them that the old right of property no longer exists. They find themselves *compelled* to respect the "national interest" or the "welfare of the community." On the other hand, they also learn that the privileges and advantages which a businessman might obtain from the State depend largely on "good connections" with State officials. Those who do not play the game but who still abide by the old rules of fair play cannot survive in this new kind of economic struggle. Businessmen must claim that everything they do, any new business for which they want a certificate, any preferment in the supply of raw materials, etc., is "in the interest of the national community." This claim is justified in so far as a business transaction or investment serves to strengthen the country's military position. Inevitably, every businessman endeavors to identify his personal and private interests with the "national interest," and it depends largely on political "connections" and influence whether and how far that claim will be regarded as justified by the State. Under such conditions, corruption is not merely a vice but an economic necessity.

Laws and decrees are issued by the State according to immediate needs and, emergencies. Officials, trained only to obey orders, have neither the desire, the equipment, nor the vision to modify rulings to suit individual situations. The State bureaucrats, therefore, apply these laws rigidly and mechanically, without regard for the vital interests of essential parts of the national economy. Their only incentive to modify the letter of the law is in bribes from businessmen, who for their part use bribery as their only means of obtaining relief from a rigidity which they find crippling. So does corruption become a liberative force under fascism!

The novel feature of corruption under fascism is that despite the magnitude it has assumed, no businessman can be sure that he will get the expected results, nor can he foretell what the party leader whom he has treated "generously" will do next. The party member is merely a cog in a gigantic machine. The authoritarian rule of the party relies upon a top stratum of old party members, an "old guard" closely connected with the executives on top through many personal ties, common interests and experiences. Nothing is so zealously watched by authoritarian leaders as the first signs of any new group arising which may endanger their supremacy.

This makes it impossible for even the most important industrialist to secure for himself and his corporation the control of the Party machine, to become the "power behind the throne."

Apparently, the businessman has no way out of this plight. New economic difficulties for the State offer no hope of a change. On the contrary, the Nazis, instead of reducing state expenditures, turn to the capitalists for sufficient funds to prevent any economic breakdown which might endanger the fascist system and the self-appointed representatives of the "racial community."

*Chapter IV*

# *THE CONTACT MAN*

"A curious new business aide . . . is now all-important."

THE business organization of private enterprise has had to be reorganized in accordance with the new state of things. Departments which previously were the heart of a firm have become of minor importance. Other departments which either did not exist or which had only auxiliary functions have become dominant and have usurped the real functions of management.

Formerly the purchasing agent and the salesmanager were among the most important members of a business organization. Today the emphasis has shifted and a curious new business aide, a sort of combination "go-between" and public relations counsel, is now all-important. His job—not the least interesting outgrowth of the Nazi economic system—is to maintain good personal relations with officials in the Economic Ministry, where he is an almost daily caller; he studies all the new regulations and decrees, knows how to interpret them in relation to his particular firm and is able to guess at what may be permitted or forbidden. In other words, it is his business to know how far one can go without being caught. He also develops special knowledge on how to camouflage private interests so that they appear to be "interests of the community" or of the State. He knows how urgent the demand of a State department or institution for a certain article may be and the effect of possible delays in delivery, and, therefore, whether it will be possible to obtain a higher price or a bonus for speedy delivery. Such a contact man knows whether, when and how it is possible to obtain a special urgency certificate for a certain article and when to complain about the refusal of such a certificate. He also knows when to be satisfied with an ordinary certificate.

Just what can be done about all this does not merely depend on decrees and official policies. Many other factors of a personal nature are important, factors which only an expert in this field understands. It is not always a question of bribery or corruption. The contact man must know, for example, whether the head of a certain raw material department is a Party man, an army man or just an "old conservative." Different arguments and facts must be used in each case. When he deals with a Party man, it is advisable to show letters and recommendations from local Party chiefs, receipts showing contributions to Party funds, or Labor Front certificates on National Socialist party activities in the factory. This may, however, have the reverse effect if the department head is by chance one of the "old conservatives" who have not yet completely disappeared. An official of the latter type is very correct, sticks to the letter of the law and cannot be bribed. It might be advisable to enter his office with the old greeting *Guten Morgen* whereas his secretary perhaps had better be addressed with a strict *Heil Hitler*. The army man, on the other hand, might be more impressed if the military aspect of the matter were stressed. Such small particulars might seem unimportant to the outsider; a contact man, however, knows that these small details sometimes have miraculous effects, assisting him and the firm he represents to obtain an urgently needed raw material, supply certificate or a price increase for an article ordered by some government department.

A large part of the advertising section in German newspapers is filled with advertisements in which the applicant emphasizes his "skill," "special ability," "good connections," or "experience" in negotiations with the authorities.

In almost every issue of the *Frankfurter Zeitung,* for example, there appear advertisements like the following:

"Corporation lawyer, Dr. pol econ., 35 years old. Party member, at present actively engaged in diversified work for a number of associations and banks, willing to assume further responsibilities for trade associations or in industry . . ." [1]

"Special tasks for a limited period performed by an economic adviser. Negotiations and inquiries at Government offices in Berlin, advice and research, organization of sales. Supply complete information, fully documented." [2]

"Technician and businessman, Party member, former officer in the air force, good contacts with State offices and authorities, etc., wants employment, if possible partnership in industrial enterprise . . ." [3]

The businessman who is in need of a "contact man" will not find it difficult to get the right person if he is willing to pay the price.

Any firm wishing to remain in business must have such a contact man, who, if possible, should be personally acquainted with some high official. If a firm cannot find a man with such qualifications, it will have to content itself with a man having contact with a lesser official, who in turn can promote the firm's interests with his superiors and inform the firm of how the wind is blowing. Should a firm fail to find a satisfactory contact man and otherwise have bad luck in establishing good working relations with officialdom, purest "Aryan" though its members be, it is likely to be forced out of business. Therefore one of the effects of the State regimentation of foreign trade is the rise of a few big concerns superseding all other competitions. According to a statement of Dr. Max Ilgner, director of the I. G. Farbenindustrie, in a lecture on January 28, 1938,[4] *one-third of the German export business is in the hands of only twenty firms.*

In no field of business is the contact man more important than in Germany's import and export trade. The early morning train from Hamburg to Berlin is so full every day of Hamburg import and export agents or their contact men going to Berlin for permits and authorizations of various kinds that it has come to be known locally as the "Permit Express." You have only to take a seat in a compartment of this train to hear, in the three and a half hours of the journey, a fair cross-section of the story of German foreign trade under the Nazis.

The experiences of Herr A. are typical. For a long time he has been the head of a wool-importing firm established for fifty-six years, with a good standing on the London Wool Exchange. Recently, after obtaining permission from the Administration for Wool Importation and Distribution, the supervisory board for his industry, and the Administration for Foreign Currency, he bought a quantity of wool from a London firm. The wool arrived in Hamburg, but the Reichsbank failed to release punctually the foreign currency to pay for it. The wool was, therefore, put in storage in the "free port," where it piled up charges. When he finally received the money from the Reichsbank, the London firm naturally insisted that he pay the storage charges, in accordance with international usage. However, to get the relatively small additional amount of foreign exchange needed, Herr A. would once more have to apply to all these offices. His application would not be decided upon immediately; there would be numerous inquiries and considerable correspondence before he would know their decisions. In the meantime the wool would be accumulating further storage charges, and if he finally received the money, he still would not have enough. This is an endless process; he is caught in a vicious circle which seemingly offers no outlet. Any profit which he might have made on the deal has already been eaten up by the cost of correspondence and the running around from commissar to commissar. After thus spending a number of days fruitlessly and aggravatingly, all he has to show for his trouble is a thick bundle of letters, application forms and introductions. He has to make a supreme effort to cut through the entangling red tape; he must go to Berlin to see the leader of his business group to get a letter of introduction to an influential official of the Reichsbank, who has close relations with the Administration for Foreign Currency, who may perhaps overcome the obstacles and help him get his wool!

Herr B., a type very often encountered in trains going to Berlin, must deal with a violation of some decree in a barter contract made by his firm. He hopes to surmount his firm's difficulties through a personal chat with an important personage in the Ministry of Economics, to whom he carries a letter of introduction from a friend in the Economic Section of the War Ministry. The ability to reach such people makes Herr B. a valuable—one might almost say, an indispensable—employee to his firm, and he knows it. Last week the simple intimation to his employer that a rival firm had offered him a higher salary was sufficient to secure him an immediate and most satisfactory salary increase.

Such is the life the Hamburg importer and exporter—formerly the most independent of German businessmen—now leads. In the old days he decided for himself what he should buy and where he would sell, without asking anybody for a permit—especially not someone residing in Berlin. Today he cannot move hand or foot without a permit or certificate, quota or allowance. He cannot make the smallest purchase abroad without first taking into account a hundred new decrees and laws and filling out a score of application forms and petitions. No longer is his the pleasure and profit of buying raw materials abroad when they are cheap; he can buy only when he can get foreign currency. If, while he is waiting for this, prices abroad go up, he must console himself with the hope that the Price Commissar might allow him to raise the price to the home consumer. Usually this authorization is forthcoming and, since there is never any difficulty in finding a buyer for imported raw materials—so scarce are they in Germany—in practice the importer who can obtain a grant of foreign currency has virtually insured himself of a profitable deal without any risk.

Turning to the wholesaler, we find a businessman whose calling appeared doomed at the time of the Nazis' advent to power; for according to National-Socialist theory trading is unproductive and should be eliminated as far as possible. Yet there are still wholesale dealers in Germany who do a good business and make a handsome profit. Just as with those engaging in foreign trade, however, this is possible only through good relations with the State authorities.

A private banker who previously resided in Germany and now has his office in the capital of one of the small independent neighboring countries is often visited by German industrialists who are his personal friends or who want his advice and assistance. This banker—whom we shall call Herr X.—told of a typical conversation he had with a German business friend, Herr Y. Herr X. once said to Herr Y., rather provocatively:

"My dear friend Y., you must have a wonderful time. No more worries about sales; the customers are running after you. What a wonderful prosperity, to judge by production figures and other economic reports in your daily papers!"

Herr Y. (rather angrily): "You are talking nonsense. Never in my life have I had so many worries as today. What do you know of the terrible job I have trying to get the necessary raw materials for the following week? Daily I have to fill out an immense number of requests, questionnaires, complaints and so on. Yes, I can sell as much as I can produce, but I can never say when it will be ready or whether I will be able to deliver at all. For better or worse, the customer has to accept what he gets. He can't blame me if I have to change production plans and produce something different from what he wanted; probably I have had to use a different raw material from the one provided for in the original sales contract. However, this is not my worst worry. How can I do anything without violating one of the thousands of new decrees dealing with prices, raw materials, preferential and non-preferential or forbidden supplies? Of course one doesn't take certain decrees seriously, but this might change tomorrow and I might suddenly be penalized. A competitor might denounce me. Perhaps I may have sold a small quantity of raw materials for a hundred marks, forgetting all about some decree on restricted sales. Or I may have violated a foreign exchange decree, a still worse crime. On one occasion a foreign customer visited me, and I invited him to supper at a fashionable restaurant. He had forgotten his wallet, and I lent him a hundred marks. Of course this is forbidden; giving credit to a foreigner without having asked the Reichsbank for permission is a terrible crime. I could not sleep that night for fear that the waiter might have seen what I had done. He knows me and might denounce me. I have not dared to go to that restaurant since. When I enter my office in the morning, I can hear my heart pounding. Will there be a letter from the Commissar for Foreign Currency about this, or a letter from the tax office demanding an additional tax payment of 100,000 marks for the year 1936? Life is difficult in Germany these days. All of us in business are constantly in fear of being penalized for the violation of some decree or law."

The tone of this conversation may sound exaggerated, yet it is typical of the experiences of the medium-sized independent manufacturer or dealer in Germany who does not happen to be connected with a high Party official.

It is the average businessman's dream to find the perfect contact man who can solve all these difficulties for him.

*Chapter V*

# *RAW MATERIAL DISTRIBUTION*

> "Wood, for example, has been used largely as *ersatz* for other more valuable raw materials, such as metals. But wood and timber in turn have become so scarce that the use of wood for numerous purposes not directly connected with armaments and not immediately necessary is *verboten.*"

AT LEAST half the time of a German manufacturer is spent on the problem of how to get scarce raw materials. These cannot be obtained without a certificate from one of the supervisory boards which distribute the available raw materials, domestic as well as foreign. Usually a manufacturer needs dozens of different materials. He cannot work without any one of them. For each one there is a special supervisory board with a different procedure, with all of which the businessman must be familiar. For example, before a builder starts work on a new building or even accepts an order for repairs, he has to make sure that the various supervisory boards will issue permits and certificates. In describing the manifold things a German builder must know, the *Koelnische Zeitung* came to the following conclusion:

"One necessarily needs a guide to get through the administrative labyrinth of officialdom. The normal human being needs an assistant who can explain the procedure to him. . . . We are experiencing an era of exuberant growth of new central authorities . . .

"The second Four-Year Plan should not create new

authorities, but the establishment of new supreme Reich offices could not be avoided; for example, the Office for German Materials (Leader: Col. Loeb), the Office for Iron and Steel Supply (Leader: Col. von Hannecken)." [1]

These supervisory boards estimate how much iron, steel, copper, rubber and other raw materials are needed by the whole country in order to carry out certain production programs. They even know how great the demand is from individual industries and plants. But this knowledge is of little practical use when it is impossible to obtain an adequate supply and to regulate the demand. The supply depends on factors which are not under the control of the supervisory boards. There are other authorities, such as the Reichsbank, the Commissar for Foreign Currency, the Price Commissar, the War Department Business Council, etc., which might nullify the policy of the Raw Material Boards. The supply and demand of raw materials change according to changing conditions in home industries—and on the world market—as well as under the influence of foreign policies which are not under the control of the commissars and supervisory boards. They might calculate at best how large a quantity of a certain raw material is actually available on the market and how much is needed in order to satisfy the most urgent and immediate demands. However, this is somewhat theoretical, for there is no way of measuring how urgent a demand is.

Many raw materials which are scarce in Germany are being imported in greater quantities than at any time before. During 1929, a year of prosperity, when barter trade was unknown, German industry had reached a high level of production. Yet in 1938 Germany had a net import of 30 per cent more iron ore than in 1929, 143 per cent more lead ore, 330 per cent more chrome ore, 50 per cent more copper ore, 140 per cent more nickel ore, 70 per cent more raw copper, 24 per cent more other copper, 62 per cent more nickel, 26 per cent more flax, 76 per cent more hemp, and so on. The greater part of these raw material imports is needed for armaments.

GERMAN IMPORTS OF RAW MATERIALS

(In thousand metric tons)

| | Iron Ore | Lead Ore | Copper Ore | Nickel Ore | Crude Oil | Raw Copper | Hemp | Flax | Textile Fibers & Yarns |
|---|---|---|---|---|---|---|---|---|---|
| 1929 | 1,683.4 | 58.1 | 439.6 | 13.8 | 518.7 | 162.8 | 17.1 | 5.7 | 802.0 |
| 1933 | 452.7 | 96.8 | 230.0 | 3.4 | 280.6 | 120.1 | 11.2 | 8.4 | |
| 1937 | 2,061.0 | 126.7 | 549.9 | 20.0 | 732.3 | 162.8 | 28.5 | 7.5 | 660.7 |
| 1938 | 2,192.5 | 141.0 | 648.3 | 34.2 | 777.8 | 272.1 | 29.9 | 8.5 | 775.1 |

(*Figures from the official German foreign trade statistics*)

Until just a few years ago, Germany's iron and steel industries were able to export large quantities of iron and steel after having satisfied the domestic demand. Since then, production has greatly increased, exports have declined, yet iron and steel are as scarce in Germany today as are foreign raw materials because of the gigantic armaments program.

Scarce raw materials are not distributed according to productive capacity, consumption or past production. Conditions may have changed in the sphere of production and consumption. Peacetime articles which were previously in demand may very well be considered of minor importance today. A new measure for estimating the urgency of any given demand has to be found. Therefore, "urgency certificates" are issued which entitle the holder to the privilege of a special supply from producers or dealers. These certificates are often graduated according to different degrees or urgency or "national interest." There are certain categories of demand which are always privileged: for example, demands for the construction of army, State and Party buildings, for fortification work and war supplies, and for export requirements. In the next category are usually to be found buildings sponsored or recommended by the Four-Year Plan Commission and by other State authorities. There are general rules as to the priority of other demands. Decisions as to the distribution of raw materials are often subject to later changes dictated by new policies or unforeseen conditions. An identical general trend, however, prevails in all fields of raw material distribution.

At first the State intervened only in particular emergency situations which seemed temporary. The private raw material syndicates or producers were instructed to give preference to customers who were in possession of urgency certificates. When the number of urgency certificates exceeded the quantity of raw materials available, special or preferential urgency certificates were issued. Firms which were unable to obtain certificates had to be satisfied with what they could get after the certified demand had been filled. This right of "free" purchase often meant nothing, especially to those who did no direct work on armaments, Party buildings, etc. This led to the introduction of "control numbers" for firms which had obtained certificates for iron and steel supplies, and quota numbers for individual firms with preferential and special urgency certificates.

Factors which are decisive for measuring the degree of urgency vary according to circumstances. During the first period of the Four-Year Plan, Party buildings or armaments production had preference on the schedule. Four-Year Plan projects for production of substitute raw materials and exports ranked second. In 1939 exports and armaments were given preference even over Party buildings.

Theory and practice, however, are far apart, especially under a system where a huge bureaucracy exists and "private initiative" tries to make official rules conform to personal and business interests. Realities have a way of peeping out from behind the façade of rules and regulations. There are many loopholes in the bureaucratic system through which private and individual interests can modify the distribution of raw materials.

Heads of the gigantic bureaucratic organizations have difficulty in controlling the demand and the urgency of the requests. "Private initiative" upsets their efforts. A whole army of investigators and office workers is engaged in checking up demands for raw material, future stocks and new requirements, with the result that a steady stream of complaints against decisions rendered arrives every day. The volume of daily or weekly applications does not indicate what proportion of the requests are genuine, nor how much they may have been purposely inflated. An extra staff of thousands of officials is necessary to investigate these cases. Millions of questionnaires are sent out in order to get a true picture of demands, stocks, etc. Questionnaires and statistical reports of thousands of firms are collected and catalogued. A vast number of office workers labors over them in order to calculate normal requirements, the volume of demand, and other figures necessary for getting a picture of the market situation. And what has been the result of all this tremendous bureaucratic work? The "urgent" demands do not correspond to the real needs and render it impossible to ascertain which cases are truly urgent and which requests should be granted first.

It is impossible for the raw material supervisory boards to meet the most important requirement for effective control and organization—issuance of purchasing permits or certificates in accordance with the quantity of raw materials actually available. The supervisory boards have neither the knowledge nor the means to adjust demand to supply. They are compelled to grant certificates according to arbitrary schedules of "urgency," only to discover when it is too late that the certificates issued are for a quantity of raw materials far surpassing the supply. Then an avalanche of complaints arrives, sent in by firms which have made strenuous efforts to obtain urgency certificates, only to find themselves in possession of sheets of paper with the seal of the authorities, but with no way of obtaining the actual raw materials.

Many special decrees have been issued, modified and modified again—all of them dealing with emergency situations and all attempting to bring order into this "organized disorder."

The scarcity of iron and steel, for instance, is felt perhaps more than that of any other raw material, in spite of the fact that Germany is the greatest iron and steel producer in Europe, and the world's largest after the U.S.A. But from the beginning it was impossible to examine every single demand for a material necessary to all industries. Therefore certain quotas were decided on for each industry. But this system did not work satisfactorily because the supply did not correspond to the sum total of the quotas. Fortuitous circumstances and special connections determined whether or not a firm could obtain its quota of iron and steel. Many firms, on the other hand, succeeded in getting more than their allotment; there are always individuals or companies willing to sell scarce raw materials secretly—in exchange for some other scarce raw material. A direct barter of scarce raw materials, without the knowledge and permission of the authorities, circumvents State control and upsets the plan; but such arrangements are quite frequent. The "contact" man who is working for the firm must be versed in such practices. He not only has to know the decrees, laws, and State authorities; he must also know how to circumvent them.

This internal barter system has attained considerable proportions. To a certain extent, it has even been legalized and encouraged. The Reich Association of the German Textile Industry, for example, organized an "exchange service for raw materials." A circular of November 5, 1937, informed its members:

"The need . . . to make available all existing raw materials has caused us to organize a raw material exchange service. . . . If for some reason a firm does not finish a repair job although repair materials have already been supplied (lumber, fittings, iron parts, etc.), it would be economically unjustifiable not to utilize these materials. . . ."

This exchange service of group organizations competes with private "contact men" or agents who arrange barter contracts among individual firms.

The commissar in charge of the supply of iron and steel sent many circulars to industrialists blaming them for and warning them against the use of non-quota iron and steel, as well as against exceeding their quotas. He appealed to their "national consciousness," pointed out the disadvantages to those firms that could not obtain their share and, finally, threatened industrialists with heavy penalties should they disregard State decrees. The firms were advised to accept new orders for manufactured articles only if and when they knew whether they could obtain sufficient iron and steel within the quota. Firms may even insist that a company desiring delivery of a certain machine should transfer to them sufficient iron and steel out of its own supply to manufacture the machine.

The following circular illustrates how raw material is distributed:

"To all members of the Building Trade Guild, Loebau, Saxony. Referring to the iron and steel quota. A.Z.: 541.

"The Reich Guild Association informs me that it has succeeded in obtaining a considerable increase in the quantity of crude steel to be delivered this month. . . . This extra quantity is to be used only to satisfy the most urgent demands. Every firm will have the opportunity of receiving a share, with the exception of metal for oven construction, the quota for which is still centrally administered.[2]

"Notify me at once as to your immediate needs for iron and steel. Kindly list them in detail and have them verified.

". . . Under no circumstances may supply certificates be used in building work when a quota has already been allotted or registration numbers have been received from the proper labor office.

". . . Nobody will receive anything unless he has

sent in the lists covering his needs together with receipts for supply certificates . . .

"Heil Hitler!

"Signed: Paul Selig, Obermeister.

There are many other raw materials which are scarce. They are arranged according to degree of scarcity so that one raw material may be replaced by another raw material which is less scarce. The ideal balance would be achieved if the degree of scarcity could be equalized so that different raw materials would all be equally scarce. This is the unattainable goal of all the planning and scheming in the distribution of raw materials.

Wood, for example, has been used largely as ersatz for other more valuable raw materials, such as metals. But wood and timber in turn have become so scarce that the use of wood for numerous purposes not directly connected with armaments and not immediately necessary is *verboten.*

The Market Association for German Forest and Wood Economy is in charge of the production and consumption of timber. Any purchase without a special permit of the Association is forbidden. New enterprises requiring a continuous supply of timber may not be set up without the Association's previous approval. Even peasants are no longer allowed to burn wood in their stoves, although it is cheaper than coal. In general, not even dead wood can be bought or sold for firewood. However, when it is absolutely necessary, the assumption is that those who have to use dead wood in their stoves are unable to use coal; otherwise scarcity of wood would merely have been shifted to scarcity of coal.

The businessman needs every bit of his ingenuity to

circumvent regulations and restrictions and to avoid interruptions in production. Rubber, for example, is extremely scarce, and it is consequently very difficult to buy a new rubber tire. It has become an officially decreed rule that no new tires may be sold unless the old tire is returned completely worn out. But this system does not work out in practice. Reserve tires are needed so badly that firms have resorted to buying entire new trucks just to obtain new tires. These tires were then removed and the new trucks sold without the tires as scrap iron. Business ingenuity in circumventing the State bureaucracy thus results in fantastic waste of materials, all in the name of preventing waste.

As a result of the raw material scarcity, certain trades are flourishing. Firms specializing in the demolition of old buildings are very prosperous. The materials which can be salvaged—from scrap iron to old bricks—are valuable and are often sold at prices not much lower than prices for unobtainable new material.

Secondhand motorcars are in great demand. They are bought by dealers who break them up even if they still are in good condition, and the parts are sold at prices which often add up to more money than the car was worth when it was in operation.

The businessman and the State differ considerably over the question of what constitutes an indispensable raw material. For example, the use of iron or steel is forbidden in the construction of garages, the installation of window frames, and for many agricultural needs. In practice, however, the restrictions are much more severe. In 1938 a rule was in force forbidding private building projects altogether if they required more than 1,500 kg. (1.65 tons) of iron or steel products. Such unofficial restrictions are relaxed or dispensed with according to the actual raw material situation.

Only an expert in dealings with the authorities and organizations knows the difference between official and unofficial rules. Outsiders who read only official reports might easily be misled. Thus, restrictions on the use of iron and steel and other raw materials have been relaxed. There are fewer decrees forbidding the use of scarce raw materials. This does not, however, indicate a relaxation of the restrictions in practice. For it is obvious that a manufacturer who obtains merely a fraction of his former supply of a certain raw material will use it only where it is most needed.

But, in spite of permits, certificates and the "private initiative" of the contact man, production often has to be held up due to the lack of one or more materials that fail to arrive on time. In factories, many different materials, tools and so on are needed. It is a question of luck whether or not all the materials arrive at the same time. Sometimes skilled metal workers have great difficulty in buying new tools, and they must remain idle even though enough raw materials are available.

Many appeals are issued and letters written to the manufacturers to persuade them to fulfill their "national duty." But the private entrepreneur is inclined to consider primarily his own and his firm's special requirements. He needs raw materials which are scarce. Special measures to "fight against waste" are expensive. Economizing on raw materials means a decline in the quality of the manufactured articles and affects sales in competition with similar articles. In the name of "national duty" the manufacturer is asked to expend his energies and money to save scarce raw materials and to replace them by more expensive ersatz materials. "National duty" against private interests—the latter would surely prevail if it were not for the many coercive measures used to prevent the businessman from acting in his own interest.

Many businessmen boast of their sacrifices in the "national interest," emphasizing their special efforts to economize on the consumption of raw materials and to support the policies of the various governmental agencies. The skill of the firm's representative in advertising its patriotism and military fervor is often more important than anything else as a means of impressing a patriotic bureaucrat who makes the decisions of the distribution board. This impairs the position of less "patriotic" competitors. Their representatives also must do something to put them in good standing with the State bureaucrats. So the out-of-favor manufacturer reports on the transactions of competitors who try to circumvent regulations. In this way a State bureaucrat obtains inside knowledge of business affairs in the industry which he is to control. This knowledge adds to the reputation of the bureaucrat, who thus proves his efficiency to his superiors. Consequently an atmosphere of mistrust and suspicion prevails among businessmen in the same trade. They may have been business friends for many years, yet they do not know what is said behind closed doors at the commissar's office. They often are surprised at the fact that the commissar has knowledge of certain trade secrets which he could have heard about only through a competitor's betrayal of confidence. One's closest business friend may be the informer. The State commissar may even pretend to know for certain what he merely suspects, so as to get more information.

The greater the shortage of raw materials, the stronger has become the pressure of different groups for preferential treatment. Many enterprises could claim that their work was of utmost importance to the State, and many State authorities were willing to certify the "absolute necessity" and the "national interest" to be served by preferential treatment of applications. There was a tendency to neglect raw material requests for undertakings which could be postponed or which were not directly related to the armaments program.

When supervisory boards for raw materials were first organized, quotas were not usually provided for repair work or for independent artisans. Usually such people maintained repair shops where they worked directly for the consumer. Consequently their work did not appear sufficiently important for the State commissar to grant them a share, especially since the leaders of this group had little influence with the Party bureaucracy. But the long period of scarcity changed the situation. At first many industries or consumers could be cut off from supplies of raw materials without any noticeable effect on the national economy. When, however, insufficient repair work threatened to result in the ruin of machinery and thousands of independent artisans were idle because they could not replace urgently needed tools, their demands for a share of iron or steel assumed greater importance. The commissar might advise firms which insisted on a share to use more ersatz. But this was not always possible; neither an independent artisan nor a big industrialist can afford to replace iron nails, for example, by nails made of wood, aluminum or other ersatz.

In 1938, years after the introduction of State control

of raw-material distribution, the "Independent Artisans" group finally obtained a share of the available iron and steel. It was only a small share, but previously they had had no quota at all.

With the growth of this control system, bureaucratic requirements have grown tremendously. Even the smallest artisan must fill out dozens of questionnaires and must read long circulars. One circular of the Reich Estate for German Handicrafts with regard to applications for a supply of iron and steel asks thirty-one questions which have to be answered with great care by all independent artisans in Germany.

The clash between different groups and authorities who simultaneously claimed to represent the most urgent and most important "interests of the State" and therefore insisted on preferential treatment, resulted in such anarchy, in such a flood of complaints, investigations and wasted correspondence, that as a final solution, a new authority was created for the most important branches of industry. Three commissars were appointed: one for the building trades, one for the machine-tool industry, and one for the iron and steel industry. These new commissars are plenipotentiaries extraordinary who can overrule decisions of all other authorities; they are responsible solely to Goering. This "reform" might have made superfluous a part of the paper war between different offices and authorities, but the relationship between supply and demand did not improve. Nor was a method found for the elimination of preferential treatment for those having "good contacts."

The clash of different groups and policies compelled the commissars to find a compromise between the various groups clamoring for preferential treatment. A plan was conceived which provided that the supervisory board would act only as a central agency fixing raw material quotas for each industry as a whole. The distribution within each industry was to be left to the industrialists themselves, or, rather, to the "leaders" of the various industries. Such a reform would have lessened the influence of the Party, which was stronger in the supervisory boards than in the industrial group associations. The latter would have gained in power considerably.

The reform was rejected by the Government. Instead, the group associations were made the go-betweens between the supervisory boards and the individual firms in the handling of complaints and general information. The supervisory board is not to deal directly with any complaints, which must be sent to, and investigated or commented on, by the group association. The decision as to the issuance of certificates or allotment of raw material quotas to an individual enterprise must be made by the supervisory board.

The group associations acquired real functions as a result of this reform. Previously, they had had no task of practical importance; now they function as intermediaries between commissars distributing raw materials and the individual firms, as complaint bureaus and information agencies. These functions have created a vast amount of office work and have considerably raised the authority of the group leader. He does not merely deal with complaints; he also maintains a kind of advisory service for group members, explaining to them the technique of applying for raw material certificates, giving them hints as to procedure so that a particular application will be granted. Especially important in the group association is the legal adviser. He is in a position to advise the membership on what is allowed or forbidden each member. He is familiar with the latest decrees. He can tell whether a contemplated business transaction is contrary to any instructions of the supervisory boards and therefore dangerous. Last but not least, the manufacturer needs a letter from his group leader in support of his request for certificates from the supervisory board; otherwise he has little chance of gaining his end.

The small manufacturer in particular is dependent on the favors of his group leader. The group leader in an industry composed of many small enterprises is more "authoritarian" than group leaders in mass-production industries.

Firms which have close connections of long standing with producers of raw materials are much better off than manufacturers who were in the habit of buying their raw materials from dealers and who had no direct contact with producers. A certificate granting a supply of a certain quantity of raw materials entitles the holder to buy that particular quantity. But it does not indicate whether and from whom the supply will be forthcoming. This becomes a matter of "private initiative" and personal contacts.

*Chapter VI*

# *PRICE DICTATORSHIP AND PRIVATE INITIATIVE*

"Effective price restrictions are impossible without complete control over supply and demand."

How cunning ingenuity and "private initiative" circumvent official rules in a country under totalitarian rule can be illustrated by the way in which a dealer bought a pig from a peasant in Nazi Germany.

A peasant was arrested and put on trial for having repeatedly sold his old dog together with a pig. When a private buyer of pigs came to him, a sale was staged according to the official rules. The buyer would ask the peasant: "How much is the pig?" The cunning peasant would answer: "I cannot ask you for more than the official price. But how much will you pay for my dog which I also want to sell?" Then the peasant and the buyer of the pig would no longer discuss the price of the pig, but only the price of the dog. They would come to an understanding about the price of the dog, and when an agreement was reached, the buyer got the pig too. The price for the pig was quite correct, strictly according to the rules, but the buyer had paid a high price for the dog. Afterward, the buyer, wanting to get rid of the useless dog, released him, and he ran back to his old master for whom he was indeed a treasure.

These "combination deals" have an interesting economic aspect. The supplementary article which is sold in order to make the whole transaction as legal as possible is not always an old dog, but, in most cases, an article which may have a certain usefulness in itself, though not necessarily for the buyer. The purchase of these supplementary articles therefore largely amounts to waste of money, made necessary to facilitate the purchase of other more urgently needed articles. Private initiative was wont to seek economies which would increase profits and the productivity of labor. Today, in a society which is laboring under great hardships as the result of scarcity of many essentials, the same goal can be achieved only by purposely arranged waste.

Other efforts of "private initiative" have similar economic results. Thus, manufacturers may introduce changes in standardized products which result in making the finished article more complicated, solely for the purpose of enabling the manufacturer to claim that the finished product is a "new article," which will not be subject to the old price restrictions. The State is enforcing more standardization of production in order to save raw materials; manufacturers must do exactly the reverse in order to defend their private interests.

The new "group discipline" which is being enforced often runs counter to the individual interests of all the group members, so that the group leaders play the role of policemen.

The *Deutsche Handelsrundschau* complained: "Those businessmen who conform to the letter of the law and instructions [of the Price Commissar] are at a greater disadvantage than those who are less conscientious." [1]

This German trade organ therefore defended stricter

police supervision of businessmen. Plainclothesmen approach traders as harmless buyers offering them higher prices than those officially set. Such "control purchases" are executed by secret police agents in order to strengthen "national discipline" among businessmen. It often happens that the plainclothesman even makes a special effort to induce the businessman to make an illegal transaction. Many businessmen therefore regard the "control purchase as a swindle maneuver and as immoral." [2]

In order to discuss illegal business transactions in a manner that makes them seem legal, businessmen in fascist countries learn to speak the language of experienced underground adversaries of the regime. They are often uncertain as to whether a prospective buyer is "reliable" and therefore talk in terms which are innocent and the meaning of which can be interpreted in different ways.

For example, Mr. A., the purchasing agent of a certain firm, inquires of Mr. Z., the manager of another firm, regarding the delivery of iron wire and receives the following answer: "I am sorry, but iron wire is very scarce and I do not know when I shall be able to deliver any. However, I can supply you immediately with screw drivers made of a new alloy." This means: Iron wire is available if an ersatz article is purchased at the same time. Mr. A.'s order might then read: "Two hundred kilograms of iron wire costing 150 marks and ten dozen screw drivers made of the alloy for 150 marks." However, Mr. Z. may insist on a larger purchase of screw drivers, and if Mr. A. fails to comply, the order for the iron wire may be turned down. But as downright refusal to accept the order would be illegal, Mr. A. a few days later might receive a letter from Mr. Z. stating:

"Unfortunately delivery of the wire you ordered must be delayed on account of general difficulties of supply. We shall be glad to get in touch with you as soon as we have a new supply available." Mr. A. would understand this perfectly: he had not ordered enough ersatz.

Combination deals are forbidden in Germany, but they will be common practice as long as the price of articles that are scarce is not allowed to rise and as long as sales of these articles are less profitable than sales of other articles.

Numerous clashes between private enterprise and the State occur as a result of price restrictions, which represent the State's most far-reaching attempt to control private economy, but effective price restrictions are impossible without complete control over supply and demand.

Such a centralized State economy has not come into existence, although numerous measures have destroyed the old private economy. The Price Commissar alone did not wield sufficient influence over competitive economy to pave the way for State economy. Other departments, besides that of the Price Commissar, have had considerable influence on the volume of production in different industries, through their distribution of raw materials. This was another step toward State manipulation of demand. The full force of propaganda and various coercive measures were used to force consumption of goods which were abundant. The same means were brought into play to prevent the use of those goods which were scarce. Medical experts were conscripted and had to prove that available foods were of greater health value than those which were scarce. But too much proof of this sort defeats its own ends, and the Price Commissar's campaign suffered such a fate.

When the government started its armament race and launched its spending program, it never intended to set up a price dictatorship. The extension of State control over prices had effects which the government did not anticipate and which were at variance with the original expectations.

A member of the "old guard," Joseph Wagner, was appointed Price Commissar. He has a huge administrative staff at his disposal and keeps in close touch with the police to insure the effectiveness of his decisions. His job is to fix both wholesale and retail prices for raw materials as well as for finished goods.

It is the duty of the Price Commissar to see that a stable price level is maintained. Price increases are forbidden and in many cases reductions are not allowed. Theoretically, at least, the authoritarian state does not allow any price changes without permission. There are, however, plenty of exceptions and much circumvention, an amusing contrast between theory and practice.

To increase his prices a dealer must have a special permit from the Price Commissar. A request for a price increase must first be certified to by the group leader; it must be accompanied by a detailed statement of necessity and other pertinent data, such as production and distribution costs.

At first, Herr Wagner did not realize the tremendous difficulties facing him. He simply decreed that after November 26, 1936, any increase in prices was forbidden. Perhaps he thought an order issued by a Party leader could suspend economic laws. He soon discovered that he did not have enough power to cope with the problem. Businessmen overwhelmed him with complaints of irregular or indirect price increases, made necessary by rising costs of production. They demanded that they, too, be allowed increases. At first Wagner stood firm and refused to make concessions. But he had no control over costs of production and it was not in his power to decide what should be produced and sold on the market.

Wagner could prevent neither the rise in production costs nor the growing scarcity of goods, the price of which he had "stabilized." Producers tried to abandon fields where low prices reduced profit and turned to production of more profitable goods. Because of the scarcity of raw materials, it was not easy for a manufacturer to make such a change. On the other hand, market conditions did not aid the Price Commissar. While he fought against price increases, other departments and governmental institutions made decisions which ran counter to his activities.

The scarcity of raw materials grew. Imported raw materials became more expensive, ersatz materials were still more expensive and, in addition, ersatz required new machinery. The huge State orders for armaments created an artificial boom for many articles and the State itself paid higher prices than before. The discrepancy between supply and demand of essential articles widened, and yet their prices were supposed to remain stable.

Within a few months after the announcement of the Price Stop Decree, the Price Commissar had to retreat; price increases were granted for numerous industries dependent on foreign raw materials, especially in view of the fact that they could not obtain ersatz materials without paying exorbitant prices. Growing taxation and increased administrative work were further factors adding to production costs.

However, in mass-production industries where only a small part of the productive capacity had previously been used, the increase in production made possible a more rational use of machinery and plant, thereby reducing overhead. But this factor was effective in these industries only during the initial period of the armament boom. Thereafter they were forced to speed up production to such an extent—often under government orders—that the means of production depreciated prematurely, with a resultant rise in production costs.

Another factor made rising prices inevitable. The State had created additional buying power by inflating the currency. State banks which had to rely on the Reichsbank paid the armament bills, in cash or credit. Under such conditions price control could be effective only insofar as it prevented an uncontrolled or excessive rise in prices. Trying to prevent it entirely turned out to be futile.

The Price Commissar's policies had unexpected results. For example, the peasants fed their cattle and pigs grain, although grain was scarce and had to be imported from abroad. The reason was that, in the interest of the big agrarians, who had a considerable surplus on hand, the price for fodder had been raised higher than the price for grain. At the beginning of 1937, 100 kg. of rye cost 16 marks, while 100 kg. of fodder cost 16 to 18 marks. Peasants were prosecuted for feeding their pigs grain, but the practice could not be stopped, until on March 25, 1937, Wagner finally conceded a price increase of 12½ per cent for rye.

Party leaders often disregarded economic facts unless these facts agreed with current Party notions. The more insistent the manufacturers' demand for price increases became, the more the Commissar extended his power and functions. Fear of inflation and hoarding—in part due to the war scare—would have led to a sharp rise in prices and to a repetition of the experience of 1923 had not the State used its totalitarian authority to ban any speculative increase and to insist on "national discipline." The rise of the price level itself could not be prevented, but it could be held in check and the relationship between different prices could be changed.

The Price Commissar's power increased greatly when he was given the right to investigate costs of production. Pressure occasionally necessitated his making exceptions to his strict rule of stable prices. But he insisted on the right to check upon the rate of profit and on costs. Often such an investigation would fail to influence his decision in any way. By a stroke of the pen he would decree a reduction in the rate of profit for an entire category of articles.

There were a number of official definitions of the "justified" price. At first the definition was that the price should be "reasonable," then that it should represent the cost of production plus a "reasonable" profit. But there was no effective control of production costs and what might constitute a "reasonable profit" remained a mystery. However, all this was soon forgotten when manufacturers started complaining about the tremendous increase in the cost of raw materials and other expenses. A new definition had to be found: the price must be "justified from the point of view of national economy." This was still more mysterious and vague. In reality it meant that the price level of any given commodity no longer depended merely on economic conditions, but also on political factors.

It is relatively easy to control prices for articles manufactured in mass-production industries. The Price Commissar ordered price reductions, claiming that an increase in production made possible more rational use of plant, thereby reducing manufacturing costs.

According to Nazi price statistics—which are misleading—many articles are cheaper than they were before the advent of the Price Commissar. In reality, prices which were officially reduced actually have risen. Cartels and syndicates formerly kept the price "stable" during a depression by granting "special reductions" to the buyers. The official or "list prices" were never changed, only the "special reductions." The advantage lay in the fact that the price could be changed according to competitive demands and no "official" price increase was necessary when market conditions forced an increase. By the simple device of making the real price identical with the "list price," it was possible to increase prices from 40 to 60 per cent on the average.

Furthermore, armaments made up the greater part of the output of the big concerns and trusts. During a period of international tension, when quick delivery of planes, antiaircraft guns or material for fortifications is necessary, there is not likely to be much quibbling over the cost sheet. But later the Government's financial difficulties made it necessary for the Price Commissar to investigate armament costs as well. He issued "Instructions on Prices to Be Charged for State Orders." When an industrialist, however, thought he ought to have more and said so, some kind of a compromise was usually arranged.

Other "model" instructions issued by the Price Commissar prevent the manufacturer from including certain items in his cost sheets, such as Party "contributions," wages above the official rates, interest charges on investments not directly connected with the item in question, etc. These "models" enable the Price Commissar to exert pressure on industrialists for price reductions on State orders, and to restrict price increases.

For political reasons, the Price Commissar tried to prevent price increases in consumers' goods. The unrest among workers, many of whom could hardly pay for the most urgent necessities of life, might have compelled the industrialists to raise wages. Therefore, manufacturers and dealers who had little political influence were forced to absorb the cost of increased raw material prices.

"When it was found necessary to allow an increase in the price of bread on account of the increase in the world price of grain, it was decided that the cost should be borne mostly by the sugar, milk, and brewing industries, which, in turn, were partly compensated by the abolition of certain taxes and regulations. It is obvious that under such a policy a price cannot be regarded as an important factor in regulating supply and demand.

"Under National-Socialist economic policy, the State determines to what extent the increased profits of industry, resulting largely, directly or indirectly, from State orders, should be used for increase of wages or dividends." [3]

The cost of the price increase in rye, amounting to some 75,000,000 marks, was thus arbitrarily shifted to other industries. The breweries had to contribute 34,000,000 marks, the sugar refineries, 29,000,000 marks and the flour mills 12,000,000 marks to an "equalization fund" so that the farmers would get more for their product without an equivalent rise in the price of flour and bread. After the introduction of this measure, the quality of flour and bread declined considerably, but the price remained "stable."

Another similar measure was the cut in fertilizer prices. One day in May, 1937, fertilizer manufacturers, much to their surprise, received an order from the Price Commissar to cut their sales price immediately by 25 to 30 per cent, retroactively as of January 1, 1937. In effect, this price cut was a transfer of income from the fertilizer concerns to the farmers.

According to the German Institute for Business Research, the total price cuts on standardized products amounted to 300,000,000 marks, or approximately 1 per cent of the total value of retail sales (31 billion marks in 1937).

The price of "luxury goods" is not so strictly supervised. In their case, supervision is rendered difficult by the fact that the processes of production are more complicated. Manufacturers, therefore, prefer these branches of industry and it is not uncommon for a concern manufacturing consumers' goods in the standardized, fixed-price category to switch to the manufacture of "luxury goods," which have a more flexible price range.

*Der Aufbau* (a Nazi periodical), expressing its resentment of such shifts in manufacture, said: "While in principle no increase has taken place in clothing prices, in practice the cheaper lines of men's and women's clothing have become very scarce and people have had to accept higher-priced goods. This is due entirely to the fact that manufacturers and dealers are too anxious about their profits. These people must be made to understand that they cannot use the raw materials distributed to them in such a way."

Most of the time it is impossible or inadvisable for the manufacturer to replace a mass-production article by a "luxury" product. In such cases the industrialist will try to reduce costs of production. He may do this by using better technique, employing cheaper labor or lowering the quality of his product. It has become a common practice to sell an article of inferior quality at a price for which an article of better quality could previously be bought. Therefore group or trade associations were ordered by the Government to issue warnings against violations of "national discipline." The Reich Association of the German Clothing Industry sent the following circular to German textile manufacturers:

NEWS SERVICE
OF THE GERMAN CLOTHING INDUSTRY
BERLIN KIELGENSTR.
BUSINESS ECONOMY—CALCULATION—PRICES
*Reference Number* 5

Lfg 45. Aug. 20, 1937
EDITED BY THE ECONOMIC GROUP AND THE REICH ASSOCIATION OF THE GERMAN CLOTHING INDUSTRY

Price Stop Decree with loopholes. Attempts to circumvent a law . . . are like desertion in war times. It is regrettable that today "businessmen" look on the law only from the point of view of whether they can circumvent it by any type of swindle. Is there any other explanation for attempts to get around the Price Stop Decree by selling a cheaper quality product instead of the higher quality? . . . Scarcity of materials is a glib excuse for such unfair business practices.

. . . Cases of "circumvention of price decrees" should be reported immediately to the Economic Group. They will be dealt with at once.

According to reliable estimates the quality of consumption goods sold in Germany has declined about 30 to 40 per cent since 1933, while the price has remained "stable."

The Price Commissar is often a silent partner in the manufacturer's practice of maintaining price by lowering quality—it is more opportune, politically, to avoid a direct price increase.

Group association leaders were ordered by the Price Commissar not to violate price decrees, so that "national discipline" might be strengthened. The following circular from the leader of such a group—the Reich Association of the Building Trades—is illuminating, as it reveals that the violation of the Commissar's price decrees has become a common trade practice.

REICH ASSOCIATION OF THE BUILDING TRADE GUILDS
(REICHINNUNGSVERBAND DER BAUGEWERBES)

District Saxony.

*Dresden—A 1, Gruner Str. Telephone 10754*

*Printed as manuscript. Reprinting or quotation forbidden.*

Druck-R. Schr. Nr. 1/1938

Br.-No. 588. 38. R./Schr. Dresden-A, Febr. 3, 1938

To the Guild Members:

As we know, there are great difficulties in maintaining a supply of lumber in our district. . . . Under the pressure of conditions our members have shown themselves willing to concede prices which are not in accordance with the decree of September 4, 1937. We urgently warn the members of the grave penalties involved. . . . Price increases without legal basis are:

1) Attempts to classify inferior qualities in higher-priced categories. . . .
2) Attempts to obtain the highest possible prices without regard to poor quality . . .
3) Reduction of the cutting of building lumber in favor of planks, in order to get higher price.
4) Combination deals . . . If a cabinetmaker has to buy additional lumber for which he has no use.

. . . We therefore decree: "Scarcity is not to be used for open or hidden price increases (see example above). . . . Arbitrary complaints and denunciations to Guilds should cease. Everyone is responsible for seeing that only reasonable complaints reach the Guilds."

The leaders issue warnings, as well as open threats, to businessmen. The following confidential circular of the Clothing Industry is typical of the relations between State authorities and businessmen:

REICH ECONOMIC GROUP
CLOTHING INDUSTRY

Strictly Confidential!
To the business leader personally!
"The accursed hoarder!"

It has been definitely established that during the last few months in a number of firms belonging to our association, inefficiency, self-seeking and misuse of capital have led to long-term orders and unnecessary stocks of materials.

Purchases which in the normal way would not have been

made until four or five months later, have been made far ahead; ridiculous orders were placed and accepted by the manufacturers during the winter of 1936-37 for delivery in February-March, 1937.

Such behavior calls for the most severe condemnation and can only be described as disgusting hoarding. As stated unambiguously by those charged with the fulfillment of the Four-Year Plan, it is also a crime . . .

. . . . . . . .

Instructions concerning stocks will be given within the next few days.

Leaders of enterprises who fail to comply with these regulations will be pilloried.

We draw your attention to the fact that under the new powers given to the State Commissar of Prices he is empowered to detain or sentence to prison evildoers or saboteurs and hoarders and that he can close down concerns entirely.

This is the last warning. We have shown you how to mend your behavior immediately. You are betraying the interests of the community.

In most cases it is impossible to know whether an indirect price increase is allowed or forbidden. It largely depends on the businessman's ingenuity, on his political influence or on the changeable opinions and policies of the Price Commissar. Political unrest among the consumers may make it necessary for the Price Commissar to find a scapegoat, and he might suddenly accuse and even order the arrest of businessmen for indirect price increases which were tolerated yesterday, but are forbidden today.

The Price Commissar has the power of the State behind him and an army of police agents at his disposal. A notice from him to the Secret State Police may mean a sudden change of status from manufacturer to inmate of a concentration camp.

The most repressed and restricted businessman in Germany will not be found in the ranks of big businessmen. He is the retailer, more especially the small shopowner; the man whose income has shrunk as the result of the steadily rising cost of raw materials and production, and the rigidly governed retail price level dictated by political exigency; the man who supported Adolf Hitler most staunchly in his fight for power and hoped to gain the most by his triumph, but instead has been the most bitterly disappointed in the development of Nazi economy.

Small shopkeepers have the least political influence, and they make the easiest scapegoats when there is an unpopular rise in prices. These shopkeepers were told that the Nazis would destroy the competition of chain stores, trusts and Jewish shopkeepers. The State was going to give them special protection. The Government fulfilled its promise to eliminate Jewish competition, but this no longer impresses "Aryan" shopkeepers. They are caught in the net of price restrictions which specifically forbid increases in retail prices, although the shopkeepers themselves have to pay higher prices and higher taxes than before.

The Price Commissar has granted innumerable price increases to manufacturers at the expense of retailers. The latters' business has been curtailed by scarcity of many articles which they can obtain only if, in addition, they buy superfluous articles or luxury goods not easily sold. They were badly off when National Socialism came to power; they are in a desperate situation today. Although theoretically still in business for themselves, they have become nothing more than distribution agents for the State, without a fixed salary or even a guaranteed minimum income. Often they survive only by illegally selling scarce articles to customers who are willing to pay higher prices or buy "luxury" articles.

Hundreds of thousands of small businessmen and their customers are forced to violate the law daily, and a whole army of policemen has been mobilized to catch these lawbreakers.

*Die Deutsche Polizei,* the organ of the S.S., issued the following appeal which graphically shows the relations between the State and shopkeepers in Germany today:

"Businessmen who are ignorant [of the new legislation] must be reminded of the price restrictions; they must know the prescribed prices. . . . Police, making their regular visits, are informed by the retailers that they were just about to put price tags on or that the goods had just arrived. As a matter of principle, this kind of excuse cannot be condoned any longer. Fixed maximum prices are ignored; shrewd businessmen mark the prescribed maximum price on one side of the price tag, and a higher price on the other side. Even when official prices are quoted, forbidden price increases must be looked for. . . . Special attention must be paid to the firm's books." [4]

This State control is not everywhere effective to the same extent. A police officer or an agent of the Price Commissar will naturally be more severe with the small shopkeeper than with the big armament manufacturer who has friends in the Party or on the General Staff of the Army. Prices have, therefore, changed income distribution, and the small shopkeepers and manufacturers have lost in the process.

The *Deutsche Volkswirt* complained of the economic absurdities which hit the small trader in particular:

"Combined sales of foodstuffs and fodder are forbidden. . . . The unwanted article is not used. . . . Extremely high penalties have been inflicted on dealers in Leipzig, Cologne and Berlin who combined sales. . . .

"Wholesaler and retailer have become merely distributors. . . . Today selling is nothing but distribution . . . without the most essential element of 'distribution'—the quota. . . .

"The retailer will not make combined sales openly on account of the strict control and heavy penalties, but there is the 'regular customer.' He will get more than his due of scarce articles if he always makes big purchases. . . . The customer with a small purse is the one who suffers. . . . Besides orderly market conditions, there ought to be market justice too!" [5]

This cry for "justice" in connection with the price policies of the State was published by a periodical known to be the organ of Hjalmar Schacht at the time when he was president of the Reichsbank. It still represents—if one knows how to read between the lines—the interests of the private trusts. They were disturbed because, with the further extension of State control over prices, the Price Commissar had entered their own bailiwick and had enforced price reductions even when big industrialists could argue convincingly that their costs of production had risen. The attempts of the Price Commissar to investigate prices paid for munitions more closely than during the first Four-Year Plan aroused the industrialists. They felt that the State had taken a sufficiently heavy toll from all classes to be able to finance itself. Prices paid by the State for armaments left a handsome profit, and the armaments business enabled industrialists to get back a part of the money which the State had taken from private economy. On the other hand, the Price Commissar regarded it as his duty to take away from the industrialists as much as possible of what they had taken from the State.

These conflicts demonstrate the financial plight of the State. They also show that price is no longer merely an economic, but also a highly political, factor. Under the totalitarian State, price control has become a matter of governmental policy.

In spite of the Price Commissar, however, price has not become solely a political matter; economic laws still influence the price level. When the lengthened workday and more widespread employment increase the buying power of the consumer without a corresponding growth in mass-consumption goods, prices will rise, no matter what the Price Commissar may do. He can merely influence this process. Price increases may not be visible immediately, but they show up in quality of goods, in "combination" sales and in direct violation of Government decrees.

Under such circumstances nearly every businessman necessarily becomes a potential criminal in the eyes of the Government. There is scarcely a manufacturer or shopkeeper who, intentionally or unintentionally, has not violated one of the price decrees. This has the effect of lowering the authority of the State; on the other hand, it also makes the State authorities more feared, for no businessman knows when he may be severely penalized.

The consumers have similar experiences. They are told by the State officials that prices have not risen and that increases in prices are forbidden. But articles of the old quality are unobtainable at the former prices; consumers have to participate in the process by making illegal offers of higher prices and by replacing articles they used to buy with "luxury products." The cost of living increases although prices remain "stable."

This whole system of camouflage to circumvent governmental decrees is carefully hidden in the official picture of the nation's economy. But sometimes the facts are revealed, as, for example, in a report for 1937-38 of the Reichs-Kredit-Gesellschaft, a Government-owned commercial banking institution, which reads:

"Just as the building index is calculated on the assumption of constant building methods, so the cost-of-living index presupposes a constant standard distribution of purchases on the part of consumers. Since 1933, however, fundamental changes have taken place in this field due to the general position with regard to supplies. The index is intended to express the cost of living for a working-class family of four. In normal times, such people, who represent the great mass of consumers, have always preferred cheaper-quality goods; but during the last few years the increasing scarcity of such goods has forced them to a growing extent to purchase goods of higher quality. In addition, the figure for housing is becoming progressively less representative from year to year since it is based upon rents payable in respect to dwellings constructed before 1918, whereas in actual fact living accommodation is more and more taking the form of houses built since that year." [6]

To take another case, the official price index for shoes has remained comparatively stable since 1933. A good pair of men's shoes cost 12.50 marks in 1933. The same quality shoes—if obtainable—cost at least 20 marks in 1938.

The *Deutsche Arbeitskorrespondenz,* the organ of the German Labor Front, was still more outspoken as to the contrast between official fiction and reality:

"With utmost conviction and emphasis the Fuehrer insisted on stable wages and prices at the Reich Party Congress. . . . The stability of wages and salaries is a fact.

". . . It is different as to prices. The price level, which had remained unchanged until recently, has been altered to such an extent during the last few months that everybody is made to feel it and this is contagious as nobody wants to be left holding the bag. From the vegetable store to the boarding-house keeper, from the butcher to the milliner, everyone says they must get higher prices, because 'everything has become more expensive.' . . . The authorities in control of prices ought to be more helpful. The Reich Bureau of Statistics would gain in prestige if it were to draw up a representative budget for the workingman as soon as possible. There probably would be unexpected surprises. Prices for the most necessary foods may have remained stable as a result of market regulation by the Reich Nutrition Estate and the fixed prices of the cartels. But this is true only to a limited extent of other articles which are in daily use." [7]

It is difficult to realize the full implications of such price control. Calculations of cost in thousands of different trades, industries and enterprises, correspondence concerning thousands of disputes over the real costs of production and "nationally justified" prices are piled up in the offices of the Price Commissar and the bureaus under his control. Instructions issued by them on comparative costs of production and distribution are a mine of information. They lay bare the workings of economic law, especially as reflected in the productivity of labor and the interdependence of a nation's industries. The Price Commissar collects data and reports which are essential for a planned society, but he does not use them for that purpose. He is interested only in proving that some industrialist or merchant is charging too high a price and can be accused of "sabotaging" government policies.

As long as industry remains under the management of individual capitalists whose interest is profits, the businessman will be in conflict with the Price Commissar, since he forbids sales at a price which is justified by market conditions but not by "national interests." The struggle of the businessman against the Price Commissar becomes a matter of life and death if and when the latter insists on a price which is unprofitable or would even result in a loss.

*Chapter VII*

# *INDUSTRIAL GROUP LEADERS*

> "Official communications now make up over half of a German manufacturer's entire correspondence."
>
> WALTER FUNK, *Reich Minister of Economics*

IF THE State were to socialize industry, the businessman would at least know, for better or worse, what his position is. Many manufacturers utterly dislike the idea of becoming State officials or agents. But there are also many managers who are tired of the risks of competitive struggle, of being dependent on the favors of the State bureaucrats. These businessmen see no chance of improving their personal position through competition. They would like to be freed from these uncertainties by becoming a part of the State machine, with a fixed salary and a pension. The State offers no economic security to the scared businessman who prefers security to the risks of business under totalitarian rule.

The only plan for complete socialization of all industries and trade branches has been prepared by the War Economic Council of the General Staff, a plan which provides for the introduction, overnight, of complete state socialism—or state capitalism—in case of war.

Measures for the immediate execution of such a plan have been carefully organized. The purpose of this plan to regulate economic life is clear: maximum production of war materials for huge mass armies and subordination of all economic activities to the specific needs of war.

The main purposes of the Four-Year Plan were: (1) extension of State control over raw materials; (2) subsidizing German production of raw materials on a mass scale in order to make the country independent of imports and to strengthen the war industries.

New bureaus were established to survey Germany's raw-material needs in peace and in war, to find the weak spots in the economic structure, to encourage national production, to replace imported goods, especially those necessary to a war economy. The chiefs of the new offices were military experts and reliable Nazi economists. Dr. Keppler was transferred from his position as head of the Economic Research Office and Economic Adviser of the Party, in which capacity he had come into conflict with Schacht; he was put in charge, under Goering, of developing German mineral resources in order to make Germany self-sufficient.

The planning work in Goering's ministry was largely work on paper, of little immediate practical importance. In fact, many activities in which the State is engaged at present are superfluous today, but necessary in anticipation of a totalitarian State during war. Millions of questionnaires, for instance, filled out by thousands of manufacturers and artisans, have been collected and filed. These statistical data are registered without any practical use being made of them. For handling these statistics, a huge staff of clerks is required; it seems to be a job intended only to keep the bureaucracy busy. But such statistics and surveys are basic materials necessary to launch "war socialism," should war be declared.

Activities which are directly concerned with preparations for war do not alter the status of the private capitalist. They are like a tax which is a burden on him but which does not interfere with the control he exercises over his business. An example of such activities is the construction of dugouts or bombproof shelters for use during air attacks.

Other types of State interference which alter or vitiate the functions of the private manufacturer are: price fixing, distribution of raw materials, regulations as to what and how much shall be produced (not applied in most industries), restrictions upon the issuance of stocks and bonds, general control of investments, etc. All of these measures encroach directly on essential functions of the entrepreneur, as does the transfer of factories from frontier districts into central parts of Germany.

This second type of State interference creates the impression that "war socialism" is already in existence in peacetime. But these acts of State interference are not part of a general economic plan; they are merely emergency measures, introduced to overcome unforeseen critical situations or weak spots in the economic system. They are largely concomitants of the armament policy, though they are not a part of the armament program. Rather are they the result of its shortcomings and deficiencies. This is confirmed by a statement in *Der Vierjahresplan,* the organ of Goering's Four-Year Plan Commission:

"The National-Socialist economic policy soon had to face bottlenecks and deficiencies. . . . It is typical of the present stage of State economic management that the great tasks of reconstruction and social order are temporarily superseded by measures destined to overcome deficiencies and which, as such, are to remain in effect only for a short period, as the economic leadership may determine. . . .

"A logically minded person might easily conclude that this kind of State interference leads to a system of State economic planning, that such a planning system will and must become more and more stringent and complete, and that increased planning narrows the economic field where competition exists. . . . Such measures [of State planning] are transitional and temporary. . . . They should not be ideal or permanent, nor should they be regarded as the goal of State economic leadership . . . as a system of total planning which replaces self-administration by State interference. . . . The National-Socialist economic leadership is not inclined to free the private entrepreneur from his responsibility for economic development, still less from his personal responsibility for his factory." [1]

Army representatives are working in the offices of many companies and trusts, watching the execution of orders for war materials. Private enterprise has to take this superintending in order to comply with the wishes of the army and to back demands for preferential supply of materials without which production could not continue.

A whole army of *Wehrwirtschaftsfuehrer*—Leaders of Defense Economy—has been appointed. Most of them are army officers who have taken special courses in economics and industrial relations. Although lacking in practical industrial experience, they are clothed with supreme authority upon their appointment as leaders. They are ignorant of the conditions peculiar to the industries over which they are to have control; neither can they estimate the importance of urgent requests for preferential treatment. They therefore have to rely on the judgment of minor bureaucrats and decide questions arbitrarily—which makes matters worse—or they have to rely on personal friendship with businessmen who are willing to give them unofficial information in return for special privileges.

The more economic difficulties threaten the prompt execution of armament orders, the more army leaders are appointed to make sure that military interests are given first place in industry. This interference of the military authorities in industry, which was not a part of the original armament plan, was necessitated by the decline in private economy which endangered important war preparations. This forced the military to take a hand in private industry, although the army had regarded the existence of a "sound private economy" as an essential element for the preparation of a sound wartime economy.

There are many State institutions which issue orders and instructions to the businessman, telling him how he should conduct his business, what is allowed or forbidden, and what he should, may, and must not do. He receives orders from and has to send his appeals and representatives to:

Ministry of Economics, and its subdivisions:
- Four-Year Plan Commission
- Foreign Exchange Board
- One or more of 25 Import Control Boards
- Price Control Commissar
- Reich Administration for Economic Expansion
- Reich Administration for Soil Exploration
- Reich Administration for Usage of Scrap Materials
- Administration for Renovation

Administration Labor Service
Special Commissars (Building Trade, Automobile Industry, Machine Industry, Power Industry)
Food Ministry and Reich Nutrition Estate, and their subdivisions:
Various Monopoly Marketing Boards
Various Compulsory Cartels of Processing Industries
Labor Ministry, and its subdivisions:
Labor Front
Labor Exchange
Regional Labor Trustees
Reichsbank, and its subdivisions:
Bank Control Board
Foreign Currency Department
Reich Economic Chamber, and its subdivisions:
Economic Groups
Occupational Groups
Regional Groups
Regional Economic Chambers
Leaders of Defense Economy (War Economic Council)
Administration for Self-Help of German Industry (in connection with the Export Subsidy Fund)

All these organizations are huge bureaucracies with headquarters in Berlin, in many cases organized independently of each other, interfering with private business and with the national economy.

The businessman has to adapt his business to the State bureaucratic system by building up a huge private bureaucracy too. Clerical work in companies and trusts and even in small enterprises has increased tremendously.

To quote from a report of Mr. A. Parker, published in *Lloyds Bank Monthly* for July, 1937:

"The bureaucracy is inevitably more bureaucratic than before. . . . Bureaucratic work occupies the semi-officialdom of numerous 'estates' and public corporations (Nutrition Estates, Organization of German Business, German Labor Front, etc.), the staffs of business undertakings which have to observe State requirements and individual citizens. It has been said that one commercial bank maintains 500 officials alone for dealing with foreign exchange regulations. The manufacturer can get raw materials (and then only a ration) only on application, which must be documented by presentation of data on past consumption, present stocks, proofs of orders, etc. The importer cannot ever, and the exporter hardly ever, initiate a simple deal without innumerable formalities. The industrial workman must take out and keep in order a work-book, and the farmer, under a recent decree, must keep certain otherwise unnecessary records for official inspection. The regulations about shop competition, which are but one branch of much wider retail trade regulation, fill 700 closely printed pages. The householder must now, as in time of war, keep margarine, bacon, and fat cards. The government has no other means of enforcing its system of vetoes, permits and restrictions than by punishing transgressors; and in fact nearly all industrial, commercial and financial transactions for which official permission has not been obtained are criminal offenses."

Since this report was published, bureaucracy in Germany has become even more top-heavy.

The greater part of every day is taken up with official conferences and correspondence with State boards, control commissions, etc. Walter Funk, Reich Minister of Economics, admitted at a meeting of economic leaders of Pomerania, a province of Prussia, that "official communications now make up over half of a German manufacturer's entire correspondence." [2]

The growth of the State agencies under the first Four-Year Plan finally resulted in such an anarchic state of affairs that the economic dictator, Marshal Goering, had to appoint special Reich Commissars in an attempt to enforce co-ordination among the manifold State authorities. According to an official statement, the functions of these new Commissars are as follows:

"He deals with factory regulations and technical problems, the process of work and its regulation, the organized employment of human beings and the retraining tasks, as well as with the distribution of materials, the flow of investments, the control of the capital market, the correct division between State finance and private financing, the elimination of superfluous offices and unnecessary regimentation, the establishment of sound relations between production of capital goods and consumers' goods, and the necessary participation of exportation." [3]

The result of the appointment of the new commissars has been a general poisoning of the atmosphere, since criticism and differences of opinion fester beneath the surface instead of being expressed openly. Antagonistic groups are neither reconciled nor satisfied.

Such commissars were appointed for the building, automobile, machine-tool, and power industries.

These new supercommissars receive direct from Goering their orders as to the tasks of the particular industry which they control. To carry them out they must disregard the interests of particular groups and the decisions of minor Party leaders. But for the manufacturer, the result of this reform is: more decrees and instructions and more uncertainty as to what is allowed or forbidden.

Mention must be made of still another bureaucratic machine, the "corporation," "group," or "estate organization." These had lain dormant but have now been revived in order to facilitate collaboration between the bureaucrats and the businessmen.

Neither the "group organizations" in Germany nor the "corporations" in Italy have developed according to official theories. After the solemn introduction of "corporations" at the Congress of Corporations in Rome, in 1929, corporations either did not exist or were unimportant for several years. In Germany, manufacturers and small producers thought that the "group organization" (or "estate") might be used to build up an entrepreneurial system of self-administration. They expected to control their "group organizations" and they thought that these organizations would safeguard their specific interests, as the former trade associations had done. They were disappointed. The application of the principle of "authoritarian leadership" in these "group organizations" transformed them into tools of the Party bureaucracy, although in some groups—especially those of big industrialists—the members still exerted a certain influence upon their leaders.

During the first period of existence of the "corporate" or "group" organizations, they were mainly concerned with collecting data, etc., for a wartime economy having no practical influence on the existing economy. However, the situation has changed, as a result of unexpected trends which have upset the original national schemes for economic State interference. "Group" organizations began to function as important links between the State and private enterprise, although they were not intended to function in such a way in a peacetime economy.

The group or corporate organizations have become the go-betweens of private enterprise and the State organizations which distribute raw materials, decide price policies, etc. The manager of a factory who wants to protest against curtailment of his allotment of raw materials, or who wants to obtain a permit for a price increase, acts wisely in not going directly to the proper State office, but in going first to the leader of his group organization, from whom he demands a certificate backing the firm's request and certifying that it should be granted in the interest of military preparations or in the interest of the Party.

The secretariats of these group organizations have also become a kind of legal information office. This is of great importance, especially for small manufacturers who cannot maintain a legal department of their own to study all decrees and the legal aspect of business affairs. Each business move has become very complicated and is full of legal traps which the average businessman cannot determine because there are so many new decrees. The group organization has a large legal department and can advise a manufacturer as to what he is allowed to do and what is illegal or inadvisable.

This development has turned the leaders of the group organizations into important personalities who are held in high respect by the manufacturer, especially by small and medium-sized industrialists who are much more dependent on their "group leader" than is a big concern or trust.

The group leader today is a contact man between firms

of a given trade and the State authorities. He is no longer the mere representative of one specific trade; he is appointed by the State and has to act according to Government instructions. His task as a Party member and State representative is to maintain "national discipline" among the businessmen of his group—in addition to collecting data, questionnaires, etc., about technical conditions, raw material demands, productive possibilities of all group enterprises and statistics.

The group leader is "authoritarian," appointed by the State, yet he is supposed to let the membership vote each year as to whether they want him to continue as their group leader. This vote is merely a test of the sentiment of the members; the State does not necessarily comply with the result of the vote.

Such a leader is often in a difficult position. On one hand he is the representative of the State, watching the individual entrepreneur for any lapse in fulfilling his "national duties"; on the other hand, he must be willing to sponsor or advocate the special interests of his group in so far as they do not conflict with the policies of higher authorities. Generally a group leader will at least try to demonstrate his good will, aiding group interests, as well as exercising his authoritarian power against firms which behave too independently or do not conform to Party interests.

*Chapter VIII*

# *THE "FACTORY LEADER" AND HIS FOLLOWERS*

"I urgently need some mechanics, but I am not allowed to engage anyone unless he can show me his 'labor book' and a permit from the Labor Exchange to change his job."

IN ONE of the uncensored letters a German industrialist wrote to a friend of his, he described industrial labor relations in Germany today. His views are commonly held by many other German industrialists.

My dear Mr. . . .

I really wonder why the Nazis have not succeeded in winning over the workers. After all, there are more jobs than workers now and we find it very difficult to find the workers we need. In general, we have to be more polite now than formerly to our workers.

This is especially true of office workers, whose position both economically and insofar as prestige is concerned has improved. These workers now have an opportunity to make occasional trips to the seaside in conformity with the "Strength through Joy" movement. Sometimes they accompany a member of the management when they go on these trips. There is always plenty of beer, and in general the outings are well organized.

In our factory, we are on excellent terms with the "confidential man" [*Vertrauensrat*]. He has a job with good pay and little work, and with him we can discuss in complete confidence all the difficulties we may have with our workers. Sometimes the Party instructs him to make certain demands "against the firm," demands that are designed largely to bolster the prestige of the Party. He comes to us and together we discuss the best way of handling this demand.

The workers celebrate the new Nazi festivals, and on their "community evenings" get all they want to drink. Yet they do not believe in the stability of the regime, and they oppose going to war. They often talk about the impending collapse of the regime.

I spoke to one of our chauffeurs, for example. He has quite a good income and should have no cause for complaint. When I talked with him, he must have believed that I was a 100 per cent Nazi. Yet he was not afraid to say quite openly:

"Hitler was lucky that war did not break out when he took Czecho-Slovakia." I answered: "But militarily we are very strong."

"Wait and see . . . when we [the workers] get arms in our hands, many things might happen . . . Everybody is dissatisfied and grumbles. I am not surprised that there is so much grumbling."

"But don't forget Ostmark [former Austria] and the new protectorate of Bohemia. After all, these are real successes," I replied.

"These conquests will not help us either. These countries are industrial countries, too, and nobody knows at present what we still have to pay for those conquests."

I became a little ironical and said:

"Well, we won quite a lot, in particular supplies of arms and of workers. Of course, these workers were formerly better fed and got higher wages. But as recompense, we have given them the new National conception: 'communal welfare precedes individual welfare' [*Gemeinnutz geht vor Eigennutz*]. What I would like to know is: do all the workers in my factory think as you do?"

"No, not in our shop. There are still at least 25 per cent Nazis."

You should know that we engage a relatively large number of office workers, and you find more Nazis among these groups than among factory workers. Wages have not been changed, but prices have gone up considerably. Cheap goods tend increasingly to disappear from the market. The government has a name for this—"steering of consumption" [*Verbrauchslenkung*].

Recently I gave a job to a worker who came from a small provincial town. He was a 150 per cent Nazi when he arrived. But he rapidly conformed. Shortly thereafter I asked him what had made the greatest impression on him since his arrival. He said: "I was amazed to hear so much grumbling, and I was also amazed that I didn't find one single informer. One evening I was drinking beer with some fellow workers. One of them who had drunk a little too much shouted: 'Hitler should be choked!' A policeman was standing near the bar drinking beer, too. But he looked the other way, pretending not to hear."

The new gigantic and luxurious buildings of the Party, in particular those belonging to Goering and to Hitler, are really provocative for the people. My general impression: only a relatively small number of fanatics and very young people, and perhaps also a certain percentage of office workers, really believe in the stability of the regime.

At the beginning of this year I was conscripted to a regiment in order to refresh my military knowledge. I lost some of the illusions I had had about the efficiency of our anti-air raid measures. The military machine appears to be excellent. Anti-air raid guns can shoot with accuracy at great distances. But after a short while (I think after half an hour) the instruments which are to spot the enemy's planes no longer function with accuracy. Something goes wrong. I heard about similar experiences with anti-air raid cannons in foreign armies.

The next war will be decided by the relative industrial capacity of the contestants and by their relative command of raw materials. I agree with what I heard from high army officers: "Does Hitler really think he can risk a war with the materials we have at our disposal?" Don't believe everything you hear about the effectiveness of the German Army. When I had finished my military service (two months), our major told me: "We have to appeal to the soldiers to be very careful with the only uniform we can give them. In 1914 every soldier had two uniforms, and three others were in reserve. Today, there is only one uniform for each soldier."

Workers grumble a great deal about the time they have to spend in the Army (two years) and in the labor service (one year). I don't dare to think how another war will end for us.

All the best,

*Signature*

The totalitarian State seems to hold out the promise of a paradise to the industrialist who hates the interference of trade unions in his business. Yet capitalists who are fully satisfied with the social peace which fascism provides for them are rare in Germany. The real picture of labor relations does not conform either to that painted by Nazi propagandists nor to that imagined by those who see only the destruction of the labor movement.

The amazing experiences of a Berlin industrialist illustrate the new position of the "boss" under fascism.

Herr A.Z. is an extremely efficient and skillful executive. He was one of the managers of the I.G. Farbenindustrie A. G. (Germany's largest chemical trust) and could have had a lifetime position with it. He was esteemed because he never indulged in superfluous talk and his instructions were given without any unnecessary show of authority; instead, he impressed his subordinates with the correctness and objectivity of his decisions.

When a certain Berlin concern got into financial difficulties, Herr A.Z. was asked to become chairman of its board of directors. Having had dealings with the firm as representative of the chemical trust, Herr A.Z. had so impressed the firm's board members that they regarded him as the one man who could save the business from bankruptcy.

Success meant brilliant possibilities for advancement; failure, the end of his career. Herr A.Z. took the chance. Within a short time he had reorganized the firm, closed one plant which was unprofitable and modernized another.

But real success depended largely on the firm's highly skilled workers who were well-organized in a trade union and who refused to sanction the dismissal of any fellow worker. Herr A.Z. succeeded in doing what all the other board members had regarded as impossible. He came to an understanding with Herr R., the trade-union secretary. As time went on, Herr R. had many opportunities of meeting Herr A. Z. They often clashed over matters of labor policy, but they grew to respect each other's frankness and ideas.

At the time Hitler came to power, the enterprise was on firm financial ground once more and for the first time was showing a profit. During the first year of the new regime nothing changed, except that a few highly skilled workers disappeared—and also Herr R., the trade-union secretary. Some unemployed S.A. men had to be given jobs, which increased expenses and decreased efficiency. Yet this was a minor change. Herr A. Z. remained the "boss." He was a conservative rather than a Nazi, although he was quite willing to accept the new regime as an improvement in comparison with the former liberal or radical governments. He felt that under the old regime Germany could never have prospered again and he welcomed the re-establishment of the German Reich as a world power.

However, this did not prevent him from gradually becoming more and more dissatisfied. He received orders to supply certain munitions factories, but difficulties in obtaining raw materials compelled him to deal with dozens of bureaucrats and State institutions. Official demands overwhelmed him. He had to establish a new department in order to deal with them. When, in spite of all his efforts, he was unable to fulfill his contract, a representative of the Four-Year Plan Commission appeared. This representative was followed by an army officer, who took full charge of the plant. The latter received the highest salary of any director or employee. He had access to all correspondence; Herr A. Z. had to ask his permission before making any important decisions, although it was well known that the army officer knew practically nothing of business management. Knowing that insurmountable obstacles and fruitless disputes would result if he tried to increase efficiency, Herr A. Z. naturally lost interest in making the attempt. Difficulties increased and the bureaucracy grew. Party representatives, who interfered with his management, assumed more and more authority. Never a talkative man, Herr A. Z. now lapsed into complete silence.

When the Nazis came to power, Herr R., the former trade-union secretary, had gone to live as an émigré in a small town in a neighboring country. By accident, Herr

A. Z. learned from a friend, who knew a member of the Gestapo, the whereabouts of the former trade-union secretary. One Sunday morning, some six years later, Herr R. was surprised by a visit from Herr A. Z., who had come from Germany over the week end for the specific purpose of seeing him. He had six hours before the train which he must take back to Germany would leave. During the entire time, Herr A. Z. talked, almost without interruption, as if he had to make up for five years of silence. The burden of his conversation went something like this:

"I must talk once more to someone whom I can esteem as a person and to whom I can speak frankly. I cannot stand it any more, always keeping silent when young Party men who are completely ignorant interfere with my management and issue instructions which I must follow without comment.

"Yes, I am the 'leader' in my factory; my workers are my 'followers.' But I am no longer a manager. You will remember that we fought over the right to hire and fire workers. In principle I stuck to the rule that if a worker was efficient and knew his job he had a permanent position in my factory. Certainly I never asked what party he belonged to; that was his business. Today I cannot apply this rule.

"There are no longer factory councils elected by the workers, or trade-union secretaries who can interfere. I have to appoint my own 'Confidential Board.' The idea is not so bad, but I would like to be able to appoint workers who can influence their colleagues and with whom I can talk frankly, as I did with you. Unfortunately, all the workers who are efficient and who can readily influence their fellow workers are either former trade-unionists or otherwise not in good standing with the Party people.

"The secretary of the Party cell is a former clerk in my office. It was he who told me what men were 'reliable' from the Party point of view. These people were to become my 'Confidential Board.' Mostly they were workers with no special skill or ability to recommend them. Of course they had Party cards. I tried to appoint one other man. The Party secretary told me that he was a former socialist and made me understand that such an appointment would be regarded as secret support of 'Marxist elements.' He suggested that I might be on better terms with the Labor Front secretary if I appointed someone they trusted. Naturally, there was nothing for me to do except follow this advice. These Party people are very unpopular; they are feared as spies, and the workers feel that they are responsible for the dismissal of former trade-unionists.

"After our army marched into Prague, a member of the Hitler Youth, whom I employed as an apprentice, came to me and denounced several workers. He had listened to a conversation in which one of the workers had declared, 'The Czechs will never become German. Hitler has broken his word and it can't come to a good end.' The other workers had agreed. I did not transmit the denunciation because I did not want to lose my best workers, but the boy spoke to a leader of his Youth League about the incident and he informed the Gestapo. A whole detachment arrived at the factory. The workers said that they remembered nothing of the matter. Finally the worker who had been denounced for making the remark was arrested. Obviously many workers must have thought that I was the one who had informed the Gestapo and I did not dare tell them the truth.

"Once I was told that I was not fulfilling my duty to the Party. I was not employing enough 'old Party members.' So they sent me twenty-five 'old Party members' and S.A. men. Without exception they had had no real training and were inefficient, but I was simply forced to take them. Accidentally one of them overheard me grumbling about some new bureaucratic regulation and he immediately denounced me to the Party and to the Labor Front office. Another Party member came and told me about it and warned me that I had better be careful in the future. So it has got to the point where I cannot talk even in my own factory. Incidentally, he added that the Party secretary did not really believe I was devoted to the Fuehrer. It seems that the Party secretary once heard me answer a 'Good morning' with 'Good morning' instead of emphatically replying 'Heil Hitler.'

"Something had to be done, so I tried to compromise. The Party members who were on my 'Confidential Board' were given easy jobs with good pay. After that they agreed that I could dismiss some S.A. men who had ruined valuable machinery because they neither knew nor cared about learning the work.

"However, things are still bad. I cannot employ the workers I want. There are no trade-union secretaries insisting that I employ only union members, but the present situation is worse. Now I urgently need some mechanics, but I am not allowed to engage anyone unless he can show me his 'labor book' and a permit from the Labor Exchange to change his job. If I were to offer a worker a job at a higher wage, just because I regarded him as competent, I hate to think of the trouble I would have and the fines I would have to pay.

"On the other hand, when I need new workers and apply for them, the Labor Exchange is always sending me workers wanting jobs, all of them either S.A. men or Party members. I am really put to it to invent excuses for not hiring them. Naturally, I suspect them of being in the Party just because they are inefficient and need Party backing in order to make a living. They themselves know this, so, if I give them jobs, they will spend a great deal of their time making themselves indispensable to the Party secretary by sending him reports on gossip and grumblers. One of them is enough to poison the entire atmosphere in the factory. And I should have to be more careful than ever so that I won't be denounced for an incautious remark.

"Although I am the 'leader,' I cannot decide what is allowed or forbidden in my own factory. Recently the Labor Trustees advised me to introduce 'factory regulations' corresponding to the 'model rules' now in force in the airplane factory at Dessau, which declare:

" 'Applicants are employed only if they are suitable for the work, irreproachable, racially sound, of Aryan origin, German and members of the Labor Front. . . . Reasons for immediate dismissal are . . . any obvious offense against the National-Socialist movement and its conceptions. . . . It is not permissible and a defamation of the work community to discuss matters which might damage the work community with outsiders.'

"If I were to put such regulations into effect in my factory, it would mean that I would have to fire all my best workers. So I didn't change my 'factory instructions.' Other factory leaders also ignored the reforms suggested by the Labor Front. Thereupon the Labor Trustee sent us a circular:

" 'The general picture of factory regulations is not pleasant; it reveals little initiative, much copying of what someone else is doing, much formality, too much similarity with previous work regulations, nice phrases on occasion, but little real National-Socialist spirit within the work community.'

"In August, 1938, before the 'Munich crisis,' the Labor Exchange informed me that 10 per cent of my workers must be released for work on the fortifications in western Germany. Simultaneously I got urgent requests from the Junkers aircraft people at Dessau and from various military authorities that the delivery of articles previously ordered must be made without any further delay. The workers resented the idea of having to work on the fortifications and I was opposed to it, too, because I could not replace them. Consequently I did what most businessmen do today. I paid no attention to the communication from the Labor Exchange. Suddenly a delegation from the Labor Exchange appeared, accompanied by an army officer. These people ordered me to take them through the factory. It was the first time they had seen my factory, but they picked out a number of workers and said to me: 'Prepare their papers. They will leave for western Germany tomorrow morning.' None of them even thought to ask me whether I could spare these workers and what effect it would have on the work.

"Recently I was delayed in filling urgent army orders because I did not have enough mechanics. I was afraid to apply at the Labor Exchange. Anyway, there is such a scarcity of skilled workers that I would probably have had to wait at least a year before I could obtain any. I explained the situation to the army representative in the factory when he insisted that I speed up production. So he arranged that I should get some mechanics who are held as political prisoners by the Gestapo. Every morning a patrol wagon arrives with twenty prisoner-mechanics. They work in a special place in the factory under the guard of S.S. men. In the evening they are taken back to prison. Do you think that this situation helps to create the right atmosphere in a 'work community'?

"A year or so ago I was ordered to spend social evenings with my 'followers' and to celebrate with them by providing free beer and sausages. The free beer and sausages were welcome enough, but the 'work community' parties have not been successful. Drunken workers, or workers who pretended drunkenness, would start a fight with some unpopular Nazis. One worker, who had had somewhat more than one glass of beer, told me that beer parties were a poor substitute for a wage increase. Fortunately the whole idea of such compulsory beer parties has been dropped.

"The Labor Front secretary tries to increase his popularity, and I have to pay for it. Last year he compelled me to spend over a hundred thousand marks for a new lunchroom in our factory. This year he wants me to build a new gymnasium and athletic field which will cost about 120,000 marks. Now, I have nothing against sports. But, as a matter of fact, the workers nowadays don't care much for sports or things of that kind. They work ten, eleven or twelve hours daily—at least sixty hours a week—and they complain that they never get enough rest. More often than not they take a nap during their lunch hour. Really, no worker is interested in the gymnasium and athletic field. Yet I shall have to build it in order to satisfy the Labor Front secretary.

"I am opposed to mass meetings artificially staged to show how harmonious things are in the 'work community.' Neither do I care for all the demonstrations my workers and I must attend, where we must march for hours, shouting 'Heil Hitler.' I was an officer in the German Army during the World War, and I am in favor of discipline, efficiency and social distinctions. After all, I am supposed to be the 'factory leader.' But at such a demonstration I am likely to be ordered to shout and sing by some Party member who doesn't know the meaning of decent work. I must behave as though I were his orderly. Next morning, however, I am again supposed to be an 'authoritarian leader.'

"Most of the workers try to avoid going to these demonstrations and quite often they are successful. This is distinctly embarrassing for me because I have to appear as the 'leader' of a 'work community' with only a small fraction of my 'followers' present. The next day work will be slowed down and the workers will complain that they are still tired from all the marching the day before and that they have not had enough sleep.

"A couple of months ago work in one of my key departments suddenly slowed up and the filling of urgent orders for the Junkers plant at Dessau became impossible. I got into considerable trouble trying to settle this affair. Obviously there was some resentment among the workers over the wages they were receiving. Not long before higher wages had been granted in a nearby factory, so I was told. I consulted the 'Confidential Board,' but their only suggestion was to call in the Labor

Trustee. Naturally, I didn't want to do that. From experience, I knew that his interference would do nothing to improve the situation. He would merely come and make a speech to the workers, and if they were not sufficiently 'convinced' by his words, he would send for the Gestapo. And in any case he would insist on my giving the names of the 'hostile elements' responsible for the trouble. Then I would be faced with another worry—are my most efficient workers going to be arrested? A few weeks later I might very well have the same trouble all over again. After all, the work is complicated and the slightest misstep may ruin valuable machinery. I certainly can't take that risk. Consequently, I tried to have a private talk with one of the workers in the department where the work had slowed down, so that we could arrive at some sort of understanding. I could tell that he was annoyed, because he told me I ought to know that he could not act as spokesman for his fellow workers and that I should consult my 'Confidential Board.' Obviously he did not trust me, and I could not make it clear to him that I wanted a frank talk with him about the demands of the workers.

"Sometimes I am really afraid of what might happen if new rush orders should arrive. My 'followers' would be forced to work faster and it would really be disastrous if this should happen to coincide with a decline in their living conditions. Everyone knows about things that have happened in other factories. In the Siemens glass factory at Dresden, sixteen workers recently shut down four furnaces. Similar incidents occurred in two large print shops in Leipzig, in the Linke Hofmann Works at Breslau and in a Silesian steel mill. I have often heard that foremen in the coal mines, attempting to execute an order to speed up production, have had fatal accidents underground. In the M.A.N. Works [one of the leading machine-tool plants in Bavaria], an engineer who was very unpopular with the workers charged a metal turner with unsatisfactory work. The latter defended himself against the charge and the engineer threatened to fire him and make it impossible for him to find another job. He thereupon hit the engineer with an iron bar, injuring him seriously. During the fight, none of the bystanders came to the aid of the engineer.

"Really, I would prefer to grant a wage increase—certainly rather than get into such difficulties. After all, the cost of living has gone up. And besides, it does not matter. I need efficient workers and can't keep them in the long run unless I make some concessions. In all probability I could get higher prices from the Army authorities if I had to pay higher wages. Once I tried to attract efficient workmen by offering them higher wages. The Labor Trustee sent me a threatening letter which read:

> Without my special permission it is forbidden to pay wages to newly-employed followers which are higher than wage rates for other workers doing similar work . . . The reason for this decision is that it is impossible to agree on higher wages (and salaries) with newly employed workers . . .

"I had to reduce the wages again. The following month there was another collection for the Winter Help. The workers refused to give an hour's pay to the fund and most of them contributed only a few pfennigs. I did not dare to send in such a small amount to the authorities on whose recommendations I depend in order to obtain State orders or raw materials. Obviously I cannot afford to be regarded as the 'leader' of workers who are not enthusiastic about National Socialism. Consequently, I myself made the greater part of the contribution, reporting to the authorities and to the Labor Front that every worker had given a full hour's wage.

"As difficulties mount, the activities and organizations of the Labor Front multiply. In every German factory there are Labor Front secretaries, committees, and auxiliaries, sections of a huge, top-heavy, bureaucratic machine. We, the factory leaders, are responsible for the following committees, deputies, etc:

"The Council of Trusted Men, appointed by the factory leader; the National-Socialist Party cell with a secretary and a representative in each department; a Hitler Youth committee; special boards for National-Socialist education, for sports, women, 'Strength through Joy' activities, and professional training; a 'work guard' which is armed for emergency situations; and several other committees. The Labor Front had instructed me to see that all the young men starting work join a special 'work guard.' A great many refused to do so, claiming that they could not afford seventy-eight marks for the uniform. The same thing happened in other factories. Nothing is heard any more about the 'work guard.'

"Don't think that the Labor Front and the 'work community' are my main worries. The greater part of the week I don't see my factory at all. All this time I spend in visiting dozens of government commissions and offices in order to get the raw materials I need. Then there are various tax problems to settle and I must have continual conferences and negotiations with the Price Commissar. Besides which, I have considerable traveling to do; in fact, it sometimes seems as if I do nothing but that, and everywhere I go there are more leaders, Party secretaries and commissars to see. All of this just to settle day-to-day problems.

"Not long ago the Labor Trustee warned me that I did not spend enough time in 'work community' meetings and that evidently I didn't really care for National-Socialist principles since I never spent any time teaching them to my workers. There have been cases where managers were removed by the Party or Labor Trustees and replaced by 'commissars.' At present I am considering whether I should appoint a 'representative' as factory 'leader.' He could deal with the Labor Front and Party secretaries. But I still hesitate. I do not know anybody whom I would trust completely . . ."

The final words of Herr A. Z. were:

"I do not know what will happen. But things cannot come to a good end."

The Nazis could never duplicate the labor policy of Mussolini during the early period of his regime. At that time, fascist labor policy did two things: first, it deprived the worker of his means of self-defense, and then it offered him fascist labor organizations as a weapon against excessive exploitation. But Mussolini later had to follow the example of Hitler's labor policy—against any kind of trade-union. The Nazi Labor Front was never able to play the role of self-appointed mediator between workers and manufacturers. The bureaucracy would have preferred to blame private manufacturers for the excessively bad labor and wage conditions and to preserve its role of a neutral third party. But the system needs increased production so badly and has made economic conditions so much worse that the State itself has to urge manufacturers to speed up production and to economize on wage expenditure.

Few German manufacturers have much respect for the Labor Front bureaucracy and its work. Like their workers, they are compelled to make large contributions to the Labor Front and its auxiliary organizations. They feel that this money is wasted. Neither the workers nor their employers dare protest, however. A strange situation has arisen in which the majority of the workers as well as many, if not most, employers regard the Labor Front as a parasitic bureaucracy. It must be endured silently because it is backed by the Nazi party and its orders reinforced by the Secret State Police. Certainly the Labor Front has failed in its promise to create an ideal "work community" of social peace and happy collaboration among all classes.

The factory leader is compelled to be an agent and propagandist of the Party in his own factory. The State makes it a rule that those factory leaders who excel in work for the Party shall be privileged in the distribution of State orders and subsidies. Therefore many factory leaders regard it as good business policy to obtain Party badges as a means of getting good results from Party organizations.

The Party organizes yearly "efficiency competitions" in order to select the best factories. Some of the official rules of this "efficiency competition" are:

"A positive attitude toward the National-Socialist movement . . . will be demonstrated by promoting the aims of the N.S.D.A.P., of its sections and subsidiary organizations, propaganda and education work. . . .

Therefore it must be asked: 'Does the factory leader participate in collective educational work?' 'Does he make participation of his followers easy by compensating them for wage losses [on account of Party work], payment of fares [to Party meetings] and similar measures?' The factory which wants the prize has to prove by its unfailing support of National Socialism that it has identified itself with the aims of the Fuehrer and his movement. . ."

The position of the manager or "factory leader" is contradictory in theory and in practice. On one hand, he has more authority than before within his factory; he can rule his business by issuing orders which must be obeyed by all his "followers." On the other hand, he himself is only an infinitesimal part of a gigantic State and military machine. Party and military authorities will interfere with his management, while at the same time making him responsible for difficulties in fulfilling his production program and for dealing with labor troubles, should they arise. He may even be declared unfit for "leadership" if he is not on good terms with Party authorities.

"The manager has been promoted . . . to the rank of leader by the racial State order which has equipped him with a power previously attributed only to State institutions. . . . The State leadership leaves it to the leader of the factory to establish discipline among the workers . . . He is no longer merely the business leader and responsible for the technical process of production, but is, to a great extent, the representative of the State." [1]

"The manager practices his functions primarily as a representative of the State, only secondarily for his own sake." [2]

In principle, Party authorities, especially those in the Labor Front, can insist on removing a manager because he does not have a suitable "leader personality"; they may replace him by a "reliable" Party man. In practice, this right of the Party is not applied against factory leaders who are in good standing with Party authorities and who are protected by supreme Party leaders in case of a conflict with minor Party people.

The contradictory position of the factory leader is aggravated by circumstances which are a result of State policies, but it remains the private affair of the factory leader to deal with them and manage his work in spite of an insufficient supply of skilled labor, dissatisfaction of the workers with rising prices and general conditions, numerous anti-air raid exercises and Party or Labor Front activities which interfere with work. Under such conditions, the manager will try to deal with his management difficulties by establishing strict military discipline. But in that case, he will need the closest collaboration with Party and Labor Front authorities. He will become more dependent on their support and interference, the more authoritarian his behavior toward his workers. If, on the other hand, he tries to create a better atmosphere among his workers and improve relations with them, he will have to grant wage increases which are forbidden, and be on good terms with workers who are trusted by their fellow workers and who are not Nazis. This is still more dangerous, for he might easily be accused of sheltering anti-Nazi elements and might be made responsible for any trouble in his factory or for a stoppage of production.

Skilled workers in ammunition factories are relatively

well paid, but on one hand the buying power of money has considerably decreased as a result of price increases and the scarcity of cheap articles, and, on the other, they must work at terrific speed at least ten hours a day, and often much longer, so that they have neither time nor energy to participate in social life.

In modern industry, especially where technical skill is necessary, excessive length of working hours easily results in a decline in the quality of work and great waste of materials. Many factory leaders are already complaining that it does not pay to let the workers work more than eight hours a day. It is much more profitable to work with fresh labor forces than with workers who are worn out by overtime. The result is a considerable rise of accidents and of waste of materials.

Even the army opposed excessive overtime for workers who, it realized, were rapidly becoming exhausted and even ill. The army feared that they would not be able to man the complicated engines of war when the time came.

At the end of January, 1939, General Thomas made a speech to the N.S.D.A.P.'s Commission for Economic Policy in which he said that the sixty-hour week would lead, in the long run, to reduced production and that the eight-hour day, according to extensive scientific investigations, is the optimum working day. These members, who are most influential in formulating the economic policies of the Third Reich, had to learn this from a general in the army.

Even the *Deutsche Wirtschaftszeitung,* an organ of German business interests, wrote:

"It is obvious that working time can no longer be

increased to any extent without exhausting the labor potentialities of German workers. In addition, there is the danger of a decline in the quality of the work." [3]

The shortage of workers in Germany seems to be an achievement often admired in countries suffering from extensive unemployment. Shortage of labor is a phenomenon well known in wartime. The Third Reich is not yet engaged in war, but its system includes many features of a wartime economy. This also applies to the labor situation.

Modern industry needs labor discipline. Such discipline may be established by voluntary agreement, through workers' trade-unions, or by compulsion. The Nazis attempted to create a new scheme of labor discipline by destroying trade-unions and substituting the Labor Front, a gigantic propaganda machine promising everything to all classes in the "work community." This scheme could have been successful only if these promises had been fulfilled.

Under liberal capitalism the private owner of a factory can establish his authority over his workers either by voluntary agreement with the trade-unions, or by a system of strict supervision and enforced discipline. When State authorities interfere they generally appear as a "third party." Under a fascist system, labor discipline and "social peace" in industry cannot be maintained without the eternal, overt interference of State authorities, to such an extent that they often supersede the manager. He himself is "authoritarian," but he is rarely master in his own house. Increased taxation, scarcity of raw materials, and the use of expensive and inferior substitutes have added greatly to business expenses, especially in view of the fact that price increases are forbidden. Consequently many industrialists, especially in industries which profit less than others from the armament boom, seek to reduce production costs by wage cuts and the speed-up. Thus they become increasingly dependent on assistance from the Labor Front and the Gestapo. In such factories an atmosphere is created which makes the factory leader continually fear that labor troubles and sabotage will occur at the exact time when labor peace is most urgently needed.

The old type of conservative employer who tried to establish some kind of patriarchal relations with his workers and who could afford to pay a relatively high wage to those workers he needed most, cannot survive under fascism.

A new type of fascist entrepreneur is emerging and prospering—the capitalist who is a trusted Party member. He contributes generously to Party funds, carries out orders faithfully, and has an increased authority which his American or British colleague might envy. He has more power than the old German businessmen and bankers ever enjoyed. He is not the rather liberal-minded, cultured businessman who believed in fair treatment for his employees or in paternalism, nor is he the conservative capitalist accustomed to give, not take, orders in the conduct of his business. He is more nearly like the old Prussian official, a man who likes to be part of a military, authoritarian regime, an officer who can take, and give, orders.

"The soldier at the front has grown in stature as compared with the entrepreneur type. . . . The entrepreneur has become small, while simultaneously the soldier has become big." [4]

Some of the big corporations prefer to hire as managers or factory leaders men who were army officers, accustomed to manage men in the military manner. The military managers enjoy greater authority in relation to the Labor Front bureaucracy and cannot be accused of failing to behave as "leaders" should. But militarization of factories does not improve labor relations.

## Chapter IX

# INDUSTRIAL INVESTMENT POLICIES

"Not even from Krupp would Goering take 'no' for an answer."

BACKED by the General Staff of the army, Nazi bureaucrats have been able to embark upon schemes which compel the most powerful leaders of business and finance to undertake projects which they consider both risky and unprofitable. The building-up of German war economy takes precedence over everything, including the opinions of private capitalists and their scientific research staffs. The hasty preparation for war, made necessary by the foreign policy of the fascist powers, has left no time for their leaders to consider what might happen in the more distant future; they have had to prepare for possible immediate emergencies. The viewpoint of private investors and industrialists who think of the ultimate safety and soundness of investments has been disregarded.

This is particularly true of the big industrialists who earned huge profits from the armament boom and who have large amounts of capital to invest. Their liquid funds do not escape the attention of State commissars, who are searching for means to finance new State-sponsored plants.

To illustrate the point, let us consider the case of Herr Krupp von Bohlen und Halbach, head of the

Krupp concern, Europe's largest armament works. The Krupp properties are as much a family affair as the Ford Motor Company. The Krupp family was, and still is, the leader of Germany's industrial aristocracy. The elder Krupp was a personal friend of the Kaiser. His heir, Krupp von Bohlen und Halbach, enjoyed undiminished respect under the Weimar Republic. The Fuehrer, in turn, paid his respects to Krupp soon after coming to power. On the eve of the famous purge in June, 1934, before ordering the execution of his own closest friends, Hitler consulted Krupp von Bohlen und Halbach at Villa Huegel, the latter's family residence near Essen.

Krupp's firm profited more from the armament boom than any other industrial enterprise in Germany. Yet even Herr Krupp is grumbling because he is no longer the absolute master he used to be.

This is reflected in the investment policies which the Krupp concern pursues—or, rather, is compelled to pursue. In common with all big industrial concerns in Germany, Krupp wants to make financial preparations for the time when the armament boom will slow down and when it may once more be difficult to find enough profitable work for his plants. He therefore sought to put aside reserves against an uncertain future and to avoid risky investments. But here he ran counter to the policies of the regime. In such a clash between the totalitarian State and private business, Krupp was bound to lose, in spite of his name and political connections.

In 1936 Goering's Four-Year Plan Commission intimated to the Krupp concern that it was planned to erect a new plant for large-scale production of synthetic rubber, or "Buna," extracted largely from coal and lime. The Commission further suggested that Krupp might finance this project out of his enormous armament profits, adding it to the manifold interests of his concern. After having spent considerable time in investigating the probable costs of production and the commercial possibilities of synthetic rubber, the research department of the Krupp concern answered the Government's proposal with an emphatic refusal.

But not even from Krupp would Goering take no for an answer. A few weeks after its negative reply, the Krupp firm was summarily informed that, on a given date, a meeting would be held of the founders of a new company—Buna G.m.b.H. At the meeting arrangements would be made for the financing of a plant to produce Buna. The Krupp concern was directed to send a representative with authority to assume a share in financing the project. There was no room for argument as to the merits of the idea, certainly none for rejection of it. The matter had been decided in Goering's office, and Krupp was left only the choice of a representative. At his leisure he might calculate to what extent his liquid assets would be reduced after his firm had subscribed its share to the synthetic rubber project.

Even Krupp can no longer insist on his formerly unchallenged independence when the all-powerful Party "requests" sacrifices in the "interests of the community." He cannot fight singlehanded against the ruling Party. It is necessary to understand this political background in order to appreciate the story of how Krupp came to the rescue of a bankrupt relative in Austria.

There is a branch of the Krupp family in Austria, owners of the Berndorfer Metallwarenfabrik Arthur

Krupp A.G., a large machine-tool plant. This enterprise did not prosper under the Austrian Republic, partly because of the general decline of Austrian industry and partly on account of the personality of the Austrian Krupp, who preferred the leisurely, extravagant life of the old aristocracy to that of an active businessman. While Austria was still independent, the Austrian Krupp had approached his German relative for financial assistance. After thorough investigation, Krupp turned down the request, believing neither in the ability of his Austrian relative nor in the wisdom of the investment. However, the owner of the Berndorf factory was no fool; before and during the days of Austria's "deliverance" he cultivated Nazi leaders at drinking parties. When Anschluss had become a fact, his bankrupt company was recommended as one deserving aid "in the national interest." The available subsidy funds proved insufficient, so the Party approached Krupp, suggesting that his family interests, as well as national interests, demanded the rescue of his relative. Krupp had to make the investment, whatever his misgivings.

Other private concerns and trusts had similar experiences. Among them was I. G. Farbenindustrie, which maintains a synthetic gasoline plant in Leuna, where new methods of producing gasoline from coal are tried under varying conditions, and large-scale experiments conducted, in a constant effort to find means of reducing production costs and of testing theory in practice. The chemical trust was reluctant to make further large investments in the production of synthetic gasoline before all the practical aspects had been thoroughly explored. They did not want to build new plants unless they could be sure that the new product would be able to compete successfully on the world market and would not have to rely permanently on State subsidies. According to reliable sources, this stage had not been reached when the State notified the chemical trust and all other owners of soft-coal mines in central Germany that they must finance the establishment of "Brabag," or Braunkohlen-Benzin A.G., with two large plants at Boehlen and Magdeburg, each with a capacity of 170,000 tons of synthetic gasoline yearly.

Nor were Fritz Thyssen and his Stahlverein, the largest steel trust in Europe, given any consideration when, in 1939, Goering established a new mining and steel concern and decided that important properties of the Stahlverein should be incorporated in this new enterprise, to be known as the Hermann Goering Reich Iron Works.

All private iron and steel concerns in the Reich had declined to finance new plants for extracting iron from low-grade domestic ore. Thereupon Herr Keppler, Hitler's former economic adviser and a personal antagonist of the former "financial wizard," Schacht, was placed in charge of the exploitation of Germany's mineral resources. He was full of wonderful schemes for opening up new sources for the raw materials so badly needed in Germany. Iron deposits in Franconia and Baden (particularly Salzgitter) had been neglected because the iron content of this ore was less than 25 per cent and smelting of ore with an iron content of less than 30 per cent has been regarded as uneconomical. The iron and steel companies were unanimous in advising the government "experts" that the costs of production would be prohibitive and that too great an investment would be required. Furthermore, this ore could not be used in existing German furnaces because of its excessively high content of silicic acid. If the same smelting process were to be used as for other ore, this would necessitate greatly increased consumption of coke, and expensive technical changes in the furnaces, with the result that costs of production would be considerably increased. Hence new furnaces would have to be constructed.

All this scientific advice was disregarded and Goering's office announced to the iron and steel masters that the Hermann Goering Reich Iron Works was to be founded. New furnaces were designed to cope with the low-grade ore. British and American experts were hired. Goering had enough foreign currency at his disposal to buy the experience and technical assistance of H. A. Brassert & Company of Chicago, which had subsidiaries in Europe. This American firm made available the best technique for smelting iron from low-grade ore. Mr. Brassert, the American expert, is an international figure, of German stock, born in England and naturalized in the United States. Most of his experience has been in the American steel industry.

The new iron and steel plants are being erected in great haste. The big industrialists who had provided Hitler with funds in the days when they thought that he would remain their willing puppet could not avoid contributing to the new project of which they disapproved. The State, however, generously arranged to supply the major portion of the necessary liquid capital.

The total capital is 400 million marks, of which 270 millions are represented by common stock, the majority of which is held by the State. A minority share of the common stock was presumably given to owners of mines taken over by the State. The remaining 130 million are preferred stock *without* voting rights. Of these, 10 million are allotted to (i.e. have to be subscribed by) the Reich's Group of German Artisans (on the theory that artisans such as plumbers, etc., are interested in an increased supply of iron and steel), and 95 million are allotted to the member firms of all industrial groups interested in the iron and steel supply. Each such firm has had to subscribe to 50 marks of these preferred shares for each worker employed by them as of July 31, 1938—that is, a firm employing 1,000 workmen must subscribe to 50,000 marks, etc. The remaining 25 million have been offered for public subscription.

The Alpine Montanwerke, Austria's most important iron and steel concern, was a subsidiary of the Stahlverein, which counted on enjoying a virtual monopoly in Austria after the Anschluss. But Party leaders and the War Economic Council demanded that new iron and steel mills be erected in Austria, where they would be less exposed to air raids from France than the steel trust's plants in the Ruhr district. The Stahlverein hesitated to expand its Austrian subsidiary beyond regional requirements, the more so as such a venture did not promise to be very successful financially, because of competitive disadvantages resulting from geographical conditions. What was the result of this hesitation? The State, through the Hermann Goering Reich Iron Works, simply assumed control of the Alpine Montanwerke and proceeded to establish a new production center in Linz on the Danube.

The construction of gigantic new foundries in Salzgitter and Linz (in former Austria) will greatly increase Germany's production of iron and steel. After the completion of the "greater production program" in 1942 or 1943, an estimated 21 million tons of domestic ore will yield approximately seven million tons of iron and steel. This will be a substantial addition to Germany's present supply of about 21 million tons of iron ore, imported primarily from Scandinavia, France and Spain.

The rise of German iron-ore production is quite impressive: from 6.37 million tons in 1929 and 2.59 million tons in 1933 to 7.57 million tons in 1937 and 11.15 million tons in 1938 (including the Saar district). In 1938, domestic iron-ore production surpassed imports of iron ore. This fact, however, is misleading. The quality of German iron ore has greatly declined, so that in 1938 the share of iron produced from German ores amounted to only 22 per cent of the total iron production. *Die Wirtschaftskurve* emphasized the difficulty of producing iron from German ore—not merely as a result of the low iron content, but also because of its chemical composition. "It is probable that at present crude iron and semimanufactured iron products can be bought at a price which is below costs of production—" despite the fact that German iron and steel prices are kept on a relatively high level by the German iron and steel syndicates. If consumption remains at the present rate, iron produced from domestic ore should constitute close to 60 per cent of total production in 1942-43, as against 19.0 per cent in 1937. If, however, the demand for iron should continue to expand, and imports should be allowed to continue at approximately the present levels, the share of production from domestic ore would increase to only about 45 per cent of the total. It is doubtful whether this goal will ever be reached.

A number of factories in Ostmark—formerly Austria—were incorporated into the Hermann Goering Reich

Iron Works. These factories—for the mass production of automobiles, machinery, freight cars, etc.—had been expropriated from "non-Aryans" and are of considerable military importance.

There are other enterprises where investments are too risky or undesirable for private capital. Consequently, State institutions, having large liquid funds at their disposal, helped to finance such undertakings. The projected plant for the mass production of a cheap "people's automobile" *(Volkswagen)* is such an undertaking. The idea of the new automobile plant is supposed to have originated with Adolf Hitler himself, who has a penchant for spectacular, monumental projects.

In 1935, at a time when butter and meat rations were at a low level, Hitler promised every citizen an automobile. He wanted a car cheaper than the Ford, a factory larger than Ford's Detroit plant or the Russian Gorki plant. The German automobile manufacturers —Opel, Daimler-Benz and others—were consulted and displayed no enthusiasm. They advised Hitler that there would be no market for such a car—the workers and middle classes could not afford to buy and maintain even the cheapest automobile. Gasoline in Germany is about five times the world market price. Repairs cannot be made without using scarce materials which cost several times more than they would on the world market. Therefore the maintenance of a car is three to four times more expensive than in the United States. The "people's automobile" will compete with the Opel and the German-built Ford cars. Thus the scarcity of raw materials and skilled labor will increase, while the new State-sponsored factory is privileged at the expense of the privately owned automobile factories.

Daimler-Benz A. G., one of the largest corporations in the automobile industry, stated in its annual report for 1938:

"Production in the automobile industry does not depend on the demands of the public. The limitations inherent in supplies of raw materials, spare parts and labor are decisive."

The objections of private manufacturers to the new automobile plant were overruled. The War Economic Council voted for the project, not merely to please the Fuehrer, but to increase Germany's capacity for the production of armored cars, trucks, etc.

An effort will be made to imitate Ford's mass production methods. Some technical details on the projected automobile may be of interest: the weight will be 650 kilograms (1,170 pounds); it is to be capable of carrying four to five passengers, and it will be equipped with a 24 h.p. motor; the consumption of gasoline is supposed to be six to seven litres ( a litre is approximately a quart) for each hundred kilometers (about 62½ miles). It is doubtful, however, whether the new car will be as good as it is promised, especially in view of the fact that it will have to be built largely with ersatz. Yet the new mass production automobile has a good chance of successful competition with other low-priced cars, especially those on the markets of southern and southeastern Europe.

The construction of the new factory was started in 1938 in Fallersleben, after the establishment in 1937 of the "Gesellschaft zur Foerderung des deutschen Volkswagens" (Society for the Promotion of the German People's Automobile), with a capital of 50 million marks. The capital is being raised partly by the Labor

Front and partly by individual weekly subscriptions of five marks as advance installments on a car. The Fuehrer's hope that hundreds of thousands would respond eagerly have not been realized. Boys and girls were therefore enlisted and entitled to sign the contracts providing for a monthly payment of five marks each. The car is to be delivered in four or five years, but only to those who have paid the installments without fail for about three years. No provision has been made for reimbursing those who will have paid a part or even the greater part of the installments but may have had to interrupt their payments because of the loss of their jobs or for other unforeseen reasons, although in a few exceptional cases eighty per cent of the money already paid may be returned. There are no definite arrangements as to the time of delivery. "The important question of the time of delivery has not yet been cleared up," said *Die Deutsche Volkswirtschaft* of August 3, 1938, in a semiofficial statement after the propaganda campaign for the purchase of these cars had been initiated.

The new car will be extremely cheap compared to other automobiles. It is to cost 990 marks (about $240) and is supposed to be delivered after 750 marks have been paid on account. Yet even this cheap price—especially considering the high costs of maintenance of an automobile—is beyond the means of both workers and the overwhelming majority of the middle classes. Strong pressure on the part of the Party, especially upon State employees, has succeeded in obtaining a considerable number of subscriptions. However, though it had been hoped to obtain half a million subscriptions, the total number received by February 17, 1939, amounted, according to an official statement, to only 170,000. This would mean a weekly payment of 850,000 marks, and more, because subscribers sometimes pledged themselves to pay at a higher rate.

Public opinion has been skeptical as to whether the cars would ever be delivered, either because the State would not fulfill its contract or because the buyers would be unable to complete their payments. Among the better paid bureaucrats and employees, however, the projected "people's automobile" has become popular.

This and other such projects of the Four-Year Plan Commission do not reveal the full scope of State interference in industrial investments. In many other industries, State and Army commissars have insisted upon rapid extension of plant capacity and increased production, the construction of dugouts as shelters in case of air raids, etc. At the insistence of the commissars, out-of-date machinery, discarded in order to reduce production costs, has been put back in operation in industries producing scarce products.

Because of work on the fortifications, demands for cement in western Germany have increased to such an extent that, according to 1938 plans, the cement industry, previously suffering from overexpansion, was to increase its production from eighteen to twenty-four million tons per year.

Private concerns are reluctant to enlarge their plants, merely to meet temporary demands for fortifications and other emergency needs. They have sought to avoid the heavy expenditure involved in building up an industrial reserve capacity needed only in the event of war.

The *Frankfurter Zeitung* of February 1, 1939, carried this concealed threat to any industrialist who might object to extension of plant capacity to meet the State's emergency demands:

"In several branches of industry, subject to emergency State orders, industrial firms have no choice but to adapt their productive capacity accordingly, unless they wish to run the risk that new independent factories—backed by authoritative State customers—will arise. They will become uncomfortable competitors when demand declines. If new factories must be erected for emergencies to meet the present increase in demand, it will mean that expenditures will be much greater in the long run. If the methods of planned economy are to be applied anywhere at all, they must be applied in this industry."

Many foreign observers, who do not know the inside picture, wonder why German industrialists should be dissatisfied notwithstanding increased production and greater profits. A special source of dissatisfaction springs directly from this increased production. Industrialists who produce urgently needed materials must speed up production, often more than is economically sound.

". . . The optimum scale of output (i.e., the most favourable relationship between expenditure and receipts) is reached before activity is fully up to the level of capacity . . . That rising costs have already made their appearance in a number of branches of the production goods industries is shown in the balance sheets . . . e.g., in the mining industry at the middle of 1938. As early as then the necessity was felt to increase depreciation allowances (owing to the over-employment of machinery) and to make additions to plant, while the need was already urgent for extra labouring power which was either not available at all or could only be obtained in comparatively inefficient forms. . . .

"Business is therefore now confronted . . . by the opposing movements of increased costs and on the other side relatively shrinking returns—lower prices in the home market, losses on the export trade, etc." [1]

A machine which runs day and night at top speed will depreciate much more quickly than one that operates at a normal speed, one shift a day. Additional replacements and renewal of technical equipment are necessary in order to avoid a shrinkage of industrial capital.

Increased production and sales should enable the industrial enterprise to accumulate sufficient liquid funds for the renewal and even extension of the plant. This is however, mere theory. In practice, there are many obstacles to the reinvestment of capital.

The Dyckerhoff Portland Zement Werke, A. G., one of the largest cement concerns, stressed the rapid depreciation of machinery, as a result of too much production, in its report for 1938:

"The depreciation rates established by the tax authorities are not in accord with economic necessities. The value of plant installations largely depends on whether machinery runs day and night throughout the year or whether sufficient time has been allowed for renovation and repairs."

The London *Statist,* in its issue of May 13, 1939, called the "overstrain" of human beings and of machines the most serious feature of Nazi economy. It said:

"Food shortage and signs of inflation are not the most serious indications of the excessive strain to which the Reich's national economy has been subjected during the last few years.

"Much more serious is the overworking of men and machines which is probably without precedent in peace-time. . . . This overstrain . . . merely additional evidence of the well-known fact that in the course of her gigantic rearmament effort Germany has exhausted those very resources in man-power and industrial capital which normally would be considered the 'iron reserve' to be drawn upon in case of war. . . . Industrial machinery is exposed likewise (like workers) to abnormal and excessive strain. Not only is the wear and tear of machinery in general appalling, but in the building industry concrete mixers and other machines operated in some instances without stop and adequate repairs for 24 hours are being quickly ruined. . . . The normal depreciation rates have proved utterly inadequate under present conditions."

In 1938, about 44.5 per cent more "capital construction" was produced than in 1929, yet "replacements" were less than in 1929. These figures indicate more production, more depreciation of machines, and less replacements.

GERMAN CAPITAL CONSTRUCTION"[2]

(In million marks)

| | *Total* | *New Construction* | *Replacements* |
|---|---|---|---|
| 1929 | 12,800 | 5,850 | 6,950 |
| 1933 | 5,060 | .... | 5,060 |
| 1934 | 8,185 | 2,360 | 5,825 |
| 1935 | 11,600 | 5,600 | 6,000 |
| 1936 | 13,800 | 7,500 | 6,200 |
| 1937 | 16,000 | 9,500 | 6,500 |
| 1938 (estimate) | 18,500 | 11,700 | 6,800 |

"Normal Replacements": 5,800 million marks.

A considerable part of the liquid funds of all companies is requisitioned by the State either for the financing of State-sponsored industrial projects, or as tax payments. The latter have risen to such an extent that many industrial enterprises have had to reduce their reinvestments.

At the end of the first Four-Year Plan period the tax bill of German business had increased enormously. Even the large firms, which had to finance new armament factories, were not exempt.

Typical tax bills of German concerns are as follows:

| | Taxes paid: | | | |
|---|---|---|---|---|
| | *1934-35* | *1937-38* | *1934-35* | *1937-38* |
| | *(in thousand marks)* | | *(in per cent of net profits)* | |
| Gute Hoffnungshuette (heavy industry) | 4,130 | 16,500 | 80.9 | 343.7 |
| Kloeckner (heavy industry) | 43,733 | 79,198 | 85.7 | 165.0 |
| Mannesmann (heavy industry) | 6,624 | 22,643 | 194.8 | 205.8 |
| Daimler-Benz (auto industry) | 4,191 | 22,758 | 102.2 | 1083.7 |
| I. G. Farbenindustrie (chemical industry) | 41,400 | 125,100 | 81.1 | 229.1 |
| Zellstoff-Fabrik Waldhof (textile industry) | 2,893 | 9,439 | 144.6 | 393.3 |
| Bremer Wollkaemmerei textile industry | 1,309 | 3,439 | 77.0 | 286.6 |

The annual report of the Dresdner Bank for 1937-38 complained:

"The additional tax payment has completely wiped out the additional gross income. Added expenses, especially for personnel and social purposes, had to be financed by other means. They have been covered by a reduction in the contributions to the pension fund and the official reserve fund amounting to one million marks each."

Vereinigte Glanzstoffwerke A. G. is the largest manufacturer of artificial silk in Germany. The tax bill of this company rose 578 per cent within three years (1935-38), the number of employees, 35 per cent. The State received 180 per cent more than was distributed to the shareholders in dividends.

Many German concerns are afraid to reveal large liquid reserves because it might mean an invitation to the tax collector. The experience of one of the most important German textile concerns, the Kammgarnspinnerei Stoehr A. G. in Leipzig, is a case in point. Stoehr had pursued a cautious financial policy, preparing for an eventual recession. In 1938, the firm had considerable liquid funds at its disposal—1.2 million marks in bank deposits. In August the authorities took action. The Price Commissar came to the conclusion that certain price decrees had been violated. A "penalty" of 1.5 million marks was imposed on Stoehr, obviously on the basis that there must be more liquid assets where such considerable cash reserves existed.

The fact that there have been so many additions to the nation's industrial plant makes it appear that there is a genuine industrial prosperity. But often these investments are made merely to replace machinery which is unsuitable for production with ersatz. The rubber goods manufacturers, for example, were compelled to find money for extensive new equipment, because Buna —synthetic rubber—is much harder than natural rubber. Therefore heavier machinery had to be built to replace what was obsolete.

Will these new investments pay or must they be written off immediately? In this connection a Nazi magazine, *Die Deutsche Volkswirtschaft,* stated:

"We have to consider that the risks in the rubber industry are at present very high. . . . We must anticipate that these risks will be higher in the future, as the manufacture of Buna will certainly result in losses."

Most textile manufacturers have had to buy new machinery in order to work with German cotton and wool ersatz. According to the official figures on new investments and production of capital goods, Germany's industrial capital has increased greatly. But these reports do not indicate the amount of "capital goods" used for armaments; they say nothing about the extent to which machinery must be replaced so that ersatz may be used.

The boom in many German industries indicates that the whole industrial structure is undergoing a rapid transformation at the hands of the State in order to meet present emergency situations and in preparation for a future wartime economy. New factories arise for the satisfaction of special demands, springing from unforeseen raw material shortages. No one knows how long such emergencies will last. Industrialists, therefore, feel that they should be prepared for future losses and the probability that much machinery will soon have to be renewed or may, in a relatively short time, become obsolete. Consequently they try to recover the money spent on new plant investments as rapidly as possible. This is often impossible, because the State has so many investment schemes of its own. It has created new technical difficulties which can be overcome only through new investments.

The Krupp concern summarized the effects of its "forced" production boom and its anxieties about the future in its annual report for 1937-1938 (dated March 1939): [3]

"The tempestuous upward development of the German economy during the past few years has forced us to use our plant to its fullest capacity and to wring the ultimate from our factories. So far it has still been possible to overcome the difficulties of obtaining sufficient manpower and the necessary materials. The increase in turnover thus achieved was rendered possible by extensive overtime and double shifts . . .

"In a number of plants earnings no longer kept step with the increase in turnover as reserve capacity was called into use to a point where production costs were adversely affected. Earnings were furthermore affected unfavorably by lower profits from foreign sales and the lesser yield of coal, the latter due to well-known causes. In the production of iron and steel the increased use of domestic raw materials involved large additional expense. If we were nevertheless able during the fiscal year to attain satisfactory results, this is due less to the increase in turnover than to the mechanization of our plant. However, the trend toward increasing cost of production continues. We will have to make increased efforts to combat it. This will require considerable means during the years to come.

"The fact that the new issue market continued to be pre-empted by the Government necessitated most careful handling of our finances. We sought to devote reserves for depreciation and net profits to renewal of plant. The excessive strain on our production plant caused depreciation at an extraordinary rate, necessitating more extensive renewal. . . .

"For the current fiscal year we have a large backlog of orders which safeguards full employment of our plant for many months. We therefore hope to be able again to obtain satisfactory results. It is true that we have to reckon with heavy additional expense, resulting especially from the still-continuing fall in export proceeds, from the increased use of German ore, from the decreasing yield of coal and from the increase in corporate tax rates. . . ."

Private firms cannot sue the Government for not paying armament bills. In April, 1939, German building firms were surprised by a Government decree announcing that all German contractors had to accept forty per cent of the payments due for armaments in two types of "Tax Certificates": type A, which can be used to pay taxes six months after their issue; type B, to pay taxes at 112 per cent of their face value after three years. Building contractors tried in vain to pay their own raw material suppliers with these "Tax Certificates."

Private business in Germany still has its own investment plans. Whether they can be put into practice or will be profitable depends much more on decisions of the Government than on circumstances under the control of the capitalist. Long-term investments, in the nature of things, involve a certain element of speculation.

"The question of whether newly invested capital will be productive can only be answered in the future. Certain reserves must be maintained in order to finance a possible transformation of the economy to a peacetime basis." [4]

The investment plans of the industrialists must not conflict with Government decisions and policies. But what the next decisions of the Government will be is largely unpredictable. There is no plan which prescribes what a manufacturer should produce and invest.

Most acts of State interference in investments and output are negative in character. To make new investments or to increase productive capacity is forbidden in many industries. In nearly all branches of industry the erection of new factories or the establishment of new firms is proscribed. Most State agencies and commissars start functioning by issuing prohibitions. One is forbidden much more often than permitted. A workshop cannot be closed without a special permit. However, it is permissible to change from the production of one article to another, although this is often of little practical importance, for if State offices do not grant the necessary supplies of raw materials or labor to produce the new product, then the right to increase production or make changes is worth very little.

There are two general principles which guide the State offices in making decisions on investments: military interests and the "interests of the Party." Often the decisions are dictated by a sudden shortage of raw materials or demands for a huge quantity of military equipment —unforeseen and at complete variance with previously planned schemes and projects.

The individual manufacturer seeks to protect his own interests against decisions of State agencies or commissars. To further them, he tries to exert pressure, individually, through Party connections, through group or estate organizations and—last but not least—through personal friends among the State bureaucrats.

The absence of hard and fast rules has its advantages. It serves to avoid schematic generalizations and additional bureaucracy. However, the laws of competition are no longer in effect. There are so many institutions and offices, representing group or particular Party interests, interfering and planning, that confusion concerning the plans of the various State agencies is the inevitable result, and an ever-recurring doubt as to what is allowed or forbidden whenever a new investment is to be made.

Unforeseen changes in State regulations often force industrialists to change their investment plans. This can perhaps be illustrated best by the experience of a big German firm with a famous trade name.

World-wide advertising has made Kaffee Haag, a caffeine-free coffee, a name familiar to nearly everyone. This German firm has spent large sums on research in analyzing foods and in studying methods of production with a view to improving the taste and quality of its product and decreasing costs. For years this company had investigated the possibilities of producing denicotinized cigarettes which would satisfy the smoker. After extensive research, a factory was started. New decrees on construction and equipment added to production costs. Other decrees affecting the distribution of tobacco and sales of cigarettes made it impossible to obtain the necessary raw materials and sales quotas in quantities sufficient to make the enterprise profitable. Finally Kaffee Haag had to abandon its plans, which had been based on mass production. Work on the half-finished plant was stopped. The funds originally set aside for this project were invested in a factory making newsprint.

The Schultheiss Brewery, one of the largest in Germany, sought to invest its considerable liquid funds in fashionable restaurants, bars and similar luxury establishments in Berlin. With this aim in mind, the concern entered upon a program involving considerable building and construction work. Then new decrees were issued forbidding the use of iron, steel, cement, etc., for new projects without special certificates, which Schultheiss was unable to obtain. The capital already expended went to waste and the firm had to look for other fields of investment.

No longer is it possible for a concern having large resources at its disposal to construct a new factory in order to drive a competitor out of the market. This would all too evidently be sheer waste of capital, unless technical improvements could be introduced which would lower the cost of production or increase the productivity of labor.

The author is reminded of a visit he made to the Ford Motor Company in Detroit in the summer of 1938. The vast potentialities of this truly gigantic organization were mostly unrealized. Yet an immense building was under construction, a factory for the mass production of automobile bodies. When this plant starts operating, Ford will cease buying bodies from independent manufacturers. No reply was forthcoming to the question as to what would happen then to the independent producers of bodies and their factories. There was also no answer to another question—does the Ford Motor Company intend to remain faithful to Henry Ford's original policy of reducing the price until sales have increased so much that all machinery is working at full capacity? The author was promised an answer in writing to these and other questions. The written reply said only that no answer could be given.[5]

In Nazi Germany, Ford would not be allowed to build a new body plant when other body plants were idle or not completely in use. Insofar as such government interference avoids waste of capital, it may be regarded as progressive. However, a genuine national investment board to plan Germany's investments does not exist. New investments are planned only from the point of view of military necessity. Without war the new investments planned by the State will, to a large extent, also be a waste of capital.

The flow of capital is no longer regulated by a capital market which directs it into industries that are particularly profitable. The State has supplanted the capital market. It compels private capitalists to make investments in a future wartime economy and creates economic conditions which cause old investments to decline in value. Thus the State makes drastic preparation for a still greater scarcity of raw materials and labor supply —all this in the expectation that wartime economy is not far off.

A visitor to the new industrial districts in central Germany is impressed by the many gigantic establishments. He does not see that simultaneously industrial life in other parts of the country is decaying. The new factories do not signify a genuine development of the country's productive forces, but an intensified one-sided growth of certain branches of production at the expense of other industries. Thus heavy industry—important for wartime economy—continues to increase disproportionately within the economy as a whole. Funds for renewal of technical equipment in industries not directly involved in the production of armaments are insufficient, because the maintenance of factories which do not satisfy the most urgent needs of a wartime economy has become relatively unimportant. For reasons of military strategy many plants in frontier districts have had to close down. The *Frankfurter Zeitung* of September 11, 1938, carried this account of the decay of industrial life in Germany's eastern districts.

"Idle factories—near the Polish border—were not reopened. The workers emigrated to prosperous industrial districts. Towns like Kuestrin and Landsberg in Silesia lost 15,000 to 20,000 workers, and in some small provincial towns the populations had declined ten to twenty per cent in recent years. . . . The list of industrial losses in the frontier district is moving indeed. Three big machine-tool plants in Landsberg, Kuestrin and Schwiebus, with over a thousand workers each, have disappeared. Also two enamel factories in Kuestrin and Reppen. Six out of eleven lignite mines east of the River Oder have been closed. The seventeen shoe factories have completely disappeared. The same is true of the factories manufacturing musical instruments and tobacco products, in the Frankfurt (Oder) and Schwerin districts. The number of workers in the textile industry in Landsberg declined from 3,000 to 2,000. . . . Efficient young workers emigrate because they have no opportunities in their home provinces. In certain respects the frontier district is similar to a colonial country exporting men and raw materials."

Even sectors of German economy which are most essential to national well-being, particularly in wartime, have experienced a deterioration in their technical equipment. The State has pre-empted the capital market for rearmament purposes to such an extent that for years the State-owned railway system, Germany's most important means of transportation, was unable to raise funds for maintenance and repairs.

A confidential report on the technical condition of German railway equipment vividly portrays a process which never before had been witnessed in German railroad history, except during the World War.

"Most of the rolling stock is in need of repair. The condition of the locomotives is worse than it has ever been. The larger yards are congested, because there is a lack of shunting engines to clear them. In certain districts the State railway is compelled to work with oil-burning engines borrowed from private companies. Locomotives stand about in the repair shops, because there are no raw materials with which to repair them properly. Formerly, axle bearings, piston rods, crank pins, coupling pins and bolts were lined with a mixture of lead, tin and antimony, but all available stocks of these metals were put at the disposal of the shipyards, because the Third Reich is rearming at sea as quickly as possible. Good bearings are even removed from locomotives and trucks and they are relined with substitute metal. This substitute is a mixture of brass, copper and lead; it is hard and brittle and 'eats' oil; when pressure is increased it breaks, and if the lubricant used is an inferior one, the bearings become hot and 'grab.' There is also a shortage of good lubricating oil. When bearings have been lined with substitute metal, the locomotives are compelled to reduce speed on the curves, and the working speed generally is reduced. In order to overcome the disadvantage of poor lubricating oil and inferior bearings, the bearings are no longer made airtight, and the result is that the axles, etc., whip and destroy the bearings."

During the winter of 1938-39 the accuracy of this confidential report was confirmed by many official Nazi reports. In the News Service of the Reich Railway Company the following statement appeared:

"There were congestions at freight stations resulting in temporary traffic tie-ups.[6] Cars were overworked. Open freight cars became particularly scarce, making severe measures necessary in order to have any available."

Compared with 1928, traffic in 1939 had increased by 10 per cent, but the rolling stock had decreased by no less than 4,000 locomotives and 80,000 cars. As an inevitable result, the safety of transportation was affected.[7] The Anschluss with Austria and with the Sudetenland increased traffic difficulties.[8]

THE DECLINE OF RAILWAY EQUIPMENT IN GERMANY[9]

| | *At the end of* | | | |
|---|---|---|---|---|
| | *1929* | *1931* | *1938 Old Reich* | *Greater Germany** |
| Number of locomotives | 25,017 | 23,066 | 22,172 | 25,206 |
| Number of freight cars | 660,112 | 647,097 | 577,060 | 629,693 |
| Number of passenger cars | 68,248 | 70,428 | 61,309 | 68,942 |

GOODS TRANSPORTED
(Monthly Average, in thousand tons)

| *1929* | *1932* | *1938* | *Greater Germany* |
|---|---|---|---|
| 36,334 | 20,170 | 37,305 | 44,000 (Jan.-March) |

These figures were commented on by the German Institute for German Business Research itself as follows:

"The demands made on the rolling stock last fall were so great that it seemed questionable whether the Reichsbahn [Reich's Railways] could take care of any further increase in transportation. This question was justified especially by the fact that the increase in performances last year could only be attained by utilization of all resources. The increase in transportation and the rising

(*Includes Austria and Sudetenland)

frequency of special problems had led temporarily to a great overburdening which had unfavorable effects on the operation of the railways. A penetrating examination of the present situation shows that the difficulties of assuring business a sufficient amount of loading room have not been completely overcome. . . .

"The Reichsbahn must reckon in the coming autumn —the seasonal peak—once again with a number of special problems. . . . The new demands will at first be all the more difficult to overcome since also in the past year . . . it was not possible to increase the available freight room to any great extent." [10]

Funds for renewal of railway equipment were made available only when transportation difficulties called forth protests from many industries and alarmed the Army leaders. Because the Government was unable to provide sufficient funds, it was compelled to satisfy the financial demands of the railroads at the expense of other branches of the economy. Investment plans for these industries were thereby disrupted.

In a country where all State activities are dedicated to war preparations and where the armament program has resulted in a scarcity of raw materials and capital funds, industrialists seek a refuge for their surplus funds in fields of investment which are unproductive and even unprofitable but whose comparative safety renders them more attractive than State-recommended investments.

In their almost panic-stricken search for safe investment opportunities, many German capitalists resort to the purchase of real estate, the value of which cannot depreciate as a result of inflation. This also explains the prosperity of certain speculative and luxury trades; for example, the paradox that Germany, notwithstanding all the emphasis placed on sacrifices in the national interest, is one of the few countries where the jewelry business is flourishing. Even cheap trinkets find a ready market at a good profit. The "Aryan" proprietor of the largest jewelry store in Berlin, a Mr. Markgraf, was arrested by the Gestapo under suspicion of having smuggled jewels into the country. He had been selling more than he could legally have obtained. Thus Germany, the country with the greatest scarcity of foreign currency and gold, is importing jewels to meet the demand of people who prefer diamonds and platinum to State loans.

The Government is unable to create conditions which make the investment policies of the State sufficiently attractive to capitalists. A few concerns may obtain such extensive privileges that they feel the totalitarian State has brought them prosperity—largely at the expense of other industries and enterprises. However, even they must modify their investment plans in accordance with the decisions of government agencies, because the absolute power of the State exacts compliance. Private initiative has not been completely suppressed, but it impels industrialists and investors in directions which run counter to the desires of the State.

*Chapter X*

# *BANKERS AS STATE OFFICIALS*

"The totalitarian State will not have an empty treasury so long as private companies or individuals still have ample cash or liquid assets."

THE manager of a big German bank sometimes goes abroad to visit foreign bankers, but bankers in Amsterdam or Zurich have ceased to wonder why their German business friends no longer dare to visit them alone. The German banker is often accompanied by somebody else—a Party man—who has to see that no private business is arranged without the knowledge of the Party. The Dutch or Swiss banker will be reluctant to invite his German friend for a social evening because the German banker would be afraid to come without the Party man. Otherwise Party authorities might be suspicious and troublesome after his return to Germany. He has to give a detailed report to the Government authorities about everything he discussed or heard. He would not be trusted if he declared that he talked with his foreign banking friends only about the weather or his own health.

Within Germany itself, the banker's activities are likewise circumscribed. He plays a dual role, a fact which creates many unpleasant and even risky situations for him. He is the head of a "private enterprise," yet he must always act like a representative of the State. A private investor would be naïve if he continued to rely on the advice of "his banker" whom he has known for many years and who formerly advised him how to invest his money. The advice he would get now would consist only of the instructions the banker gets from the Government. The banker must urge his customer to buy State bonds or bonds of Four-Year Plan enterprises, and he must always pretend to hold the most optimistic views about the financial situation of the State, contrary to his real opinions. If a private investor dares disregard the advice and pressure exerted to force him to invest his funds in State bonds, the bank manager might tell him that he had better leave his money on deposit and not invest it at all. It is not illegal to refuse, but inadvisable. If he withdraws large funds for private investments or otherwise remains stubborn, the banker will have to send a report to Government authorities informing them about the case. They will then check on how the money is used. The local Party leader will keep in touch with the bank manager, too, and learn of withdrawals or of the existence of liquid assets and make use of this knowledge when there is a new Party drive for funds.

Under fascism, big bankers, formerly independent—except, of course, "non-Aryans"—have become State officials in everything but name. They are often in high and influential positions, but they are all members of the compact, centralized State machine. Their independence, their individual initiative, their free competitive position, all the principles for which they once fought fervently, are gone. They no longer lead in society. They used to be the most influential and independent capitalists, more powerful even than the bankers in England or in the United States. For in Germany big banks were not mere deposit banks like the "big five" in England which are not allowed to grant long-term credits or to participate in issues of stocks and bonds. A few big banks in pre-Nazi Germany were in much more complete control of the capital market and had eliminated banking competition to a greater extent than the big banks in the United States or in Great Britain. There were no antitrust laws in Germany which prohibited the rise of huge nation-wide banking trusts. They could, and did, grant long-term credits and participate in issues of stocks and bonds. The executives of the big banks were the financial advisers of the industrial trusts, which were largely financed by the banks. The steel trust controlled by Fritz Thyssen, who helped Hitler come to power, arose from the financial debacle during the stabilization crisis of 1924-25 as a result of the financial skill and support of the Jewish banker Jakob Goldschmidt, then managing director of the Darmstaedter-und Nationalbank. The big banks distributed the major part of the foreign capital which went to Germany during the prosperity era of 1927-29. This was a contributing factor in making their position untenable during the banking crisis in 1931. They had to apply for State assistance. When the Nazis came to power, the State owned or controlled most of the share-capital of the large banks, with the exception of the Deutsche Bank & Disconto-Gesellschaft.

These big banks are today again under private ownership. This fact easily misleads the foreign observer. For under fascism "private banks" are as much under State control and are as co-ordinated as ordinary State banks.

The transformation of the big banks from protectors and pillars of private enterprise to the whip of the authoritarian State to be used in controlling private enterprise gives a certain degree of opportunity to small private bankers. They may be financially weak, but they have one asset which the larger banks do not possess: they are not directly Government controlled.

The private capitalist who visits such an independent banker can, however, never be sure whether he can trust him. Ths banker may be a personal friend, but he would not be allowed to exist as a banker unless he were trusted by the Party leaders, too. He must prove his "reliability" by disclosing trade secrets. He would be suspect if he did not do so.

Such a banker is really in an embarrassing position. He should be on good terms with the Party authorities and yet he must be trusted by the private investor, a combination which obviously is difficult.

Such a privileged position seems to be that of Dr. Christian Fischer, who decided to establish himself as a private banker in the spring of 1939. He resigned from the executive management of the Reichs-Kredit-Gesellschaft, a very influential State bank which controls the financial affairs of most State enterprises. Dr. Fischer is an "old-line conservative" rather than a Party man. He has a chance to succeed in his new career, for he has good connections with the State bureaucracy, plus the reliability of an "old conservative." On the other hand, the Government would not have allowed Dr. Fischer to act as private banker unless it had made sure that he would act in full accordance with the policies of the State.

The fusion between the State and the banks has developed as a result of forces which were miscalculated by all former leaders of the banks as well as of the Nazi party. During the first period of totalitarian rule, Dr. Hjalmar Schacht was given a chance to reconstruct the old banking system. Many bankers who had to rely on State support before the Nazis came to power had hoped that fascism would mean a return to the old prosperity, with private banks taking advantage of new possibilities for private investment and of the increase in savings capital. The Nazi Government did not seriously attempt to abolish private banking as demanded in the Nazi program and did not try to create one large banking trust owned and administered by the State. The German bankers cannot complain that they were "betrayed" by Hitler. A chance was given them when Schacht became president of the Reichsbank in 1933. Private investments were encouraged by the State. Taxes which seemed to be an obstacle to prosperity were reduced. Profits which were reinvested became tax exempt. State credits and subsidies were granted for repairs of houses. But real prosperity failed to emerge from these measures.

In the meantime, Dr. Schacht tried to reconstruct a private banking system. At the end of 1933, an inquiry on banking was staged. Its results could have been foreseen. The Commission of Inquiry was against any kind of socialization of banking advocated by Nazi radicals. It only recommended measures for the supervision of private banks. And as a result of the inquiry, the Government decided upon a vague "control of all credit institutions." New credit institutions would no longer be allowed unless they obtained special State permits. Other measures were quite in accordance with banking laws in democratic countries.

Many ruined Nazi manufacturers who had taken seriously the Party program against "interest slavery" and "unproductive banking capital" went to "Jewish bankers" requesting credits for themselves without offering guarantees and refusing disclosure of their financial status. Against these ultra-Nazis was decreed the Reich Law on Credits of December 5, 1934. This made it compulsory for all private bankers to grant non-secured credits of over 5,000 marks (about $1,200) to individuals or firms "only after obtaining full information on the financial affairs of the debtor." Another decree, of December 13, 1935, provided that credits of over one million marks must be reported bi-monthly to a Reich commissar. This measure was to establish a better control of the credit policy of the banks as well as a control of the indebtedness of industrial concerns.

On the whole, these measures provided for a recovery of the private economy under the leadership of the banks. But the armament policy and the huge spending program of the State subjected the machine built up by the private banks to the demands of the State.

When this new policy began, Dr. Schacht still was president of the Reichsbank and subsequently was even made Minister of Economics. He must have foreseen that the huge financial deficit of the State could not continue forever. But Dr. Schacht did not expect that a financial crisis would endanger his position as economic dictator. On the contrary, he no doubt felt that in line with his previous experience, financial difficulties of the State would strengthen the position of the Reichsbank and would make the Government dependent on the wishes of those who controlled the capital market. This had been his experience under the Weimar Republic. But now the financial difficulties compelled Schacht to create a bureaucratic machine which enabled the Government to replace him at a moment's notice by somebody more docile than he was.

Dr. Schacht tried to restrict State expenses, to keep at a minimum the regimentation of economic life under the Party bureaucracy, to encourage the revival of private initiative and competition, to end credit inflation and the growth of taxes. With Schacht were allied high Army officers who shared his point of view, who opposed the control of the armed forces by the Party bureaucrats and the Gestapo. But the Party would not tolerate restriction of its spending and curtailment of its authority by "outsiders."

Dr. Schacht and the "conservative" leaders of the large corporations thought in the old terms of a "strong state" which would insure the smooth operation of an economic system under which they would remain in control of the capital market. They had witnessed many governments they did not like. Their influence had never failed them, for the State needed credits to meet its financial demands, especially during periods of depression when capital remained idle and the State had to spend more in order to temper the effects of the depression. In such a situation the Government had to appeal to the capital market.

Under the Nazis, Schacht could no longer apply the old methods of compelling the Government to fulfill the wishes of private corporations. The Reichsbank was no longer a central bank defending the interests of the private banks or of the "capital market" against the demands of the State. On the contrary, it had to function as an arm of the Government, issuing instructions to the "private" banks and to the corporations, directing them how to invest their funds. Dr. Schacht, who had attacked parliamentary government for its increased expenditures and its deficits during the depression, had to help the Nazi Government increase its expenditures and its deficits to such an extent as to necessitate the closing of the capital market to any but the demands of the Government.

"The Government decided to fleece the short-term money market on a gigantic scale. German capitalists, like those abroad, showed little confidence in the development of German economy, and they were in consequence loath to invest money on long terms. They were, on the other hand, eager to employ their capital somehow, and the Government exploited this situation by issuing so-called work creation bills, with which a large percentage of its expenditure was met. The industrialist, or whoever received these bills in part payment, kept them as a short-term investment. A relatively small percentage he sent to his bank, which in its turn kept them as a short-term investment." [1]

When Dr. Schacht realized that he was no longer the president of an autonomous institution, he openly attacked Party leaders as "frivolous dilettantes" in a speech at Koenigsberg on August 16, 1935. The publication of this speech in the press was prohibited by Goebbels, the Minister for Propaganda, so that Schacht decided to have it printed and distributed by the Reichsbank. The speech was rather the statement of a resigned old man than of somebody who expected to succeed in the internal struggle.

"These frivolous dilettantes have not the slightest notion of the immense efforts required in guiding financial and economic policy for the fulfillment of our task. Is there any person whose heart would not be warmed by such phrases as 'The flag is more than a bank account,' 'The nation comes first, not its trade'? Such phrases are disarmingly true, but what practical use can a sensible man make of them? Recently I pointed out in a public statement that German trade must be kept free from disturbing influences; immediately thereafter I read that any argument over whether a measure disturbs trade or not was a Jewish and liberalistic one. I pointed out that our national rearmament demands the concentration of all economic and financial reserves; and when I said all, I meant all. The reply I received was that only old wives would throw up their hands and ask, 'Who is going to pay for the whole thing?' At the risk of being set down as an old woman, I want to say quite plainly that the question of the practical execution of the task set us is one over which I have racked my brains day and night. My comrades and fellow-Germans, to dismiss the gravity of the situation and our task as Germans with cheap phrase-mongering is not only silly but damned dangerous."

Dr. Schacht retired from the Reichsbank when he had already lost any real influence on Germany's financial affairs. The complete loss of the independence of the Reichsbank, which had become a mere tool of the Government, was not yet quite clear to the first successor of Dr. Schacht. As vice-president of the Reichsbank, Dr. Rudolf Brinkmann became the real head of this central banking institution, taking over the duties previously performed by Dr. Schacht. Soon after his appointment, however, he retired, according to the official Nazi version, as a result of a "nervous breakdown with loss of memory."

Commenting on Dr. Brinkmann's mysterious "nervous

breakdown with loss of memory," the French periodical, *Agence Economique et Financière,* published a report of a meeting in Berlin of civil service officials and Nazi leaders at which Dr. Brinkmann, then still State Secretary and Vice-President of the Reichsbank, said: "We have been paying in Germany for one gun the normal price of ten, and that gun is of inferior quality. Our currency is exhausted, and we know that no more money can be raised by taxation." Three days after this speech Nazi papers reported Dr. Brinkmann's retirement.

The totalitarian State reverses the former relationship between the State and the banks. Previously, their political influence increased when the State needed financial help. Now the opposite holds true. The more urgent the financial demands of the State become, the stricter measures are taken by the State in order to compel these institutions to invest their funds as the State may wish.

It happened in the spring of 1938 that the Reichsbank refused to rediscount any further issues of State bills. As a result, the banks stopped buying these bills from the industrialists. This almost created a panic, leading to sales of securities and a consequent fall of prices on the Stock Exchange. The banks were then ordered to intervene. Thus the Nazi State hinders the operation of the "economic laws," which can make themselves felt in democratic countries.

Dr. Schacht stressed the fact that there was no longer any idle industrial capital. Further extension of production must therefore be financed from an increase in national income. In other words, private industrialists would be unable to replace their depreciated equipment and to make new industrial investments if the

State continued to monopolize the capital market and to absorb all liquid funds.

The totalitarian State will not have an empty treasury so long as private companies or individuals still have ample cash or liquid assets. For the State has the power to solve its financial difficulties at their expense. The private banks themselves, the financial institutions which previously dictated the terms on which they were willing to lend money, have built up the system of siphoning off liquid funds. This financial system is now utilized by the totalitarian State for its own purposes.

The State has the supreme claim on anything private citizens or private firms own. These would have to go bankrupt first, before the State goes bankrupt. This, however, is not possible either. For the State can always free itself from financial commitments by a simple decree. It may refuse payment and make levies on individuals or whole groups of citizens in order to raise money, ordering them to turn over a part of their fortunes to the State without compensation. Or it may suspend payments of private debts in order to enable the State to raise fresh credits. This may be achieved by cancelling debts or by reducing the interest rates for loans. Early in 1935, for instance, a general reduction in the coupon rate of all bonds, with the exception of industrial debentures, from 6 per cent or whatever higher rate they carried, down to 4½ per cent was decreed, effecting a total indebtedness of about 10 billion marks. This was not a conversion as the term is understood in democratic countries, that is, a reduction of interest rate by voluntary agreement between debtors and creditors. The State compelled the creditors to renounce one-fourth and more of their interest claims on a total debt of over 10 billion marks. Private owners of mortgages and of industrial bonds were "advised" to follow the example; they had to reduce interest rates to 5 per cent or less.

Liquid funds which were freed by the cancellation or reduction of financial obligations were taken by the State. In practice, all institutions which usually have large funds for investment and for granting credits at their disposal had to buy State bonds. The suppression of private issues strengthened the position of the State on the capital market. In addition, insurance companies, savings banks, and municipalities possessing liquid funds were compelled by special decrees to buy State bonds or Treasury bills.

NEW ISSUES OF SECURITIES IN GERMANY
(In million marks)
(Compiled from reports of the German Institute for Business Research)

| | *State Loans* | *Industrial Loans* | *Stocks Shares* |
|---|---|---|---|
| 1926 | 1,163 | 322 | 988 |
| 1928 | 633 | 294 | 1,339 |
| 1932 | 248 | 10 | 150 |
| 1933 | 71 | 2 | 91 |
| 1934 | 75 | 4 | 143 |
| 1935 | 1,636 | 3 | 156 |
| 1936 | 2,670 | 47 | 395 |
| 1937 | 3,150 | 258 | 333 |
| 1938 | 7,744 | 107 | 822 |

A decree of the Reich Minister of Finance, issued on October 29, 1938, compels all municipalities to invest at least 75 per cent of their liquid funds or reserves in State bonds or Treasury bills. Before this decree, the municipalities were able to use such funds for special local purposes.

Insurance companies must ask the Reich Minister of Economics for a permit before they may grant a loan to a private company even though this loan be secured by a first mortgage. When the decree making this procedure obligatory was issued, it was intended merely for the supervision of the insurance companies. Because of the compelling need to direct the flow of capital of these institutions as well, the Reich Ministry of Economics came to use its supervisory power as a brake on such credits.

"These measures were sufficient, until the middle of 1938, for a satisfactory supervision of the capital market. . . . In June and July, 1938, however, a special situation arose as a result of political events. . . . The Western fortifications created great financial demands. Therefore, every cent of the capital market had to be at the disposal of the Reich. As a result, on August 12, 1938, savings banks, State and private insurance companies were prohibited from granting new mortgage loans . . . except for the construction of army buildings and houses necessitated by the Four-Year Plan, apartment houses for workers, and replacements of tenement houses in Berlin, Hamburg and Munich." [2]

The resources of the German capital market, formation of new long-term capital, are estimated at 2 to 2½ billion marks yearly. Dr. Karl Schwarzkopf, managing director of the Landeskreditbank Kassel and former State Secretary, estimated that "the capacity for the formation of new capital . . . is less than one-third of the pre-War level. . . . At present one might estimate the new formation of long-term capital at 2 to 2½ billion marks." [3] The estimates of new capital amount to 350 million pounds, or 7 billion marks, in England (1935), and 30 billion francs, or five billion marks, in France (1935).

The German Government expects to be able to issue at least 2 billions in new State loans annually for a number of years; that is, 80 to 90 per cent of the available new capital will be required by the State.[4] The rest will not, however, be "free." It will have to be used in those projects considered essential by Goering's Ministry, to make Germany "self-sufficient." Other issues of shares or debentures will not be permitted; they would be in competition with the State.

Many businessmen who previously left their money on deposit with the big banks turned to savings banks and insurance companies after the experience of the banking crisis and out of general anxiety to avoid any investment risk. It is tragic and grotesque that these funds which have been accumulated as a result of the desire of investors to avoid any risk are almost completely seized by the State and spent for armaments. Insurance companies and savings banks as well as commercial banks have to accumulate State bonds and Treasury bills. State debts increasingly become their assets, the "earning power" of the State—taxation of the nation—their chief source of income.

"The State could take the decisive role in the formation of capital. . . . This explains the fact that the heading 'securities,' in the balance sheets of insurance companies has changed . . . and has become the most important form of investment for new funds of the insurance companies. . . . Among 'securities,' of course,

State loans and Treasury Bonds are of prime importance. . . . In addition, there are the bonds of State corporations for special purposes." [5]

The insurance companies fear that the investment of all their funds in State paper is very dangerous for them. They are in the position of a businessman who foresees that the debtor will be unable to fulfill his financial obligations and who, worse yet, knows that the creditor will be powerless in respect to the debtor whenever there should be any disagreement.

The leader of the Reich Group of Insurance Agents and Representatives stated the position at their Congress in Hamburg in October, 1938, in cautious and occasionally obscure words, the meaning of which is clear only to those with inside knowledge of the Nazi regime:

"The attempt to change the structure of the insurance business would be an extremely dangerous experiment. . . . It would be an irresponsible step to replace one economic form by another. It is true that the form is not the decisive thing, but rather the underlying philosophy. This is undoubtedly partially true, but not entirely. . . . A warning against total centralization. . . . Instead of working with knowledge based on practical experience, one works with general slogans which do not become significant by frequent repetition. . . . Competition must be orderly, but it should not be wiped out or replaced by compulsory cartels. The rules of competition should not be so severe that they protect lazy, inefficient enterprises which are inimical to progress and therefore a liability. . . ." [6]

A comparison of the trends on the American and German capital markets will startle the observer who pays more attention to statistics than to social facts. In the

United States, private issues have shrunk and public issues have overshadowed them since the depression. American capitalists who held liquid capital funds did not find opportunities for private investment which adequately satisfied their demand for security and profit. Therefore, American investors (especially banks and insurance companies) preferred the purchase of Government bonds, thus rendering possible without difficulty the financing of the huge State deficits. The reader might conclude that in Germany the private capitalist looking for reinvestment of his capital would have encountered greater difficulties in finding satisfactory private investment possibilities and would therefore have bought State bonds anyhow, with or without coercion. Such a conclusion, however, would be contradicted by the fact that private banks and insurance companies made strenuous efforts to free themselves from the strict State control and to escape measures for compulsory investment of their funds in State bonds. This drive for private investment possibilities was not a result of new prosperity or of an at least partial recovery of private economy. Rather were these attempts to avoid the purchase of State bonds due to fear that it was too risky an investment, and that the State might devalue the currency. Therefore the obligations of the State were and are unpopular investments, although there is no alternative in the field of private investment. The main concern of private investors in Germany has been the safety of new investments rather than their profit possibilities.

In former times this problem could be solved easily. Under the old system of private banking, any enterprise could raise capital by selling shares or debentures, provided buyers could be found for the newly issued securities. If this was not possible, a banker might advance cash in the expectancy of a later issue of securities which would serve to repay the banking credit. This is "sound" finance as long as interest or dividends can be paid and as long as a capital market exists which will absorb new issues of securities.

The Nazi State was unable to find enough capitalists willing to buy State debentures. Yet it raised huge short-term credits and even loans by compelling capitalists and financial institutions, unwilling and unable to risk their money in new investments, to invest their capital in the riskiest form of large-scale, short-term financing of State "investments."

This explains the impressive ability of the Nazi State to spend and spend extravagantly, to finance huge deficits without an immediate breakdown of the economic system.

The Nazi State takes advantage of the fact that Germany is a highly industrialized country where the savings of several generations have accumulated in the form of gigantic investments and in an industrial machine bigger than that of France or even England. In comparison with Germany, Italy is a poor country; its technical equipment and industrial capital is merely a fraction of such investments in Germany. Mussolini, therefore, finds it much more difficult to finance excessive State deficits than does Hitler, and Mussolini's deficits have a greater and more immediate effect upon private economy than Hitler's. Yet the final consequences of living at the expense of the savings of the past are more fatal for a system which can feed its population only by means of a highly industrialized economy and not entirely or mainly by means of agricultural labor.

This living on the capital of the nation finds expression in the growing indebtedness of the State to private economy. It has been authoritatively estimated [7] that in Germany today direct and indirect State indebtedness in all forms—bonds, other securities, bank credits and so on—amounts to over 55 per cent of the total indebtedness, with private debts accounting for the remaining 45 per cent. Excluding mortgage debts, the indebtedness of the State amounts to something like 75 per cent of the total.

If traditional relations between creditor and debtor prevailed, the debtor should be under the control of the creditor—in receivership—if there were any difficulties in paying interest and amortization charges. Figures and words have changed their meaning. Many private enterprises have managed to pay off debts under the Nazi regime. The fight against "interest slavery"—a propaganda slogan of the Nazis before they came to power—has in part been successful insofar as private debts are concerned, and interest payments have shrunk. But this shrinkage of debt and interest payments has been more than offset by the growth of debt and interest obligations of the State, and also by a tremendous growth of taxation. Yet this does not mean that the State as a debtor is "enslaved" to its creditors—the bondholders. For the State has the power, at any time it pleases, to refuse fulfillment of its obligations as a debtor.

"National Socialism does not allow either the level of interest rates or the distribution of new money capital to be determined by the free play of demand, supply and quotations. The present interest rate is the result of a number of planned and carefully adjusted economic measures which are not based on the impracticable idea of giving interest laws the character of police orders but which are based on the desire to control all factors which influence the rate of interest." [8]

There are, however, obvious limits to the State's power to draw on private funds and the State budget must be limited accordingly. But these limits are very elastic, since they are not set by the net income of private economy. The State can spend much more by levying tribute on all private property and by eating up part of the capital which several generations have accumulated.

Unfortunately, the State deficit has grown so tremendously that it even surpasses the total liquid funds at the disposal of the capital market. The new State loans were used to pay for current State expenses—new deficits—not for transforming the short-term into long-term debts. A large proportion of the short-term State bills had been turned over to the Reichsbank or to other State banks, so that the State had to finance a large part of its own deficit.[9] This would have led to inflation on a much greater scale than really occurred had not the totalitarian State reserved to itself the power to tighten control of all financial developments in an emergency. In 1939, the Government was no longer able to pay off the armament bills and compelled the industrialists to accept partial payment in the form of special bills which can later be utilized for payment of taxes. In order to overcome the difficulties of the moment, the tax revenues of the future are mortgaged.

The tremendous rise of the short-term indebtedness of the National-Socialist State has been often regarded as an indication that the regime would be defeated by a financial debacle. Those who stress this point underestimate the ability of the fascist State to exercise stringent control over private economy.

Only a fraction of the State deficit has been financed by inflation. The fact that an inflationary process has started is not so remarkable as the fact that it has not gone much farther. Despite a yearly State deficit of about five billion marks from 1934 until 1938, the financial means derived from inflationary expansion of money in circulation cannot exceed 2 to 4 billion marks, that is, they constitute only a small fraction of the total deficit. In February, 1939, the volume of "money in circulation" [10] was 68.6 per cent greater than in 1929, industrial production (including armament production) had increased about 30.1 per cent, production of consumption goods only 17.0 per cent. But money circulates more quickly, so that the inflationary process has probably gone further than the above figures reveal.

Such figures are not symptoms of an early breakdown of the system, but foreshadow more coercive acts by the State and indicate the impossibility of a return to the old kind of private economy.

"The present financial position is unsound, but it is not dangerous in the sense that Germany—as so many people believe—is headed for a financial collapse. It is true that under normal conditions the existence of a floating debt—that is, inclusive of creation of work bills —of as much as 16,000,000,000 marks would constitute a most dangerous potential inflation. At the first sign of financial or political disquiet the bills held by private capitalists and the banks would be rediscounted with the Reichsbank, and the note issue would be doubled or trebled at a moment's notice. In Germany this danger can be ruled out. The means of control of the totalitarian State are so complete and powerful that it is well within the power of the government to nip such a danger in the bud. The government could, in fact, quite easily refuse to grant rediscounting facilities and thus transform the bills into a kind of perpetual loan." [11]

The most serious financial problem for the Nazi State is not the danger of a breakdown of the currency and banking system, but the growing illiquidity of banks, insurance companies, savings institutions, etc. The bulk of the funds entrusted to these institutions by depositors and holders of insurance policies is now invested in State bonds or bills which cannot be turned into cash. Germany's financial organizations are again in a situation where their assets which should be kept liquid have become "frozen." From the purely financial point of view, the situation is more serious than in 1931, the year of the banking crisis. But the totalitarian State can tighten its control over the whole financial system and appropriate for itself all private funds which are essential for the further existence of a private economy. Yet the institutions which still exist as private enterprises are not allowed to go bankrupt. For an artificial belief in credits and financial obligations has to be maintained in open conflict with realities.

## *Chapter XI*

# *STOCK EXCHANGE AND SPECULATION UNDER FASCISM*

"The 'Aryan' members of the Berlin Stock Exchange have lost much more than they gained by the removal of the 'Non-Aryans.' "

THE Berlin Stock Exchange still exists—as a building, as an institution with large offices, with brokers and bankers, with a huge organization for daily announcement of stock and bond quotations. But it is only a pale imitation of its former self and of what a stock exchange is supposed to be. For the Stock Exchange cannot function if and when the State regulates the flow of capital and destroys the confidence of investors in the sanctity of their property rights.

The glorious days when millions of marks daily poured into the Stock Exchange, when the bonds and securities of foreign countries were handled, when new concerns and trusts were promoted and exciting speculative maneuvers were staged—those glorious times have long since departed, and even the doorkeeper who vividly remembers the excitement of the "good old days" does not believe that they will ever return. Yet the decrepit machine still runs. The office staff, brokers and bankers have been reduced in numbers as a result of the enforced removal of all "non-Aryans." But the pure "Aryans" who remain members of the Stock Exchange do not enjoy their privileges under totalitarianism. Some of them may have expected to prosper after the exodus of the Jewish brokers and bankers, by having inherited their business. But the "Aryan" members of the Berlin Stock Exchange have lost much more than they gained by the removal of the "non-Aryans." They do not have much to do and feel strongly that they have become superfluous because the Stock Exchange no longer functions as such. It has become an empty husk. Sales amounting to a few thousand marks are great events and may easily cause wild fluctuation in the price of securities unless the State Commissar intervenes.

The commission a Berlin broker can charge a customer is much less than the commission charged by a broker on the New York Stock Exchange. Commissions are calculated differently in Berlin than in New York, yet a rough comparison is possible. And not only does a Berlin broker receive on each specific transaction a smaller commission than does his "opposite number" in New York, but there are far fewer transactions; the volume of sales is infinitely less in Berlin than in New York. Thus in every respect a member of the New York Stock Exchange occupies a far stronger position than does a member of the Berlin institution.

Slack business is not a peculiarity of the Berlin Stock Exchange. Wall Street, too, has experienced it. But the Berlin Stock Exchange represents a phenomenon of its own—a State regimentation quite different from the supervision of the Stock Exchange as it existed before the Nazis came to power. A State Commissar for the Stock Exchange already existed in pre-Hitler Germany. This State Commissar daily visited the Stock Exchange but he was without real influence. His role was merely supervisory, similar to the Federal Government's control of the New York Stock Exchange, which is intended to prevent private groups from controlling or manipulating the market. In Nazi Germany, however, the State itself manipulates the capital market and therefore also the Stock Exchange.

When, in 1937, the New York Stock Exchange experienced a new recession, the Berlin Stock Exchange, which formerly followed the lead of Wall Street, remained almost unaffected. This was not a sign of strength but of effective Government manipulation. It prevents market fluctuations. When, for instance, German capitalists wanted to increase their investments in stocks of private corporations rather than to buy State bonds, the Government interfered. The fear of inflation made stocks an attractive investment. But as this would have been harmful to the State's credit, Dr. Schacht warned German capitalists in an address in Koenigsberg, in August, 1935, that "all Germans were in one boat" and they all had to share the risks of the depreciation of the mark. Sales of stocks were curbed. Furthermore, the Government created an artificial demand for State bonds and bills at the expense of foreign holders of German securities. They are not allowed to withdraw their capital from Germany. Yet they cannot make use of the Stock Exchange in order to buy German stocks in an effort to protect themselves against the risk of a devaluation of the currency. An order of the Foreign Exchange Board of December 9, 1936, provided that the foreign owners of blocked marks are allowed to buy only bonds.[1] The expropriation of Jewish capital would have led to large-scale sales of stocks and bonds with resultant price disturbances if the Government had not stepped in.

"Another new situation arose in November, 1938, affecting the movement of capital. The restriction of Jewish business activities, if previous experiences were repeated, would have led to a new wave of sales. . . . This would have had an undesirable result because investment capital would have gone into buying cheap securities from Jews, when it was urgently needed for other purposes. Therefore, credit institutions were instructed by the Ministry of Economics to refuse acceptance of any selling orders of securities from Jewish owners. On account of the extraordinary emergency, this order was issued to the directors of the economic groups orally on the morning of November 14, 1938, before the opening of the Stock Exchange. . . . It is quite possible also that it may become necessary to put under control those methods of finance which today are still free." [2]

A foreign visitor to the Berlin Stock Exchange would easily be deceived. There are announcements of daily quotations and price changes as though a free Stock Exchange still existed, but nowhere would he find the former "public"—private buyers and sellers—as represented by independent brokers, bankers and "visitors." [3] In former days the floor of the Exchange was crowded with people, rushing to and fro. There was noisy shouting from all sides, typical of the floor of a free stock exchange. Today, the floor is quiet and looks peaceful. Plenty of empty space makes it appear like the dignified anteroom of a government office rather than the old-time Stock Exchange—as it still exists in New York, London or Paris. A "big day" at the Berlin Stock Exchange today is no longer marked by excited discussions of industrial finance. It is more important to hear what is whispered about new Government actions and policies.

Brokers, banking representatives, "visitors" at the Berlin Stock Exchange, all play a new role. Everything is under the control of the State Commissar. He has his advisors and informers among the brokers and "visitors."

Private speculation has not disappeared, but it operates almost entirely outside of the official Stock Exchange. The greater part of the sales and purchases of stocks and bonds is executed at quotations which depend on individual arrangements and which often differ greatly from the official quotations on the Stock Exchange. State Commissar Martini of the Berlin Stock Exchange complained that instructions for control of the sales of securities "turned out to be ineffectual in practice."

The office for the listing of new securities, he said, is of no use if "an increasing number of the most respectable companies fail to have their securities listed because they fear the inconvenience of a far-reaching disclosure of their situation, and want to save the cost of listing on the Stock Exchange. . . . Disadvantages of not having an official listing are so slight that they are disregarded. . . . There are innumerable independent brokers for transactions in unlisted securities . . . satisfied with market reports, the publication of which is not yet forbidden. The securities business has therefore largely circumvented the Stock Exchange Law and follows its own easier course. Even companies of high standing are willing to sell their securities in the free market without official listing on the Exchange. The embargo on new issues has favored this development. There is still a third kind of securities business, the so-called telephone business conducted over the telephone. It avoids all control. The volume of business done by telephone sometimes exceeds all other securities transactions." [4]

Commissar Martini sought to outlaw all transactions in securities outside of the Stock Exchange. The periodical, *Die Bank,*[5] termed this proposal unworthy of discussion.

The Stock Exchange still retains the function of evaluating the "earning power" of private companies, as well as of the State's credit, as expressed in price quotations for stocks and bonds. Therefore the Stock Exchange is a necessary institution for the fascist economic system. It cannot be discarded, although the program of the Nazi Party called for the abolition of "anonymous" capital, and in particular, of the Stock Exchange. The Government is utilizing it in support of the regimentation of the capital market. Private investors as well as corporations are compelled to accept quotations of stocks and bonds as true market values, although they may be based on State guarantees and artificial optimism.

Newspapers still publish reports on the "tone" of the Stock Exchange, with quotations of stocks and bonds as of old. But the changes which really have occurred cannot be discerned in these newspaper reports. Yet a comparison of the stocks and bonds listed in newspaper reports on the Stock Exchange in former times and at present reveal some interesting changes. The *Frankfurter Zeitung* listed in its reports on the Berlin Stock Exchange at the end of May, 1929: 23 Government bonds, 57 bonds of provincial and municipal communities, 640 stocks; at the end of May, 1939, however: 64 Government bonds (including "special tax bills"),

238 provincial and municipal bonds, 471 stocks. The number of Government bonds listed rose 178 per cent, the number of provincial and municipal bonds 210 per cent, the number of stocks declined 26 per cent.

These figures indicate a trend which had already begun during the world economic crisis. Investors turned from private investment fields to State-guaranteed or protected investments. Today, under totalitarianism, a certain reversal of this tendency can be observed. The interest in private investments has increased, not as a result of greater confidence in them, but due to the loss of confidence in State guarantees and as a result of the desire to escape State control, inflation, and measures of expropriation by the totalitarian State.

The Dresdner Bank, for instance, sold the bulk of its own stock, 120 million marks, which had been owned by the State, to the public. This was easily arranged through the bank's 165 branches. The clients obviously preferred the stock of a private corporation to State bonds. The result of this transaction was that the Government obtained funds of private investors and yet did not lose control over the "privately owned" Dresdner Bank. For the State has organized and rigorously maintains supervision of all security issues and in general of the credit policies of the banks.

Because of this preference for private issues, the Government decided upon certain changes in its investment policies when the second Four-Year Plan was announced in 1937. Some private issues were again to be permitted. However, State control over the capital market was not relaxed. Any such hopes that conservative capitalists might have harbored were disappointed. The armament race as well as the urgent need for homemade raw materials made it necessary to finance new factories for the production of ersatz materials. Private investors tried to avoid investments in armaments works and State projects. An ingenious compromise was made. A number of leading mining, steel and chemical concerns founded new "Four-Year Plan Companies." The shares are mostly property of the mother concern. The greater part of the capital, however, is raised by the issue of bonds—part also in the form of stocks. These issues appear as "private issues" on the Stock Exchange and are therefore more attractive to the investor. But these investments were not made quite voluntarily by the concerns and trusts which are the official owners of the new works. They acted under order of Goering's Four-Year Plan Commission.

"Investments in private industry were not lacking. They probably increased considerably in comparison with the previous year; but they were not for the most part freely made and did not originate with the private initiative of investors; they were without exception created to serve the purposes of the Four-Year Plan." [6]

*The Economic Review of Foreign Commerce of the United States* also declares:

"While there has been a certain amount of privately financed industrial expansion, such investments . . . were determined exclusively by the objectives of the Four-Year Plan." [7]

The transformation of the Stock Exchange from a mere market for stocks and bonds into an instrument of the State was not accomplished because the Nazi Party program was hostile to the Stock Exchange as such; other planks in the Nazi platform calling for economic changes were simply forgotten after the Party came into power. The ground for the transformation of the Stock Exchange had been prepared a long time before fascism came to power—even before the world economic and banking crisis had taken effect. The Berlin Stock Exchange—like most stock exchanges in eastern Europe—had never acquired such a relatively independent position as the stock exchange in New York, London or Paris. Greater amounts of capital were available in New York, London and even in Paris, than in Berlin. This, however, was only one of the reasons for the secondary position of the Berlin Stock Exchange. In Germany a few big banks actually had controlled the Stock Exchange, although this control was indirect and unobserved by the casual visitor. In England deposit banks are not allowed to trade in securities on the Stock Exchange. This is the privilege of the brokers and jobbers. A New York deposit bank cannot underwrite issues of stocks and bonds. In Germany, however, the big banks used to be, and still are, both deposit banks and discount and merchant bankers as well as dealers in stocks and bonds. They grant loans and participate in security flotations.

These big banks largely replaced the Stock Exchange by acting as buyers and sellers of stocks and bonds. The banks bought and sold on the Stock Exchange only when there was a differential between sales and purchases of customers or for some special reason—sometimes in order to "support" a slack market. The Stock Exchange was of importance to the banks, even if they did not require it for their own transactions, because its existence served as a guarantee to the investor that he could buy and sell stocks and bonds at market prices.

The Stock Exchange obviously could function only as long as numerous investors existed who were willing to buy stocks and bonds. But the inflation of 1923 in Germany had wiped out the greater part of the savings of the middle classes. The ruin of many capitalists as a result of the world economic crisis and the terrific losses sustained by most speculators had a devastating effect upon the business on the Stock Exchange. In former times, a depression was usually followed by prosperity, which enabled many small- and medium-sized investors to recover. The armament boom, however, had no such effect. The middle class did not improve its position.

A few figures are illustrative:

The total number of corporations dropped from 11,690 at the end of 1928 to 9,634 at the end of 1932, and 5,518 at the end of 1938. The number of corporations with a share capital of five million marks and more declined proportionately much less, from 750 in 1928, to 679 in 1932 and 616 in 1938.

DEATH OF BUSINESS
(Dissolution of Firms in Germany)

| | *Corporations* | *Limited Liability Companies* | *Other Firms* |
|---|---|---|---|
| 1928 | 932 | 8,384 | 22,227 |
| 1929 | 804 | 6,779 | 19,263 |
| 1930 | 678 | 4,728 | 19,559 |
| 1931 | 736 | 4,671 | 17,428 |
| 1932 | 904 | 4,777 | 16,260 |
| 1933 | 600 | 4,367 | 14,188 |
| 1934 | 602 | 4,890 | 13,611 |
| 1935 | 856 | 8,892 | 15,713 |
| 1936 | 749 | 7,513 | 16,266 |
| 1937 | 1,167 | 9,820 | 17,829 |

*(Compiled from figures published by the Statistisches Jahrbuch fuer das Deutsche Reich, various volumes)*

The following figures are even more interesting: the total share capital of all corporations registered in Germany declined by about 34.8 per cent from 1928 to 1938. But whereas the large companies with a share capital of five million marks or more accounted for only 55.8 per cent of the total capital of all corporations at the end of 1928, they represented 74.6 per cent at the end of 1932 and 77.2 per cent at the end of 1938.

The comparison afforded by these figures is somewhat distorted by the effect of the Law for the Transformation of Joint Stock Companies of July 5, 1934, which, in accordance with Nazi philosophy, was designed to foster the transformation of "anonymous" corporations into other, more personal, forms of corporate organization. Two thousand and seventy companies, or 22.3 per cent of the total number, were thus eliminated from the roster of corporations. Their aggregate capital, however, was only 1,557 million marks or 7.8 per cent of the total, due to the fact that the law primarily affected small corporations. Another law, which became effective on October 1, 1937, raised the capital requirement for corporations from 50,000 to 500,000 marks. Corporations already in existence at the date of enactment of this law were allowed to continue operations, but must raise their capital to 100,000 marks by the end of 1940.

The figures on the concentration of corporate capital call for yet another comment. They demonstrate concentration of control rather than concentration of ownership of corporate capital. This point is quite important. For in all advanced industrial countries, especially in the United States, a relatively small number of corporations are in control of the greater part of the corporate capital. Only 0.15 per cent of all corporations in the United States, for instance, owned approximately 53 per cent of the total corporate assets in 1933.[8] In Germany, in 1933, the corporate capital of 0.4 per cent of all corporations represented 25.6 per cent of the total; the corporate capital of 3.9 per cent of all corporations represented 60.6 per cent of the total.[9] However, in Germany, as well as in Italy and Japan, concentration of ownership of corporate capital exists to a far greater extent than in the United States.

In Italy under Mussolini, the concentration of control of corporate capital has also increased greatly. The share of the 100 largest corporations in the total corporate capital has risen from 32.1 per cent in 1922 to 38.1 per cent in 1933 and 44.0 per cent in 1936, the percentage of all assets from 30.1 per cent in 1922 to 40.3 per cent in 1933 and 46.3 per cent in 1936.

"Large corporations have played an increasingly prominent role in Italian economic life since the advent of Fascism. By 1936, 100 great manufacturing, communications and trading companies—a mere half of one per cent of all stock companies—owned almost half of all non-financial corporate assets. Concentration has become even more pronounced in the field of banking. Evidently the Fascist environment has not been uncongenial to the growth of large-scale business organizations." [10]

It seems that in the United States the concentration of the control of corporate capital is at least as great as or even greater than in Germany. But the ownership of corporate capital is more concentrated in Germany—and in Italy—than in the United States or in Great Britain. This statement cannot be verified statistically because in Germany and Italy no figures on the number of stock- and bondholders are available. But many known facts justify the assumption that the overwhelming part of the stock of practically all big corporations in Germany and Italy is in the hands of a few big shareholders, and that only a small proportion is in the hands of the "public" or of small stockholders.

In the totalitarian countries big corporations tend to become mere "family trusts," a trend which is especially typical of the large corporations in Japan, where four big family trusts own almost the entire large-scale industry and middle class investors never were of any importance.

In Germany a few "Aryan" families like Mannesmann, Friedrich Flick, Otto Wolff and Graf von Ballestrem were able to acquire additional control of numerous plants and companies. Industrial enterprises owned by "non-Aryans" became the property of these big concerns and trusts.[11] In the foodstuff industry and retail trade, however, where the small proprietor predominates, the expansion of concerns and trusts has been curbed. This indicates a trend of the disappearance—or at least decline—of the medium-sized independent manufacturer. The gap between a few big concerns and trusts on one hand and numerous small impoverished manufacturers and shopkeepers on the other hand becomes wider than ever before.

This development reduces the importance of the Stock Exchange. The disappearance of small corporations gives rise to a tendency among small investors not to risk their capital in new competitive enterprises. The larger the big corporations grow and the closer they become connected with the State bureaucracy, the fewer chances there are for the rise of new competitors.

Certain changes in corporate organization also indicate that small shareholders have become quite unimportant. The German Corporation Law, which became effective on January 30, 1937, did not even pretend to have regard for the interests of the small shareholder. The "authoritarian leadership principle" must be applied in all corporations, and this confers full authoritarian power on the managing director, who, in general, is a representative of the biggest shareholder.

"The chairman of a corporation is the organ of business leadership. . . . Up to now the chairman was subject to far-reaching control by the Supervisory Board [elected by the stockholders]. This has been changed. The Supervisory Board now only has the right to appoint and recall the chairman. Under the new law the management of the corporation becomes the sole responsibility of the managing director. He is now therefore independent of the chairman of the Supervisory Board, and is not subject to the latter's instructions." [12] There are other reforms along the same line.[13]

The structure of the National Socialist State somehow serves as an example for all corporations. An understanding of the structure of the totalitarian State, therefore, makes it easy to understand the changes in the structure of the private corporation. At the head of the Third Reich is the Fuehrer, the authoritarian executive. Private citizens may be compared to stockholders who still have a claim to dividend payments, but have no power to render that claim effective. And as the Fuehrer controls the State, so command of the corporation has been usurped by the authoritarian executive. The shareholders have lost their controlling influence and no longer have any right to insist on their claims at the shareholders' meeting. They have no right to protest and to remove directors who do not respect the property rights of the members of the corporation. On the contrary, the managers have such authoritarian power that they can refuse any dividend or interest payment, demonstrating to their creditors that any return on their capital, any dividend or interest payment, is not their due but rather a voluntary act on the part of the executive.

The world economic crisis has created widespread mistrust among investors. It is no longer possible for corporations to convince prospective investors that the future earning power of new investments is as certain as it appeared during prosperity. But the State is in a better position. It has the power to tax the people and the whole economy—more power than any private monopoly which can tax only certain sections of the economy or the consumers of its particular products.

In modern capitalism claims for interest or future profits are mortgaged and turned into "capital." Debts appear as wealth of creditors, and therefore as "wealth of the nation." State debts also are registered as "national wealth" because capitalists or investors have acquired claims for interest payments to be made at some future date. The greater such claims are, the higher taxation mounts, the greater the "national wealth" becomes. This kind of "national wealth" can be tremendously increased under a totalitarian regime, to a greater extent and at a quicker pace than under liberal capitalism, for the totalitarian State does not allow the private investor to judge for himself the kind of investment he wants to make, the reliability of the debtor and the prospect of the debtor's willingness to fulfill his financial obligations. This is the outcome of State dictatorship on the capital market.

*Chapter XII*

# "SELF-SUFFICIENCY" THROUGH ERSATZ

"Much technical genius and hard work have gone into adapting the industrial machine to the use of *ersatz*. The results have been disappointing—huge investments to produce inferior articles at higher prices."

SCIENCE, particularly modern chemistry, enables us to reproduce almost all "natural" products. Furthermore, chemistry gives us other completely new products, different from anything in nature. Today it may be economically unsound to manufacture them in quantity because of insufficient technical development; tomorrow they may well revolutionize production and consumption.

Criticism of ersatz production in Germany and other totalitarian states must not be regarded as denying the likelihood of further technical progress. It seems certain that progress will not be frozen at today's level. Already trends are discernible which indicate that we are witnessing only the beginning of a new technical revolution. To grasp the implications fully is not yet possible. Today new technical methods are used to increase the production of armaments and to give them a more destructive power, far exceeding that of any previous implements of war. This "progress" means that technical possibilities exist which might be used for a better purpose.

Synthetic materials, or "ersatz," are produced in the United States as well as in Germany. The American firm, E. I. du Pont de Nemours & Company, Inc., is in the forefront of this development. Dr. C. M. A. Stine, in an article published in the *Du Pont Magazine,* indicates the tremendous potentialities that are now unfolding as a result of present-day discoveries.

"We have entered the Chemical or Scientific Age. The Machine Age could not go beyond the limitations of natural materials, so that in the main it was limited to improving things known for centuries. The Scientific Age is taking us beyond into a realm of new materials not to be found in Nature, and from them we are creating things that did not and could not exist before.

"This new ability of man to create, and the new vision it has given us, in turn is creating a new economy—an economy that is putting wealth, in the true sense of greater enjoyment of life, within the reach of millions who never before knew it; that is, creating new opportunities for work, new leisure, new health. Above all it is creating new knowledge in the light of which almost nothing stands as impossible." [1]

But limited capacity to consume is an obstacle to further expansion on a mass-production basis. Construction of new and better plants and equipment would make existing means of production obsolete. The dead weight of the old investments hampers technical progress. The United States has the advantage of a wide internal market—wider than that of any other country—which has enabled it to participate in the development of synthetic products on a mass-production basis to a greater extent than other countries. The United States likewise has no difficulty in financing the huge investments necessitated by new chemical industries. In Germany, on the other hand, recently built plants for synthetic products would not have been created were it not for the strong pressure of the totalitarian State upon economic life. Government intervention can achieve results which would be impossible under the competitive system. But as a result of this development of new chemical industries, Germany's internal economic equilibrium has been seriously thrown out of balance.

The mere evidence of new technical developments does not necessarily mean that at the present time their application is economically justified. At a later stage they may well turn out to be a success from the economic point of view as well. The fascist State must disregard economic considerations. Its main concern is: are the new plants essential for wartime economy or for the replacement of raw materials which cannot be imported because of lack of foreign currency? This makes the State especially interested in ersatz, or synthetic production.

It has happened before that a regime which, historically, represented the extreme decay of a society, sponsored new technical developments which became effective only after the downfall of the regime that gave them life.

The comparison with feudalism in its period of decay is striking. When absolute kings strengthened their political power by encouraging what industry and commerce existed, their actions foreshadowed the replacement of individual home production by modern industrial production.

History seems to repeat itself. Frederick William, absolute ruler of Prussia at the beginning of the eighteenth century, tried to introduce local production of silk, a costly attempt which was a complete failure. The National-Socialist State has repeated the experiment. Under the first Four-Year Plan several communities in Bavaria, Saxony and the Rhineland were forced to cultivate mulberry bushes, and special associations were organized to persuade the peasants to collect the cocoons. In 1934, the Weidenwerk Spinnhuette A.G. was founded in Zelle with government capital. In 1936, 472 kilograms of silk were produced on German soil. Since then, however, nothing more has been heard of the experiment.

The absolute monarch of the eighteenth century who wanted to strengthen his power felt it necessary to introduce certain industries into the economy of his country. But society was still fundamentally feudal; it relied on agriculture and manual labor and was not yet prepared for modern industrial production. Consequently, the State factories were very expensive and did not lead to progress in other spheres. Yet they were the first signs of a new technical era in a backward country. Gigantic chemical plants turning out new or "artificial" products may well play the same role under fascism as the State-sponsored factories did under feudalism in decay.

Before going into details as to the success of ersatz production, something should be said about the character of the economic "self-sufficiency" the fascist State is trying to create.

There is widespread misunderstanding about "autarchy." Increased barriers against world trade, and particularly the development of productive forces to replace foreign raw materials, are tendencies which can be observed in all countries, but this process has reached its culmination in the fascist "have not" countries. Everywhere industries producing for the world market have declined; they relied on an international division of labor and looked forward to an indefinite expansion of markets and of productive forces.

A competitive economy can never be satisfied with what it has gained. The steady drive for world-wide expansion has been reflected in the industrial structure of those countries which supplied the world with goods. Industries producing "capital goods" or "means of production" grew at a much faster rate than those manufacturing consumption goods. However, in the end, the new "means of production" must serve to produce finished articles for consumption by human beings—except in the case of "means of destruction," which belongs to a peculiar economic, or, rather, uneconomic, category.

In the industrial economy of our times the capacity to produce capital goods has by far exceeded the capacity to produce consumption goods. In order to find a market for capital goods, industrialists have had to make investments which heightened the disparity between the two divisions of industry. When world economy was expanding, that economic disparity was bridged by the opening of new markets and fields of investment. Now that such expansion is no longer possible, the disproportion has become a tremendous problem.

On the surface, fascist economy, particularly in Germany, seems to have found a solution for the economic crisis; it has been able to employ fully every able-bodied man and woman. Nazi leaders have proclaimed "autarchy"—economic self-sufficiency—as a program to keep the nation and the industrial machine busy creating new productive forces and ending dependence on the rest of the world. The reality, however, is quite different.

The economic policy of the fascist regime does not create economic self-sufficiency. Genuine self-sufficiency would mean complete independence of world economy. The new productive forces under fascism increase the disparity between capital goods and consumption goods industries. The decline of the consumption goods industries proceeds at a quickened pace, while the capital goods industries grow rapidly. But these capital goods are largely synonymous with war materials.

In the essence of things, such an industrial policy is not independence from world economy. On the contrary, it means preparations for the conquest by force of new markets and international monopolies. These war preparations influence decisively Germany's industrial structure.

German prewar industrialization was characterized by two phenomena: the rise of German militarism, and the supplying of goods for the world market. The former entailed a disproportionate growth of those heavy industries necessary for the production of armaments. The latter meant the growth of industries producing machinery largely for export.

Prewar Germany developed a gigantic heavy industry, which produced iron and steel in greater quantities than any other European country. Iron and steel firms earned profits as a result both of the armaments race, which was started by German militarism at the end of the nineteenth century, and of German imperialist expansion (for example, the Berlin-Bagdad Railway).

While British industry developed first on the basis of textile exports, German industrial growth was based from the beginning upon huge exports of iron, steel and machinery. Hence, for German capitalism continuing industrial development of the world was a vital necessity on which her large export of capital goods depended. So long as world capitalism was expanding, Germany's prosperous industrial machine could go on working at full speed, supplying the world with the means for further industrial development.

Postwar Germany had lost her prewar position as the leading producer of iron, steel and machinery, and the monopoly of certain chemical products she formerly held. There still remained certain types of machines with which German industrialists supplied the world market in competition with only one other country—the United States of America. But after the World War the dependence of world economy on German machines and other means of production decreased as a result of industrial progress in other parts of the world. Yet immense sums were invested in the renewal, modernization and extension of Germany's industries, financed, to a large extent, by foreign loans.

From the military point of view, Germany's prewar industrial structure was a happy combination of a powerful heavy industry with big manufacturing plants which did not need subsidies in peacetime. Germany's prewar industries were privately financed and remained good businesses mainly as a result of the nation's unique ability to supply the world with complicated machinery, electrical equipment, etc.

Now there is a still greater disproportion than in prewar times in the growth of heavy industry. The totalitarian State is attempting, on a gigantic scale, to use and extend its industrial capacity in such a way as to make German militarism the strongest in the world—so strong that it will be able to conquer by force what it cannot achieve by peaceful commercial competition. From being the workshop of the world, German industrialism has become the workshop for German militarism. Therefore Germany's exports no longer expand at a rate corresponding to the growth of Germany's industrial capacity.

Reduction of exports brings about reductions in imports and a resultant scarcity of foreign raw materials. This necessitates the production of ersatz without consideration of the high costs involved. The whole industrial machine may come to a standstill unless enough "ersatz" is available. New technical processes must therefore be put into operation even before they have reached the mass-production stage.

Among the raw materials which are of vital importance to German industry, textile fibers, ores, petroleum, timber and rubber occupy first place. It is in these fields that the greatest efforts have been made to replace imports by domestic production. Without these materials German industry cannot exist and Germany's war machine cannot function. Their share in Germany's imports in 1929 was 39 per cent; in 1932, 32 per cent; in 1935, 32 per cent; and in 1938, 35 per cent.[2]

### *Cell Wool*

Cotton and wool, the major raw materials needed by European textile manufacturers, were and still are shipped largely from America and Australia. In return, Europe supplied and continues to supply the rest of the world with finished goods. But this world trade has declined. From 1932 to 1938 German imports of cotton fell almost 40 per cent in quantity and about 36 per cent in value; from 1929 to 1938 the decline amounted to 48 per cent in quantity and 77 per cent in value. Imports of wool dropped 23 per cent in quantity and 12 per cent in value from 1932 to 1938; from 1929 to 1938, the decline was 32.8 per cent in quantity and 71.9 per cent in value.

GERMAN IMPORTS OF COTTON [3]

| | *1929* | *1932* | *1935* | *1937* | *1938* |
|---|---|---|---|---|---|
| In million marks | 814.7 | 291.3 | 329.7 | 275.1 | 186.9 |
| In 1,000 tons | 476.8 | 424.7 | 397.4 | 349.6 | 250.0 |

GERMAN IMPORTS OF WOOL

| | *1929* | *1932* | *1935* | *1937* | *1938* |
|---|---|---|---|---|---|
| In million marks | 739.4 | 236.4 | 248.1 | 285.2 | 207.3 |
| In 1,000 tons | 204.6 | 180.0 | 156.3 | 128.2 | 138.9 |

Foreign sources of supply have shifted too, especially cotton imports. Germany imported only 19 per cent of its cotton supply from the United States in 1938 compared to 75 per cent in 1932 and 76 per cent in 1929. Brazil and Egypt have superseded the United States as exporters to the Reich. Imports of raw cotton were increased from those countries with which barter deals were consummated. Germany exchanged industrial goods, munitions and so forth for raw materials. Conversely, imports of raw materials were curtailed from those countries with which such barter deals could not be arranged.

The growth of synthetic production has had a very great effect upon all cotton and wool exporting countries and is of increasing importance since it indicates that the old international division of labor has come to an end. Synthetic production of textile fibers started with artificial silk or rayon [4] which resembles silk more than it does wool or cotton. Another synthetic product, cell wool, a rayon staple fiber which is made from wood or skimmed milk as the basic raw material, is a strong competitor of cotton and wool. Cell wool has become the main source of supply for domestic textiles in countries where a scarcity of foreign currency and large scale armament construction have necessitated rigorous restrictions on the import of raw materials for textiles.[5]

A recent issue of a German periodical makes the following comment:

"This [the development of cell wool] is the astonishing fact, and, as will be shown, it threatens wool. It is not the production of the 'have nots' which counts, but the interest of the entire spinning and textile-consuming world in the new fiber. For as soon as the success of the new spinning materials was made known, even the countries which did not have raw material difficulties started producing it. . . . The old cotton and wool countries, the United States and England, took up staple-fiber production on a large scale and within the last three years have greatly increased it." [6]

Since 1932, production of cell wool has been rapidly expanded in Germany. Italy and Japan, in order to replace cotton and wool. In 1937, the Reich produced about ten times more cell wool than the United States, Italy 6.8 times more than the United States, and Japan 7.7 times more than the United States.

WORLD PRODUCTION OF CELL WOOL

(In million pounds) [7]

| | *U S. A.* | *Germany* | *Japan* | *Italy* | *Great Britain* | *France* | *World Total* |
|---|---|---|---|---|---|---|---|
| 1929 | .5 | 2.4 | — | 1.7 | 2.6 | — | 7.2 |
| 1932 | 1.1 | 5.5 | .6 | 9.4 | 1.2 | 1.6 | 19.8 |
| 1937 | 20.2* | 220.0 | 174.8 | 156.3 | 32.7 | 11.3 | 623.0 |

(*Preliminary figure of the Bureau of Census)

In pressing for the mass production of cell wool and other synthetic materials, the fascist countries have been motivated neither by a desire to increase productive forces with a view to satisfying previously nonexistent demand nor by the possibility of producing such raw materials more cheaply than the corresponding "natural" products. New factories have been built, or are under construction, as a result of decisions of a government which considers only military preparations important.

In discussing the sudden rise in the production of cell wool in Germany, Italy and Japan, the German Institute for Business Research emphasized the fact that the rise had been due largely to State subsidics and indicated that it was skeptical about the future of the new plants.

The Institute report states:

"General rearmament throughout the world has naturally led to a greater demand for wool. . . . Only when world rearmament has come to an end and military needs are the normal replacement needs, can staple fiber (cell wool)—when civil demands predominate—be a strong competitor of wool. . . . Natural wool will probably maintain its position as a 'heavier' textile raw material for heavy clothing in colder climates." [8]

In spite of the skepticism expressed by experts, the German government has gone ahead with its plans of rapid extension of cell wool production. In 1935, orders were issued for the immediate construction of four cell-wool factories. They were financed partly by the State and partly by compulsory contributions from the textile companies, the latter being forced to buy shares in the new companies.[9] The cell wool industry is confined to seven companies: two of them—I.G. Farbenindustrie, the chemical trust, and Vereinigte Glanzstoffwerke, the largest rayon concern—control over 50 per cent of the total production.[10]

At the time this development was taking place, other branches of the textile industry increased their production of textile fibers, but this increase did not compare with the increase in the production of cell wool, either relatively or absolutely.

The following table gives some idea of the production of textile raw materials in Germany.

GERMAN PRODUCTION OF TEXTILE RAW MATERIALS

(Official figures—in tons)

| | *1933* | *1937* | *1938* | *1939* |
|---|---|---|---|---|
| Flax | ? | 26,000 | 28,000 | |
| Hemp | 200 | 6,800 | 10,000 | |
| Natural wool | 5,200 | 7,100 | 7,500 | |
| Artificial silk | 28,700 | 57,500 | 65,000 | |
| Cell wool | 5,400 | 102,000 | 150,000 | 225,000 [11] |
| Reworked wool | 9,300 | 55,000 | 60,000 | |
| Reworked cotton | 9,000 | 37,000 | 42,000 | |

Only a small proportion of Germany's consumption of "natural" textile raw materials can be satisfied from domestic production while the home production of artificial silk and cell wool already exceeds the domestic demand.

German production of textile raw materials in 1938 in per cent of consumption (1937)[12]

|  |  |
| --- | --- |
| Flax | 46.1 per cent |
| Hemp and jute | 4.9 per cent |
| Natural and reworked wool | 17.2 per cent |
| Artificial silk | 118.2 per cent |
| Cell wool | 142.8 per cent |
| Reworked cotton | 9.3 per cent |

According to the German Institute for Business Research, Germany had to import 94 per cent of her supply of textile fibers in 1933. This percentage fell to 83 per cent during the first Four-Year Plan, but this growth in self-sufficiency becomes less impressive if one takes into consideration the fact that even in 1938 the total production of textile raw materials in Germany amounted to only 22.3 per cent of the consumption.

Official statements declare that the quality of certain kinds of cell wool approximates that of cotton and wool. For example, the *Saechsische Wirtschaft,*[13] trade organ of Saxony's manufacturers, described cell wool in the following manner:

"This new material . . . is no substitute, no passing fancy, but a well-liked fiber. Previously it was of poor quality, but now it has a tremendous advantage over all natural fibers; its texture can be varied according to specific requirements."

Companies producing cell wool have reported the development of several types which are as permanently curly, elastic and heat-retaining as natural wool. The I. G. Farbenindustrie claims that its new fiber, "Vistralan," will react in the dyeing process exactly like wool.

From the technical point of view it may be possible

to produce artificial fibers which are superior in quality to cotton or wool, or fibers which have completely new properties. But the important question is not whether cell wool is really an effective substitute for cotton and wool but whether a good quality of cell wool can be produced to sell at a reasonable price. According to all technical experts, the production costs of these materials are so much greater than similar costs for cotton or wool that the mass production of these fibers is out of the question for many years to come. The exorbitant costs of production have been reduced at the expense of quality. But even fibers of inferior quality are more expensive than cotton or wool.

Consumers buying articles manufactured from cell wool are generally disappointed, for prices are higher and quality inferior. The government claims that the new material will soon supersede cotton and wool; that it will be cheaper in price and better in quality. But the consumers are not convinced; they stock up on cotton and wool articles, thereby increasing the scarcity of these materials.

Clothes made from cell wool are generally stiff and heavy and often retain moisture. In commenting on them, a private report declared: "A few years ago the big clothing shops were able to sell a suit made of pure wool for 35 marks. The worker could wear it for years. Today a suit, similar in appearance, costs 50 marks. The suit is no longer 'pure wool.' After a short time it looks like a sack. It soon shows wear and the threads look as if they were giving way. A few years ago one saw good overcoats in the shop windows for from 35 to 75 marks. Today the overcoats one sees cost 45 to 75 marks, but they are good in looks only. To get a coat of the former quality one must pay at least 120 to 200 marks."

In an announcement over the radio, President Kehrl, head of the Office for German Raw and Work Materials, declared that in 1938 capacity of cell wool production had reached a total of 150 million kilograms, or one-third of the previous demand for cotton and wool. He hastened to add that the public must not think cell wool clothes would deteriorate when they were washed, although he admitted that manufacturers often made statements such as, "We cannot guarantee this article as washable." In future, he declared, the police would forbid this.[14]

The quality of cell wool articles is undoubtedly higher than it was a few years ago but the price still is higher than former prices for similar wool articles. The tensile strength on which the quality of the yarn depends has been increased thirty and more per cent. In September, 1937, the Price Commissar forced a reduction of the cell wool price over the protests of the cell wool firms. German cell wool firms claimed that high costs of production plus heavy investment risks made it impossible to reduce prices. Nevertheless the price was reduced 9.3 per cent. Simultaneously the compulsory admixture of cell wool with cotton yarn in the finished product was increased from 16 to 20 per cent. Naturally the cheaper qualities disappeared from the market, while higher-priced articles were available in quantity. Unfortunately, the higher-priced articles of "better quality" were hardly as good as the previous cheaper quality had been.

Before the introduction of cell wool, Augsburg cotton yarn cost 1.33 marks a kilogram; today, mixed with cell-wool yarn, it costs 2.07 marks, a price increase of almost

60 per cent and a simultaneous decrease in quality.

Mass production of cell wool has increased the demand for wood. But "the raw materials wood and skimmed milk (likewise used in the manufacture of cell wool) are not available in unlimited quantities, and furthermore wood does not grow in a short time . . ." [15] In 1937, the Government decreed that 50 per cent more timber should be supplied from German forests than was supplied previously, in spite of the fact that such excessive lumbering is bound to have disastrous effects on German forestry.

The supply of wood from German cuttings has been increased from 25 million cubic meters annually (1925-1929) to 39.0 million in 1937, and about 45 million cubic meters in 1938.[16]

In the long run, this means the depletion of German forests, all the more so as the demand for wood as a substitute for other scarce materials increases. The Government has therefore decided that production of synthetic fibers shall not be expanded beyond the point where such fibers represent more than 20 to 25 per cent of the total textile consumption.

Yet the army needs wool for uniforms. Large subsidies, therefore, were paid to farmers in order to make sheep herding more attractive than the raising of cattle. Sheep-raisers were guaranteed a domestic price for their wool which was two and a half to four times as high as the world market price. In addition, they received long-term State credits on easy terms for the purchase of sheep. Fifty years ago the change from sheep breeding to the raising of cattle and grain was considered a sign of progress. Today the Government is paying a subsidy to those who are willing to use their land for sheep.

### *Synthetic Gasoline*

It would be futile to build a huge air fleet and construct thousands of tanks, armored cars, etc., unless sufficient gasoline were available to operate them. Consequently, the Nazis have expended great efforts in an endeavor to increase the domestic production of gasoline, and these efforts have shown remarkable results. German official reports claim that 100 per cent self-sufficiency in gasoline can be achieved through synthetic production, but this assertion is contradicted by the Reich's violent drive for control of foreign petroleum resources.

According to the German Institute for Business Research, in 1937 Germany produced 36 per cent of the mineral oils (natural and synthetic products) she consumed, as against 20 per cent in 1935. In 1939, Germany will probably produce 50 per cent of her requirements. It is, however, very significant that domestic production of "gas oil" (Diesel oil), especially important for warfare, is relatively small and amounted to only 8.7 per cent of consumption in 1937.[17]

GERMANY'S SUPPLIES OF MINERAL OILS

| | *Total Consumption* | *Production from Domestic Raw Materials* | |
|---|---|---|---|
| | (1,000 tons) | (1,000 tons) | (In % of total consumption) |
| Gasoline | 2,345 | 1,220 | 52.0 |
| Diesel oil | 1,385 | 120 | 8.7 |
| Kerosene oil | 89 | 40 | 44.9 |
| Fuel oil | 791 | 320 | 40.5 |
| Lubricants | 540 | 140 | 25.9 |
| | 5,150 | 1,840 | 35.9 |

Yet the rise in gasoline production is quite impressive in view of the fact that Germany possesses no important natural crude oil resources. It should be remembered, however, that the whole economy of the country has to pay a heavy toll to support domestic gasoline production.

The price of synthetic gasoline is four times that of the world market price for natural gasoline, despite the huge subsidies paid the producers of the synthetic product.

According to the calculations of Dr. Rudolf Regul,[18] the cost of production of synthetic gasoline from coal amounts to about four times the cost of production of natural gasoline.

The German consumer has to pay for imported gasoline:

| | *In marks* |
|---|---|
| World market price for 91.5 liters of imported gasoline (includes expenses for transportation) | 6.70 |
| Import duty | 18.35 |
| Turnover tax | .47 |
| Compulsory admixture of German alcohol (8.5 per cent) | 3.00 |
| | 28.52 |

Furthermore, the importer and salesman have to make a profit, so that the final price is more than four times the world market price.

In theory it is possible to extend synthetic gasoline production almost indefinitely. But the national economy cannot live merely on gasoline. German military experts are, however, inclined to make heavy inroads into the economy of the country in order to assure a greater supply of gasoline during wartime.

Self-sufficiency of mineral oils in peacetime would not assure self-sufficiency in wartime. According to German experts in war economy, the army air force and navy would absorb over seven million tons of gasoline or fuel per year in wartime, in addition to the present peacetime consumption of five million tons. Even this estimate has been criticized as too low. It is asserted that gasoline and fuel consumption of a "big power" waging totalitarian war would jump to three or four times its peacetime consumption.[19]

### *Buna*

Rubber is another key product needed in vast quantities both in war and in peace, as a result of the growing motorization of transport. Natural rubber does not grow in Europe. During the last World War, the urgent need for rubber compelled Germany to produce synthetic rubber and to use it despite its high production costs and the many deficiencies in quality. But as soon as the World War ended, synthetic rubber production was discontinued.

Present conditions have again intensified the efforts of German experts to solve the problem of synthetic rubber production. A new German synthetic rubber—called Buna—is to play the role in its field which cell wool plays in the textile field. Buna is supposed to be as good as or better than natural rubber, and in certain cases this seems to be true. However, the "better quality" of synthetic rubber—especially its greater hardness—tends to complicate the manufacturing process. When Buna was first introduced, German manufacturers estimated that they required nearly four times as much machinery to work with it as with natural rubber. Since then, technical developments have decreased this proportion [20] but, according to German experts, costs of production are still at least three times higher than those of natural rubber. Huge investments in plants for the production of Buna have been made, although, from the point of view of economy, the process has not yet reached the mass-production stage. Production has been made possible only by huge subsidies and "conscription" of capital.[21]

As a matter of fact, consumption of rubber has grown more than the production of Buna. Although Germany can produce over 25 per cent of her needs, she is now importing more natural rubber than formerly, before production of Buna was started. Imports of natural rubber in 1938 were 66.6 per cent higher than in 1933, at the beginning of the first Four-Year Plan. It is expected that Buna production can be extended to about one-third of Germany's rubber requirements in 1939-40.[22]

What a price has to be paid for this 25 or 33 per cent self-sufficiency! In 1937, a hundred per cent ad valorem duty was imposed on rubber imports. This yielded 160 to 170 million marks yearly. The price of natural rubber has increased more than 100 per cent, yet Buna still costs over 60 per cent more than natural rubber and nearly four times as much as rubber abroad.

Before foreign natural rubber passes the German customs it costs about one-third of the sales price in Germany. Yet three times the world market price for natural rubber is insufficient to cover the costs of production of synthetic rubber. The German producer therefore gets a subsidy of almost twice the world market price in cash from the Government—in spite of which, private producers complain that production is not profitable.

Germany spent 80 million marks for the import of rubber in 1938. Home production of this rubber would have cost about 400 million marks.

In addition, every industry using rubber has had to buy new machinery. The opinion of German capitalists on this matter was expressed by *Die Braune Wirtschaftspost* as follows: "Relative risks in the rubber industry are very high . . . because the shift [from natural rubber] to Buna means losses in many cases . . .[23]

Synthetic production of rubber might soon be resumed in all industrial countries, but it is improbable that buna will become of decisive importance. Its production is complicated and expensive and better processes might be discovered.

"Development of a process for making a synthetic rubber from butane was announced today by Dr. Gustav Egloff, director of the research laboratories of the Universal Oil Products Company, who said the process had been advanced to the stage of commercial utilization. Their synthetic rubber has wearing properties superior to those of natural rubber, and he added that its costs will enable it to compete with natural rubber for many uses.

"The synthetic product developed in his laboratories is better and cheaper than the 'buna' rubber produced in Germany, Dr. Egloff said. The German material is made by a process which starts with acetylene, a synthetic hydrocarbon which must be manufactured from calcium carbide in an electric furnace process, while the American process starts with a gas so plentiful that it is almost a waste product in some oil fields and is also produced as a by-product in refinery processes." [24]

### *Other Substitutes*

There are many other substitutes such as alloys and plastic materials to replace metal, fish skin as a substitute for leather. Much technical genius and hard work have gone into adapting the industrial machine to the use of ersatz. The results have been disappointing—huge investments to produce inferior articles at higher prices.

It is typical that the Nazis should expect the gigantic automobile plant financed by the German Labor Front to become the largest and most modern in Germany. The buyers of the new automobile are not so sure of the value of the product, however, especially when they are compelled to sign a declaration that they have no claim for compensation if the technical standards should not be up to minimum legal requirements. For the new "people's automobile," the special pride of the Fuehrer, will be built with ersatz materials.

The absolute power of the State has been used to advance the armament industries and ersatz with such ruthlessness that the decline in other branches of industry has been accelerated. Germany's capacity for obtaining foreign currency and raw materials through the medium of exports has also declined. The situation has a momentum of its own. The greater the scarcity of raw materials, the stronger becomes the pressure of the State to extend production of ersatz, regardless of expense and in spite of insufficient technical experience.

For example, at a convention of German soap manufacturers on August 30, 1937, the official speaker, Arthur Imhausen, told those present that synthetic fats would be produced from coal tar, not only for making soap but also for fine quality butter. On another occasion, at an exhibition sponsored by a State-subsidized research institute in Duisburg, a group of peasants who had eaten butter made from coal testified that this synthetic product could not be distinguished from the best natural butter. Unfortunately, realities have a way of interfering with official plans. The trade organ of the German coal experts, *Der Kohleninteressent,* issued a warning that it would be a long time before synthetic butter could possibly compete with natural butter. Their warning said: "Artificial butter made from coal is a purer fat than natural butter . . . It is better not to say very much about the question of costs of production . . ." Earlier, Dr. Bergius, outstanding German expert on synthetic production and inventor of the best known process for the production of gasoline from coal, declared at a meeting at the Haus der Technik in Essen: "The pig is still the best fat producer. We have not been able to discover an industrial process for producing fat so effectively."

*Chapter XIII*

# *FROM WORLD TRADE TO TRADE WARFARE*

"The Greeks have to accept payment in mouth organs or radio sets, and in such large quantities that their demand for these articles could be satisfied for many years to come. Optical instruments which the Nazi Reich could not export elsewhere were offered to the Bulgarian peasants."

IN THE era of world prosperity, when crises and depressions seemed merely temporary interruptions in the onrushing stream of continued economic development, international trade relied upon a scheme of generally accepted rights, laws and customs as much as upon freedom of the seas and protection against pirates and robbers. Since the world crisis of 1929, however, the old concepts have been brushed aside and new and confusing practices are supplanting the stable relations which formerly regulated international commerce. Only fragments of the fundamental principles looked upon but a few years ago as virtually immutable are still operative. A variety of new methods and conditions have profoundly affected the former freedom of international trade. The private businessman attempts to adapt himself to the new conditions and to continue "business as usual," but the changes, involving him in a variety of risks previously unknown, are so manifold and far-reaching, and they are sprung upon him with such alarming suddenness that he scarcely has time to consider any given situation before further changes upset his plans and negate his carefully laid precautions. He is compelled to take new risks unless he is content to sit still and retire from business. He may still hope that the new restrictions on his freedom in international trade are only temporary and will end with a happy return to the "good old times." But such hopes are becoming more and more remote from reality. And the end is not yet in sight.

In all of the existing confusion, only one thing seems clear, namely, that a new consolidation of world trade, of its rules and conditions, has not yet been achieved. Whether or not the foreign trader will ever again find himself on safe and unshifting ground is at least problematical.

The changeover from free trade to trade subjected to protective tariffs did not begin to compare in importance with the problems confronting international trade at the present time—State regimentation and State control of foreign trade, establishment of State boards for the handling of foreign currency, export and import quotas, State measures against "flight of capital." Such regimentation has been instituted not only in fascist States; many of these measures have likewise been adopted in those non-fascist States which were affected to an especially grave degree by the world's economic crisis.

About 25 per cent of the world trade of today is strictly subject to exchange controls. In addition, a further sizable proportion of world commerce is hedged around by other State restrictions which drastically interfere with the free flow of commerce, subordinating it to the "tasks of the State." Tariff regulations have lost in importance, for direct interference curbs imports far more effectively than protective tariffs. It is obvious that no country in the world can avoid being influenced by these changes. In the long run, all countries will be forced to adapt their foreign trade systems in conformity with the new situation.

State economic measures which affect only the internal market do not necessarily force other States to adopt similar measures. In international trade, however, a new policy and a new conception enforced by one country compels all other countries, or the traders of those countries, to transform their commercial habits so as to be able to meet the new competition. International trade relies on certain customs and conventions which must be equally effective everywhere. They must be respected by all participants. If, however, one group of traders defies them systematically and cannot be disciplined, then all other participants must change their methods and policies, too. A foreign trader who acts as a private businessman representing only his own firm cannot deal on an equal footing with a foreign trader who is the agent of the State. The U.S.S.R. was the first State which organized complete State control (State monopoly) of foreign trade in peacetime. This had an important effect upon international trade methods. In all other States where trade relations with the U.S.S.R. were of any importance special organizations were formed and measures adopted by the State and by private trade associations in order to regulate transactions with the U.S.S.R. Yet this was regarded as an exception and did not fundamentally change the traditional practices in foreign trade.

Today, however, the exception has largely become the

rule. Japanese exporters are organized in export cartels by the State. The State restricts competition among exporters and importers. The same thing is done in Germany and Italy. Moreover, it is not only in totalitarian States that payments for imported goods have become dependent on governmental decisions. Similar regulations have been adopted in certain non-totalitarian countries. Any foreign trader exporting to such a country must make sure in advance that the State involved is willing to supply foreign currency for the payment of his goods.

Furthermore, the private trader cannot compete with the trader of another country who is subsidized or otherwise supported unless he himself receives similar support from his own government. In most countries the State has now organized special measures for the "promotion" of exports. The preservation of traditional rules and the retention of the conservative spirit on the part of certain businessmen gives an advantage to their competitors whose business transactions are directed and subsidized by their governments and who do not feel bound to traditional rules and international laws.

There are, of course, many instances where the free and independent businessman has an advantage over one who is State regimented and dependent on decisions of a government bureaucracy. But in the long run the advantages are outweighed by the superior power of a State over that of a private businessman. Trading with a firm located in a totalitarian State is peculiarly hazardous because such a firm is no longer a free agent, subject only to accepted international regulations. The actions of a firm in a totalitarian State assume what appears to be a very capricious character. This is inevitable, for the

State has absolute power to modify private contracts and their execution—or nonexecution.

The situation is complicated by the extreme uncertainty and confusion which surrounds all dealings with a firm whose every activity is controlled by the State. The State-regimented foreign trader plays a dual role—he appears as a private businessman, signing contracts in the name of his "private" firm. But the fulfillment of his contracts, his buying and selling policies, depend neither on his own free will nor on the international customs and laws which were valid in a free competitive world economy. Whether fulfillment of contracts can be guaranteed or violation of contract can be prosecuted depends to a large extent on the government's decision and on the political power of the State. This factor has been recognized by many foreign traders only after experiences which have proved costly indeed. Totalitarian States still exploit regulations developed under unrestricted competitive world trade although they have already changed these rules and laws in accordance with the "interests of the State." The secret of the success of certain new trade methods of Nazi Germany is the belated recognition by other countries of the structural changes that have occurred in world trade. Dr. Hjalmar Schacht in particular recognized and exploited the inability of a competitive company to defend its interests efficiently in commercial deals with totalitarian States.

German foreign traders used to joke about the international trade methods of the President of the Reichsbank. One story ran as follows:

A deputation of South Sea natives was sent to the President of the Reichsbank and addressed him thus:

"Big chief of the money: Our magician has instructed

us to sail from our coasts over the big sea and to come to you. May we sell our Kauri shells to you?"

The President of the Reichsbank answered:

"With pleasure, gentlemen. You merely have to exchange the shells for Fiji canoes, the Fiji canoes for moss from Iceland, this moss for Chinese dog hair, Chinese dog hair for Japanese paper napkins, and the Japanese paper napkins for Argentine flax seed. We have need of Argentine flax seed in our margarine production. In payment we shall deliver to you the finest and most modern planetarium. When your big powerful magician sees the planetarium he will be delighted at this exchange and will be impressed with the progress in the world. Yes, gentlemen, the ways of modern world economy are *wunderbar*."

Hamburg and Bremen traders relate this story with a grim smile. They often are disgusted with the tricky methods used by the totalitarian State to obtain foreign raw materials without payment in foreign currency. In "payment" for the goods imported, Germany ships to her foreign customers, who are dependent on her goods, whatever articles she may happen to have in abundance regardless of whether or not the recipient wants this particular type of merchandise. Sometimes she makes no payment at all.

Primitive international trade began by barter, that is, by direct exchange of products without the use of money. These primitive practices have now been revived. When Germany resurrected barter trade, she represented it to potential foreign customers as a means of re-establishing world economic harmony which had broken down as a result of the world economic crisis. A glut of agricultural products and raw materials on the world market prevented agrarian and raw material producers from buying industrial goods. Simultaneously, industrial countries, in particular, Germany, were unable to sell their industrial products. A stalemate resulted, with Germany lacking foreign currency for the purchase of agricultural products and raw materials. Workers and machines remained idle. The finding of new ways of exchanging industrial goods for agricultural products or raw materials seemed a mere technical problem. "Barter," that is, exchange of industrial products for agricultural products and raw materials without payment in foreign currency or gold, seemed to be a remedy by which both patients—the agricultural country and the industrial country—could be cured of their ailments. Dr. Schacht, during his trip through the Balkans in 1938, as the Nazis' commercial agent, offered splendid schemes for the solution of the world economic crisis. "You need agricultural implements and industrial plants and material for railroads and armament. We are going to provide you with all these things," he said. He was asked: "How shall we pay?" The answer was persuasive: "What about the natural resources of your country? We are willing to accept all your crops and your output of raw materials in payment. We shall pay you more than the world market price. We are quite ready to come in and help you develop your natural resources to the best advantage and we are able to do this."

The solution sounded plausible. Experience, however, was to teach the agrarian and raw material producers that the world economic crisis could not be solved by reverting to more primitive methods of international trade. Barter proved extremely disappointing to Germany's customers. Barter trade made agrarian and raw material producers dependent on the totalitarian State in unforeseen ways. Barter trade likewise became an important weapon in the hands of the totalitarian State against its competitors on the world market. This development was not apparent during the first stages of barter deals. These initial transactions were private arrangements between German importers and foreign exporters. German importers, unable to obtain sufficient foreign currency to meet their payments, could now import foreign products on a barter basis, paying surpluses due their creditors in "additional" exports of German goods. The government hoped that these private barter deals would stimulate German exports and thereby relieve the scarcity of raw materials. It was not the intention, however, that barter deals should be resorted to where the customer could pay for the manufactured articles either in foreign currency or in specie. Had this system worked in practice as its sponsors hoped, Germany would have achieved her aim of acquiring both raw materials and foreign currency.

What actually happened, however, was that barter transactions tended to supplant sales for foreign currency or specie. It was more profitable for the German exporter to arrange with the foreign buyer that payments be made in materials instead of in cash. Whatever cash payment (foreign currency) was received had to be turned over to the Reichsbank. Foreign materials, however, could be imported and sold at a handsome profit. Scarcity of foreign materials and high prices in Germany made such barter business very attractive for the German exporter and often also for the foreign importer of German goods. The barter transactions, therefore, resulted in many upsets both in Germany's foreign trade and in her foreign currency position. Goods were imported which were not vital and could not be used for armament. Effective control of prices proved impossible and the flow of foreign currency to the Reichsbank dwindled. The resultant dislocations caused the Reich Foreign Exchange Board eventually to restrict private barter trade.[1] Private barter has almost been abolished, but the methods of barter trade have not been renounced. Barter transactions have become strictly government-controlled or direct State affairs.

Along with the difficulties that Germany has experienced in solving her problems by barter deals, one must also recognize that through them she has gained certain positive advantages, though these be only of a temporary nature. The exporter who is able to get cash payment for his sales abroad is no longer allowed to make barter deals. Countries with which Germany has an export surplus—for example, England—have been excluded from barter deals altogether. In countries where Germany buys vast quantities of raw materials and agrarian products, however, barter trade is used in order to compel the foreign seller to buy German products, thus stimulating German exports at the expense of her foreign competitors. American exporters of cotton, for instance, were previously paid in "Aski marks"; these could be spent only for German goods which naturally must be exported from Germany. The American exporter, therefore, became an importer and an involuntary sales agent of German goods. In spite of restrictions of barter trade, cotton could previously be exported from the United States to Germany on the basis of barter agreements. But since the introduction of "Countervailing Duties on Imports from Germany" [2] by the United

States Treasury Department, all imports from Germany on a barter basis have been prohibited.

A discussion of barter trade and the blocked mark would be incomplete without mention of another aspect of their operation. With a grand gesture, the Nazi government offered to purchase from the agrarian- and raw materials-producing countries their whole crop or output, or the greater part thereof, thus solving the problem these countries had of selling on a glutted world market. The Nazi State was willing to take care of sales difficulties. It was even willing to pay a price much higher than the world market price. Only one condition was imposed: that for these materials Germany should make no payments in foreign currency. Payments were to be made in Aski or in clearance marks (*Verrechnungs mark*) which could be spent only for purchases of German goods within Germany. The more agricultural products and raw materials Germany bought by paying in Aski or in clearance marks, the more the other country was bound to import from Germany. When no, or insufficient, compensating purchases were made, mark funds were accumulated—a foreign credit for the German State for which it paid no interest. The greater this credit became, the more the owner of Aski or clearance marks—often foreign governments—had to import from Germany, for otherwise these mark deposits were of no use. Various governments in southeastern Europe and in South and Central America were thereby compelled to import much more from Germany than they otherwise would have done.

The Nazi authorities did not regard the excessive price paid for agrarian products as a loss, for they could pay in goods which otherwise would not have found a market and could dictate the price of these goods since the agrarian-exporting State was obliged to buy German products. This put the Nazi authorities in a strong position and enabled them to raise the price for industrial export goods.

The Nazi State did not buy coffee, tobacco and other world goods merely for consumption at home. It needed gold and foreign currency and these it could obtain by selling on the world market goods secured through barter transactions (or by payment in Aski marks). The result was astounding:—the agrarian countries which were unable to obtain sufficient foreign currency to satisfy the urgent demands of their national economy found that they were in the position of having involuntarily granted credits to the Nazi State. The Nazi State, in turn, was able to dump these articles on the world market. The agrarian countries thought they had sold products to the Nazi Reich which they could not have sold elsewhere. But it happened in a number of cases that such goods were later resold by the Nazis on the world market. The agrarian country or raw material producer might have sold its products directly on the world market —at low prices, it is true, but in return it would have received foreign currency. Instead, the foreign currency went to the Reich while the agrarian producer received nothing but Aski marks for these sales.

This was the situation that developed between Germany on one hand and on the other hand such relatively poor countries as Greece, Bulgaria, and a number of the South and Central American countries which sold to Germany most or part of their crops—coffee, grain, corn, cattle, etc.—for which the Reich paid in blocked marks. In some countries—for example, Greece and

Rumania—the agrarian producer was paid by his own government in the currency of his country, and the government became the owner of clearance marks. If the government wanted to get something for the mysterious clearance marks, it had to buy German goods. But the Greek or Rumanian governments were unable to buy freely from Germany needed machinery or articles which contained a considerable percentage of scarce foreign materials. The Rumanian government was compelled instead to spend large amounts of blocked marks for the purchase of thousands of typewriters—enough to supply all the offices in Rumania for years. It had to resell these typewriters on the world market at a fraction of the cost price. Rumania, moreover, had to take the blame for dumping, although it acted only as the Reich's involuntary sales agent. Simultaneously, in order to obtain foreign currency, the Reich sold on the world market Rumanian agricultural products as well as Brazilian coffee, obtained by barter agreements.

"Germany got the advantage of a low-value currency for her imports and of high-value currency for her exports, at the expense of the foreign owners of the blocked mark. . . . At present the use of blocked marks in payment of German exports has almost completely ceased, although a large part of German trade with Latin-American countries is paid for with the so-called Aski, or compensation, marks. . . .

"Time after time during 1937 and 1938, it was announced that Germany had succeeded in obtaining orders for delivery of industrial plant or other capital goods on a long-term credit basis. This appeared all the more astonishing since Germany's banking resources did not allow for such generous credit terms. The explanation lies in the fact that in reality the credit transactions were financed not by Germany but by the governments of the debtor countries. . . .

"In general, exporters are very cautious when granting long-term credits to customers. This is particularly true with regard to Balkan customers. In Rumania, therefore, German sellers became very popular and were able to beat foreign competition because of the generous long-term credits they granted to anybody who wanted German goods. It has been made possible for anyone in the Balkans to buy a German motorcar or bicycle against a nominal deposit and on extremely easy terms." [3]

The London *Economist* called this transaction the "long-term credit trick." This "generosity" of the German seller was at the expense of the Rumanian government. The Rumanian purchaser of German goods turned over the money for the purchase not to the German seller, but to his own government. If he failed to meet his payments, the Rumanian government was the loser. Whether he paid or not, the German seller received the full price for his products from the clearance-mark deposit of the Rumanian government.

In spite of the growing foreign disillusionment with these barter deals, the Reich managed to continue its manipulations by offering considerably more than the world market price to foreign producers of agricultural products. The agrarian seller could see only that he apparently got more than he could get anywhere else.

German buyers paid about 43 per cent more than the world market price for wheat bought in southeastern Europe, and about 50 per cent more for barley. "In Poland, Germany concluded a deal for the sale of considerable machinery by signing an agreement whereby she will buy for some years agricultural products considerably above the world market prices." [4] But whether this deal will be carried out is doubtful.

Germany's clearing agreement with the Greek government showed a credit balance of 28 million marks in favor of Greece, but the Nazi government refused to settle this account—except by supplies of more German commodities which Greece did not need.

The same thing happened in Turkey. German buyers did not hesitate to buy all the mohair produced in Anatolia and all the nuts produced in Trabzon—and paid for them in goods or in blocked marks. In return, Turkey received German coffee mills, gramophones, radio sets and similar articles, although Turkey needed machinery. The German government sold the major part of the Turkish products for foreign currency on the world market.

The foreign owner of Aski or clearance marks often finds it impossible to buy those goods in Germany he wishes to buy. The German exchange control authorities excluded from the list of goods which can be bought with blocked marks for exports, according to a decision of July 19, 1938:

(a) Articles and commodities in which Germany has a virtual international monopoly to such extent that their export at the current high German prices requires no assistance.

(b) Goods of which there is a shortage in Germany so that their export is not favored by the German Government.

(c) Goods composed of foreign materials to such a large extent that their export is objectionable to the German Government because of the drain on Germany's foreign balances which would result from the purchase of the materials used in their manufacture.[5]

How rigorously this system is applied depends more or less on the political influence of the foreign State of which the foreign owner of the Aski marks is a citizen. American cotton exporters, for instance, are treated with more consideration than Greek or Bulgarian tobacco exporters. The Greeks have to accept payment in mouth organs or radio sets, and in such large quantities that their demand for these articles could be satisfied for many years to come. Optical instruments which the Nazi Reich could not export elsewhere were offered to the Bulgarian peasants. It has proved almost impossible, however, for those countries to purchase in Germany semimanufactured articles for their own domestic industries.

These methods of "barter" have enabled the Nazi Reich to make inroads in South American markets, especially in Brazil.

The Nazi State may consider the fact that the German share in the import trade of Latin America rose from 9.54 per cent in 1932 to 15.1 per cent in 1937 and reached almost the prewar level (16.5 per cent) as evidence of success. Latin America's share in Germany's import trade, however, declined from 12.2 per cent in 1913 to 8.9 per cent in 1937.[6]

The share of South America, as a whole, in Germany's exports rose from 3.3 per cent in 1932 to 10 per cent in 1938 (6.0 per cent in 1929). Germany's share of Brazil's total imports has more than doubled in the past ten years. It rose from 10.6 per cent in 1928 to 24.4 per cent in 1938. Simultaneously the United States' share of Brazil's imports declined in the same period from 28 per cent to 24 per cent. In 1938, therefore, Germany exported more to Brazil than did the United States. Mr. Eugene P. Thomas, President of the National Foreign Trade Council, in New York, commented on this development as follows:

"In her purchases from Brazil, Germany bought far in excess of her domestic requirements and resold at a profit and for cash what she herself could not absorb. In payment for these goods, Germany flooded Brazil with German manufactures which Brazil was unable to absorb as rapidly as they were dumped on her market. Many of these German goods were found to be not as suitable for Brazil's needs as American products. In her trade with Brazil, Argentina, Chile, Peru and Uruguay, Germany ran up a debit account of large proportions which she has been unable to settle. Victims of German barter methods, these Latin American countries found at the end of 1935, according to German estimates, that Germany's debts to South America had mounted to 650 million Reichsmarks. Other authorities place the actual indebtedness at about one billion Reichsmarks. Fearing that she might be shut out of these rich reservoirs of raw materials, Germany applied high pressure methods and did not hesitate to use political propaganda to attain her economic objectives." [7]

States which permitted private traders more or less freedom in the purchase and sale of German goods—the State, however, acting as intermediary and handling the financial end of the transaction—soon found that they could exercise no control over the workings of the barter or Aski mark system. They were powerless to prevent the system from serving exclusively the interests of the totalitarian State. In self-protection they therefore refused to renew those pacts or themselves established strict State control over exports to and imports from Germany.

The greater part of the raw materials the "have not" powers need cannot be obtained by barter deals or from vassal States. It must be imported from countries where the exporter insists on payment in money he can spend on the world market or in his country. This is the reason why Germany, like Italy and Japan, is in urgent need of foreign currency or gold. The principal means through which Germany can obtain foreign currency or gold is from payments from countries where the currency still is "free," that is, free to leave the country or return. In such countries, foreign trade, like trading in general, is still little supervised or manipulated by the State.

In totalitarian States, exporting is no longer the private concern of businessmen. They work for their own profit, but, more important, they also serve the cause of the State. The exporters of a totalitarian State appear very much like any other businessmen. Yet something has changed. They, in contrast to other businessmen, are State-regimented, but they also have ample opportunities to gain the financial assistance of the State in order to beat foreign competition. State control of exports has forced upon them a "national discipline"—a united front against foreign competition. Where they meet no foreign competition, they must raise prices to the highest degree possible; when they are faced with competition, they resort to dumping on an unprecedented scale. It is possible for them to do this because the State grants them export subsidies adequate to compensate them for the reduction in the selling price. The exporter of a totalitarian country is compelled to act as the agent of one big State trust, co-ordinating his policy with the sales policies of all other exporters, and getting full support—financially and otherwise—from his government. His foreign competitor, on the other hand, represents only his own private firm. This system has been organized on a grand scale, especially in Germany. The State exerts a strict control over the sales prices of all German exports. Any sale abroad must be registered with the Reich Foreign Exchange Board. This gives the government control of payments in foreign currency. It also enables the State to control the price policies of all German exporters. As a matter of fact, there exists a dual control of the price policies of German exporters. The German exporter must report the price for the sale of German goods abroad to the Reich Foreign Exchange Board, which was organized in 1935 by the then President of the Reichsbank, Dr. Hjalmar Schacht, as well as to the administration of the "Self-Help of German Industry." This harmless name seldom appears in Nazi publications. It is, in fact, the innocent-sounding title of an Export Subsidy Fund. The purpose of this fund, to which all industrialists must contribute, is to subsidize exporters who otherwise could not compete on the foreign market. Subsidies are not paid in all cases, however, and the amount of the subsidy varies greatly.

A firm which applies to the Export Subsidy Fund must prove that without the subsidy it cannot sell at a profit. The firm must also indicate at what price it can sell abroad. Officials of the Fund compare this sales price with prices for similar articles made by other manufacturers. Sometimes the officials insist on a higher price than that originally quoted because the foreign buyer cannot obtain the product elsewhere at that price.

During the first period of the Four-Year Plan, German exporters were subsidized either by being allowed to purchase German dollar bonds at depreciated prices or by being permitted to purchase scrip issued by the Conversion Office of the Reichsbank to foreign creditors in payment of debts. The scrip could be bought at a discount of approximately 50 per cent while it could be exchanged within Germany for its full mark value. The foreign creditor thus had to pay for the promotion and subsidizing of Germany's export trade. This kind of export subsidy was later superseded by the special Export Subsidy Fund. While the scrip method was widely discussed, when it was in use, only little is known about the Export Subsidy Fund. No exporter is allowed even to mention its existence during private conversations with foreign business friends. Consequently the following confidential letter from a trade group is revealing:

NEW SERVICE OF THE GERMAN
CLOTHING INDUSTRY
*Exportfoerderung*
Berlin W 68, Kielgaustr. 4
HERAUSGEGEBEN VON DER WIRTSCHAFTSGRUPPE UND
DER REICHSVEREINIGUNG DER DEUTSCHEN
BEKLEIDUNGSINDUSTRIE

Lfg. 22 Reg. no. 13
November 5, 1937.

*Strictly confidential:*

"With reference to the confidential character of the export subsidy procedure:

"Although each notice in our *News Service* containing an announcement about the export subsidy procedure is marked 'Strictly Confidential,' we have, unfortunately, observed violations of this confidence in a number of cases. Reference to 'scrip procedure,' 'compensations of the Reich,' 'export promotion rates,' and so on, have been discovered in the foreign correspondence of a number of firms. We again remind our members very earnestly that the confidential character of the promotion procedure must be preserved under all conditions and that a penalty is involved if it is mentioned in letters, especially to foreign countries.

"In order to avoid unpleasant measures against factory leaders and firms we request our members to examine carefully any letter sent abroad and to avoid any mention of the export promotion procedure even in conversations with foreign business friends. We urgently request that the situation be again explained to employees concerned with foreign orders."

The turnover tax, which is collected from all industries on behalf of the Export Subsidy Fund, yielded about 1,200 million marks in 1938, approximately 25 per cent of the total value of German exports. In the spring of 1939, the Nazi Government decided to pay a State subsidy of 500 million marks into the Export Subsidy Fund for 1939-40. This secret fund will thus dispose during the year 1939-40 of 1,700 million marks, equal to about 35 per cent of Germany's yearly exports in 1938. No subsidy is paid where the foreign buyer seems dependent on German products, as is the case where Germany has a monopoly and the foreign buyer can, therefore, be forced to pay the price dictated by the German firm. The average subsidy paid to an exporter amounts to about 40 to 45 per cent of the sales price.

The Reichsbank and other German State authorities are able to aid German exports in other ways than through the direct intervention of the Export Subsidy Fund. A German manufacturer unable to sell at a profitable price has ample opportunities for getting State financial assistance. It is impossible to determine in the case of any individual export transaction whether and to what extent it has been subsidized. The elastic evaluation of blocked, Aski, and other marks makes it possible for the Reich Foreign Exchange Board, in conjunction with the Reichsbank, to grant hidden subsidies. The foreign buyer might be accorded especially cheap Aski marks, or the German exporter might be empowered to use the foreign currency he gets from sales abroad for financing an import business. The exporter who can increase his exports above a certain volume is to receive in the future some kind of special export premium by being given a freer disposition of the extra income of foreign currency.[8] This is generally very lucrative, because foreign materials are scarce and it is easy for the German importer to sell them in Germany. Or the Reichsbank might request the Price Commissar to grant a certain firm a higher sales price in Germany for some imported raw material. The extra profit derived from this import business compensates for the loss entailed in selling goods abroad at prices far below the German costs of production.

Nazi practice of export subsidizing was described by Attorney General Frank Murphy in a letter to the Secretary of the Treasury of March 18, 1939, as follows:

"An American importer desires to import into the

United States from Germany certain German cameras. Before this can be done approval of the transaction must be obtained from the German exchange control authorities, without whose approval nothing can be exported from Germany. . . . Under an arrangement approved by the German import control authorities . . . a German agent acting for the American importer buys American cotton at the world price for $1,000 and sells it in Germany for 2,500 Reichsmarks, plus a premium of 33⅓ per cent, making a total sales price of 3,333 Reichsmarks, the equivalent of $1,333. . . . The American importer thereupon buys cameras for $1,333 (3,333 Reichsmarks) and imports them into the United States. Thus, for cameras which cost the American importer $1,000 the German exporter is paid $1,333; with the result that the German exporter is enabled to compete unfairly with, and probably to undersell, American camera manufacturers, while the exportation to Germany of American cotton is correspondingly restricted or curtailed."

The extent of the indirect export subsidies thus cannot be determined outside of Germany, without special knowledge of the arrangements between the Reichsbank, the Price Commissar, and the Export Subsidy Fund administration on one hand and German exporters on the other.

With a stroke of the pen, the German government can compel German industrialists to dump a certain percentage of their output on foreign markets.

"The authorities responsible for German economic policy laid special stress in the autumn of 1938 upon a call for further efforts in the export field. The Reich Minister for Economic Affairs issued a special order on

November 25, 1938, which emphasized in two different ways the paramount urgency of the export business. Firms with outstanding performances to their credit in this field are to be given preferential treatment in the distribution of public contracts, while on the other hand firms which are culpably behindhand in effecting foreign sales are to be put at a disadvantage with regard both to public contracts and to the distribution of raw materials. Secondly, priority was given to export orders over all home orders, public as well as private. This latter provision is particularly important in that during the last twelve months export business has often been lost through inability to effect delivery." [9]

It became profitable for many industrialists to throw a certain volume of their production on the world market, even at a price which meant a loss to them, as this loss was more than compensated for by profits derived from armament sales at home. Opportunity to obtain this latter profit would not have been given them had they been unwilling to push sales in the foreign markets.

The stringent control of foreign trade in fascist countries and in Japan is not identical with the foreign trade monopoly of the Soviet Union. In Germany, Italy and Japan, the State determines what merchandise and how much of it is to be imported. It likewise controls and "promotes" exports but, with certain exceptions, the State as such is not directly involved in the actual purchase and sales transactions. The transactions are handled by businessmen who act in their private capacity and not as officials of the State.

The peculiar coexistence of the State and private economy, of State agencies and of State control existing side by side with private enterprises run by and for private interests, which characterizes domestic trade within Germany, is found likewise in the sphere of foreign trade. Because of the special nature of foreign trade, the clash between private and State interests in this field is even sharper than it is in the purely internal market.

The importers and exporters have advantages over traders engaged solely in domestic trade. They are dealing with foreign concerns which are not subject to the control of the totalitarian State. They cannot be watched as closely as shopkeepers in a German town. They are better informed than other businessmen about conditions abroad, and have more opportunities to evade strict State supervision.

There are many subterfuges which the German exporter or importer may employ. He may try to raise his export subsidy by asking his foreign business friend to send him letters testifying that he will buy only if a price reduction is granted and asserting that he has better offers from other countries. The extra profit derived from such an artificial price reduction will probably be divided between the German exporter and the foreign purchaser, with the exporter's extra profit being deposited in a secret bank account abroad. This can be done, of course, only where the articles in question do not have an established market price, as in the case of complicated machinery. The German importer likewise may ask for a special commission from the foreign exporter and this he will hide from the German authorities, thereby also creating a secret reserve fund abroad.

Thus, if he is not rigorously watched, the German exporter or importer has a good opportunity, if he is so inclined, to circumvent the Nazi Government restrictions and, by quoting fictitious prices to foreign firms, to build up reserves in his personal account abroad. The Nazi Government is aware of this loophole, and therefore looks with special suspicion upon all exporters and importers. This causes innumerable hardships, for it is precisely in the field of foreign trade that there is the most urgent need for freedom of action and independence from bureaucratic control and interference.

Despite the manifold and extremely aggravating attempts of the authorities to make the exporters toe the line, it is evident from the following circular issued by the Nordmark Chamber of Commerce under date of November 15, 1937, to its members engaged in foreign trade, that many conflicts with the law do exist. Says the circular:

"With reference to foreign currency frauds, the Department of Foreign Trade has received the following letter from the Chamber of Commerce in Hamburg which should be studied with great care by all members:

"A number of arrests have been made recently in connection with cases of violations of foreign currency decrees. This has caused discussions and doubts among the businessmen as to whether the incidents really were so serious that arrests had to be made.

". . . Every trader must take great pains in foreign currency affairs. . . . This affair will not be discussed in newspapers or other publications.

Heil Hitler!
The Executive
Subdivision of Import and Export."

Absolute power has become a decisive factor in the relations between debtors and creditors. Dr. Schacht is reputed to have said, "It is no longer the creditor but the debtor who has the whip hand." This is only true insofar as the debtor has sufficient power to defy the foreign creditor. The southeastern European vassal states of the Nazi Reich would certainly not improve their position were they to become the debtors of the Nazi Reich.

There exists a growing tendency to respect property rights in world trade only insofar as they can be effectively protected—either by absolute power or by retaliatory measures. Everywhere, in particular in trading with fascist countries, business morale is declining. This holds true in State as well as in private deals. Contracts are still signed and promises of payment are made, but the signatures under these contracts do not guarantee fulfillment, as they did formerly. The government officials of the totalitarian State review the completed contract and decide whether or not the pledge of the private firm is to be kept or cancelled. Of course, traditional forms are preserved, and there is no open declaration of contempt for law.

In a number of cases Import Control Boards have advised German importers to cancel contracts with foreign firms because the same goods could be bought more cheaply elsewhere, or because political or other reasons dictated that they should be purchased in another country. The German firm then must say to the firm from which it agreed to purchase that it very much regrets its inability to accept the merchandise but that it is unable to do so because it cannot obtain the requisite foreign currency or because some Nazi authority has objected to the respective barter deal. The foreign firm, in turn, can do little about such a breach of contract.

Even in controversies all parties to which reside

within Germany, businessmen no longer hasten to prosecute for breach of contract. Sound as their case may be, the plaintiffs may find that the defendants have better political connections than they have, and in Nazi Germany judges are as accountable to Party secretaries as is everyone else.

When the plaintiff is a foreign firm, the German defendants are quick to avail themselves of the defense slogan "interests of the state," so that it is almost impossible for a foreign firm to win a case in a German court. Even though a decision might conceivably be rendered in its favor, the foreign firm would have won merely a technical victory, for the Reichsbank never releases foreign currency in payment of such claims. In practice, therefore, German firms may break buying contracts abroad at will (or on the order of a commissar), should the world price drop. They are then free to repurchase elsewhere at a lower price. The situation is different only if the German firm has foreign assets rendering it vulnerable to court actions abroad and is obliged to accept the decision of a foreign court.

"Conservative" German businessmen—principally international bankers and merchants—who grew up with the traditional respect for private property and who had established international contacts with foreign bankers and foreign traders, had created "good will" which was one of the essential assets of their firms. Bankers in London or Amsterdam could reveal the names of such "conservative" businessmen who still try to adhere to former business standards and to retain the good will they have established. One and all, these individuals mourn the end of sacred, time-honored principles. But they are being superseded rapidly by businessmen who are not troubled by traditions, and the concern of the conservatives over respect for private property is not shared by the highest authorities of the fascist countries. They are, in fact, contemptuous of it.

"The development of international law is not at all desirable. . . . The fixing of such a goal [sanctity of property rights] is either utopian or dictated by corresponding interests of international power groups. Jewish and liberal authors represented such an aim in Germany." [10]

The use of force to compel the fulfillment of financial obligations is not an innovation of the Nazis. They can and do claim that this principle was applied during the World War and in the Versailles Treaty. What is new is that principles customary in wartime are being applied by the Nazis to peacetime trade.

An outright return to the frank use of force is not advisable even from the point of view of those who prefer the absolute power principle to the acknowledgment of traditional rights. The open resumption of piratical methods would be a premature challenge of foreign powers. Dr. Schacht evolved an ingenious system which enabled the totalitarian State to use its power and influence abroad in varying degrees and forms, without openly disavowing traditional standards.

He introduced the system of using various kinds of marks, a system which has often been misunderstood abroad. In his "birthday" address before the Reich Economic Chamber on January 22, 1937, Dr. Schacht ridiculed foreigners who did not see the intrinsic meaning of the "devaluation" of the marks paid to them.

"When I am talking abroad about the stability of the mark, people usually laugh at me because there are so many kinds of marks, all of which have a different value. To be sure, there are many kinds of marks, all of which do differ in value, without any of them being on gold parity, since they are quoted at 20, 30, 40, 50 or 60 per cent discount. My answer to this is always exceedingly simple: 'Yes, this applies to the mark that belongs to *you;* the mark that belongs to *us* is stable.' " [11]

This system can be applied in such a way that mark debts abroad are paid back at a rate of exchange which is kept artificially low, while on the other hand payments to Germany have to be made at an artificially high value.

The Nazi State prefers to differentiate according to the rule: "To every creditor according to his power—not according to our ability to pay."

British, Dutch, Swiss and French creditors have been treated better than American creditors. The British government could effectively threaten the German government with the introduction of a "clearing system." In that event, all British importers of German goods would have paid their bills not to the German exporter, but into a special fund directly administered by the British government. This fund then would have been used to pay: (a) exporters of British goods to Germany, and (b) British creditors who have a claim for payments from Germany. Germany would have received only whatever surplus remained after all these claims had been satisfied. This system would have been effective because Germany exports much more to Great Britain than it imports from that country. Therefore the Nazi Government conceded partial repayment of debts to British creditors. Agreements for partial payment of outstanding debts were also concluded with other foreign countries which could exert similar pressure on the Reich.

The Reich Government tried to replace the Clearing Offices established by other countries by Payment Agreements. These provide not merely for payments for exports to Germany but also for at least partial payment of outstanding German debts.[12] But only those countries which could, if necessary, impose a clearing system for foreign trade with Germany have been able to conclude payment agreements.

No corresponding arrangement has been made for paying State and corporate debts due in the United States inasmuch as Germany's imports from the United States by far exceed her exports to this country. Only in a few cases have American creditors succeeded in collecting their German debts—or at least partial payments in acknowledgment of the obligation—by effective counter-threats. The creditors of the Norddeutscher Lloyd Shipping Company, for example, were able to make an arrangement with certain German debtors as a result of a threat to attach German liners on their arrival in New York.

On March 7, 1939, the German Foreign Debts Conversion office applied to Washington for a registration statement covering a proposed issue of $70,000,000 of 3 per cent refunding bonds. The Securities and Exchange Commission insisted on having certain information in the registration statement. When this was refused by the Nazi Government, the SEC suspended the registration statement, and declared:

"The registration statement does not disclose the entire amount of floating debt of the German Government or an adequate history of defaulted obligations. . . . No statements of the balance of international payments of

Germany for any year since 1935. . . . Furthermore, the registration statements have not been adequately amended to set forth requested information vital to American investors respecting present German resources of gold and foreign exchange."

The Nazi economists claim that they are compelled to apply their new methods in world trade because the Versailles Treaty robbed them of the means with which to buy sufficient raw materials and foodstuffs. They refer to the fact that prewar Germany, like Great Britain, imported more than it exported. The import surplus was financed by "income from abroad," mainly dividends and interest from foreign investments. Postwar Germany lost its foreign investments. It even had to pay "reparations" as well as interest and amortization on foreign credits.

This could be done only by increasing exports of industrial goods—in competition with the exporting interests of the victorious powers. Extension and modernization of Germany's industrial machine was necessary and was made possible by the influx of foreign credits. But the world economic crisis reduced the greater part of Germany's industries to idleness. In Germany itself, forces arose which rebelled against the loss of industrial capital which was of value only if production could be resumed. It so happened, however, that many industries which had been producing for the world market could also produce armaments for the home market. This is one of the advantages an industrial country has compared to an agrarian country. Corn, grain and fruit have value only as food. They cannot be used as bullets. Raw materials, other than foodstuffs, are useless unless manufacturing industries exist which consume raw materials. An industrial country, on the other hand, can produce peacetime goods for the world market or, if necessary, it can switch to the production of armaments which strengthen the military power of the State. Evidence of this change in Germany's production can readily be observed by a traveler. He will easily discover the contrast between the depression in the trading ports of Hamburg and Bremen on the one hand and, on the other hand, the boom in construction in central Germany where new armament works are being erected. A world armament race completes the disruption of the international division of labor on which our world economy relies.

When State control of foreign trade was inaugurated, imports were restricted because of a lack of foreign currency and gold. Germany's rearmament policy, however, increased her demand for foreign raw materials, and likewise decreased her ability to export industrial goods.

The major part of the raw materials imported by the Third Reich are used in such a manner that it is impossible to pay for them through increased exports. We must recall here the structural changes of Germany's industry under the Nazis, described in previous chapters, namely, the decline of the export and consumption goods industries and the greatly increased production of armaments. The rise in capital goods production thus was due to armament manufacture and not to the increased production of machinery for export.

Germany's industry used to rely largely on the importation of foreign raw materials and the export of manufactured goods. One of the best German economists, Professor Max Sering, who is still living in the

Third Reich but who does not understand the new times, has written:

"The powerful structure of this new industrial society [prewar Germany] relied essentially on foreign countries. Germany was rich in coal, sulphate, iron and zinc ores. But the textile industry worked almost exclusively with foreign raw materials. The metallurgical, electrotechnical and rubber industries, the oil, fat and timber industries, as well as the manufacturers of leather goods, were dependent on large supplies from abroad. . . . Therefore a large section of Germany's industrial population worked for foreign countries and was nourished by them." [13]

Postwar Germany depended to a greater extent than prewar Germany on the export of manufactured goods to finance imports of raw materials and foodstuffs for its industrial population and to service payments of foreign debts.

A reconstruction of Germany's industries on the pre-War pattern took place during the period from 1925 to 1929. Foreign credits were used at that time to reconstruct and extend Germany's industrial machine, equipping it again with the most modern technical means so that Germany might regain its privileged prewar position. The world economic crisis and the consequent depression made it clear that Germany could never again become the hub of industrial world production it had been previously. The futility of its attempting to do so was not recognized by those who believed in the possibility of a new world prosperity. Industries which depended on a return to the "good old days" became idle during the depression. They could not be reawakened without a new world prosperity. Fascism seemed to give them a new chance—mass production for the State, in an effort to make the State so strong from a military point of view that it might take by force what was unobtainable by peaceful competition.

Germany's former exporting industries became part of a gigantic military machine, prepared to turn out armaments on an unprecedented scale.

"The supreme guiding principle of foreign trade is neither a maximum volume of exports nor the exploitation of every chance for foreign trade that may be advantageous from the point of view of [comparative] costs, but primarily the satisfaction of the demand for imports as a necessary supplement to domestic production." [14]

There is a definite trend in world trade toward the formation of "blocs" of imperialist powers which draw or try to draw into their "spheres of influence" countries producing food and raw materials. The decline in Germany's foreign trade with the United States is, therefore, rather a result of that general tendency than of a special discriminatory policy toward the United States. Moreover, there is a general tendency toward a decline of Germany's foreign trade with industrially developed countries.

GERMAN EXPORTS AND IMPORTS [15]

(In per cent)

| | "Industrial Countries" | | Southeastern Europe | | South America | |
|---|---|---|---|---|---|---|
| | Imports | Exports | Imports | Exports | Imports | Exports |
| 1929 | 39.4 | 49.3 | 4.6 | 5.1 | 8.3 | 5.8 |
| 1934 | 33.8 | 51.3 | 7.3 | 5.6 | 6.4 | 4.6 |
| 1938 | 28.9 | 36.7 | 10.5 | 13.1 | 11.1 | 8.0 |

(All 1938 figures included only January to September)

These figures indicate: less foreign trade with "industrial countries," more foreign trade with "agrarian countries," in particular, with southeastern Europe. However, the figures do not disclose whether Germany's trade with nations in these categories is growing or decreasing; they show merely what percentage of German trade goes to each category listed.

The Reich Minister of Economics, Walter Funk, wrote in Goering's organ, *Der Vierjahresplan:*

"The United States will lose Germany as a customer. . . . We shall find a substitute for orders from the United States in the Balkans and in Turkey, whose economic structure is better fitted to natural exchange of products with Germany." Neither the Balkans nor Turkey, however, can export cotton or copper to an extent comparable with the United States or nearly adequate for Germany's demands.

In spite of large subsidies, enforced export drives, and political pressure, the Nazi export offensive has scarcely enabled Germany to hold its own in world commerce, even in countries where it has expended much energy and money.

Certain of Germany's export industries have been especially hard hit, for example, toys and leather goods. But this has not been decisive in Germany's general decline of foreign trade caused by the world economic crisis. This decline has been intensified by Germany's preoccupation with the production of armaments and with the production of goods for the home market. Thus we have a situation where exports have declined while industrial production has risen. German exports, in percentage of Germany's total industrial production, have fallen from 30.9 per cent in 1931 and 22.5 per cent in 1933 to 13.1 per cent during the first half of 1938.

GERMAN EXPORTS IN PERCENTAGE OF TOTAL INDUSTRIAL PRODUCTION [16]

| | | | |
|---|---|---|---|
| 1928 | 22.0 | 1935 | 15.2 |
| 1931 | 30.9 | 1936 | 16.1 |
| 1933 | 22.5 | 1937 | 16.2 |
| 1934 | 15.9 | 1938 | 13.1 |

The economic policies of the State have made it more difficult than before to pay for the increased importation of raw materials by increased exports of manufactured articles. It is much more profitable for the German industrialist to work for the State, manufacturing war materials, than to work in an industry manufacturing export goods and competing on the world market.

Imports which are still vital, however, must be paid for, and in most cases without delay. There are now fewer opportunities than before for the totalitarian State to finance imports through foreign credits or loans. In addition, the Nazi State has actually obtained less foreign currency from exports than the trade figures would indicate.

The German Institute for Business Research complained that "several countries took advantage of the monopoly they practically have in certain articles and would only deliver their articles against payment in free foreign exchange. As a result, Germany, despite extensive use of bilateral payment agreements, must always be intent on securing a sufficient amount of foreign exchange." [17]

"Only about one-fifth of the total income from exports has accrued to the Reichsbank in the form of foreign currency. Out of this amount had to come expenses for amortization and interest payments on foreign credits, expenses of foreign representatives, travel costs abroad, charges for foreign trade, transport costs and commissions." [18]

According to official trade figures, the Third Reich had an import surplus of 433 million marks in 1938. The deficit in foreign currency must have been much greater. Exports showed an actual decrease, yet imports of raw materials, urgently needed for armaments and as wartime reserves, had increased.

"Taking Greater Germany as a whole, moreover, the passive balance was far greater still. Imports into Ostmark [Austria] from foreign countries rose even more sharply in proportion, while exports experienced a more than average decline owing to the problems of transition and readjustment. Furthermore, in considering the special foreign exchange position of Ostmark, it must be remembered that the invisible items by means of which Austria had in previous years made good the (somewhat smaller) passive balance in respect to her commodity trade—viz., tourist traffic, transit traffic, and interest on foreign investments—probably fell during 1938." [19]

From 1937 to 1938, the volume of imports of the basic materials rose as follows:

| | |
|---|---|
| Wood | 35.2% |
| Cotton | 11.0% |
| Building and industrial timber | 22.0% |
| Iron ores | 10.3% |
| Copper | 39.7% |
| Fuels and lubricating oil | 16.5% |

Imports of wool, however, have considerably declined.

The Nazi State was unable to raise a foreign loan. Still, it succeeded in financing the increased imports it needed for armaments. This was made possible by the various means that can be applied only by a State which regiments and controls all economic activities. Imports of foodstuffs, for instance, were largely curtailed. This did not mean that Germany had become self-sufficient in foodstuffs, but that consumers in Germany had to reduce their standards of living. "Guns are more important than butter," according to Goering.

Secondly, all foreign assets held by Germans ("Aryans" and "non-Aryans") were conscripted and, in most cases, expropriated. The German owners were compensated, but with German marks at artificially high rates. They had to hand over the assets to the Reichsbank, which sold most of them abroad between 1936 and 1938. Some foreign investments were sold at a great loss due to the fact that the State bureaucrats handled the sales and that the foreign buyers were fully informed of the Reichsbank's precarious condition. In some cases only one group of foreign capitalists (for instance, Dutch) was interested in a given German investment. Taking into account the general risk of new investments in Europe and the Reichsbank's inability to play for time, only a portion of the ordinary value, therefore, was paid for some of these investments.

It is interesting to note that German capitalists are not generally allowed to keep the profit accruing from the artificial devaluation of the mark. A German industrialist who wishes to pay off a foreign debt has to pay the full amount of his debt to the Reichsbank, and the Reichsbank in turn deals with the foreign creditor and makes an arrangement with him providing for a "discount" varying from 20 to 80 per cent on payment in foreign currency. The profit derived as a result of this discount is kept by the Nazi State.

State officials, for example, sold German holdings in foreign shipping companies which are largely engaged in transporting German and other European goods. A foreign partner in these companies bought from the Reichsbank at a low price the shares previously held by German iron industrialists, and German capitalists no longer have a voice in their management or share in their profits. Previously, the German industrialists who were part owners of these companies received dividends from them which partially offset shipping charges. In addition, they were in a position to influence directly the rate policies of the companies in their own interests. This situation no longer obtains. Thus, in instances of this type, the Reichsbank's sale of German holdings abroad resulted not only in a real loss, but even in increasing the deficit in the Reich's international payments. German industrialists not infrequently felt a secret pleasure at this result, because they were angered by the enforced expropriation of their foreign holdings for the benefit of the Reichsbank. But this does not pave the way for a return to the old system of free foreign trade.

These various marks and "discounts" enable the totalitarian State to pay each foreign creditor on the basis of an individual arrangement. For this reason the Nazi State is not anxious to resort to general devaluation of the mark. Strict control of foreign currency and foreign trade keeps the domestic mark at a value different from that of the foreign mark. General devaluation of the mark would mean that every foreign creditor would be treated alike.

Clearing systems and State measures for the control of foreign trade are becoming increasingly a feature of the foreign trade of our times, but they create no new organized system of world economy.

*Chapter XIV*

# *FASCIST EMPIRE BUILDING*

"'Something for nothing' is a dominant principle in the methods of imperialist expansion adopted by all 'have not' powers."

A British businessman, visiting Germany during the first years of the Nazi regime, would have been welcomed as a "pure Aryan" and as a representative of a sister nation. Such an attitude arose from Hitler's views as expressed in *Mein Kampf*. Today the situation is different. In present-day Nazi propaganda, Great Britain is pictured as the most covetous bourgeois "have" power and the ringleader of those countries who seek to prevent the rise of "young" nations like Germany and Japan. Every newspaper reader in Germany is fully acquainted with the most unsavory aspects of British imperial policy. Nazi propagandists harp on the fact that the Britons, like all other empire builders, employed brute force in creating their own empire. Germans are repeatedly told how British imperialism ruthlessly destroyed India's domestic textile industry in the interests of the Lancashire textile manufacturers. They are also reminded of the fact that Great Britain has repeatedly denied self-rule to the Indian people. The Germans are also fed with numerous statistics illustrating the tight control that the "have" powers exercise over the raw materials needed by German industry, such as copper, tin, rubber, crude oil and so on. They are informed of the huge incomes that British capitalists receive from abroad as well as of the enormous investments that the British have made in their colonies. So insistent has this propaganda been, that the German businessman generally is better acquainted with the early history of British imperialism than even the British businessman.

This being so, it would be vain to attempt to counter the propaganda of the Nazi regime by moralizing about Germany's desire for absolute power and her declining respect for international treaties. As a matter of fact, in Germany, as well as in Italy, anti-British propaganda has proved much more effective than propaganda for the crusade against Bolshevism. The Nazis constantly utilize Germany's scarcity of foreign currency and raw material to popularize and justify her struggle for the creation of an empire.

Since the foundation of the British Empire, however, world conditions have changed. There are no longer "uncivilized" countries—that is, countries in which pre-industrial economic systems predominate or which are sparsely settled—free from imperialist control. With only minor exceptions, the entire world has been staked out and claimed. New colonial empires can be created, therefore, only by the destruction of rival empires—and of the U.S.S.R.—through a new world war.

Previously when an imperialist power gained control of a "backward" country, new and large-scale investments were made in order to open up the undeveloped natural resources of the country. This process took a certain period of time—frequently many years—to bear fruit. Fascist imperialism, however, is unable to wait for the slow economic penetration of new territory. It cannot use the methods employed by the older imperialists, namely, the establishment of "spheres of influence" through the export of capital. The precarious economic situation and the pressing military needs of the "have not" powers make it necessary for them to gain immediate, not deferred, economic advantages from the new territories that come under their influence. Nazi Germany, therefore, in each of her conquests has rushed to appropriate to herself all tangible resources of capital, foodstuffs and raw materials available in the new territory, largely without compensation to the former owners.

New methods of exploitation must be used where the conquered country already has fully developed capitalist property relations and established industries belonging to native or rival foreign capitalists. Since the lack of raw materials and of exchange has been a motive power in forcing fascism to take the road of imperialist expansion, the economic exploitation of the conquered country must be made completely subordinate to the urgent needs of the "mother country." Native and rival foreign capitalists must be expropriated on a large scale so that the conquerors can acquire without compensation the accumulated wealth of the country. The principle of "the sanctity of private property" derived from capitalist property relations becomes embarrassing. Therefore the prospective "mother country" must proclaim new principles in order to justify the wholesale expropriation of capital and the destruction of competitive enterprise. These new principles, as employed by the Nazis, have been called "racial principles," "national interests," and the like.

Neither Japan in China nor Nazi Germany in Czechoslovakia began the economic penetration of their "protectorates" or new colonies by large-scale investments which would have created new industries within the boundaries of the vassal state. Only those enterprises which could supply the "mother country" with urgently needed materials were encouraged.

When the Nazi Reich embarked on its expansionist drive, stocks of raw materials, foreign currency and gold were at a low ebb, and it was impossible to replenish them with sufficient speed in the normal way. The military machine might have collapsed had it not used its power to obtain these vital necessities.

The immediate cause for Germany's expansion was not her need of finding an increased outlet for industrial products, but there were internal difficulties which were intensified by her need of gold, foreign currency and raw materials. The Reich had no means of paying for these in quantities sufficiently large to keep the industrial machine at work, because its "free capital" had all been invested in strengthening its military power. In a sense, Germany was in the position of having to utilize its military power to prevent the capital invested in it from becoming obsolete.

The first act of the Nazi Reich after the occupation of Vienna as well as after the occupation of Prague was symbolic. Gold and foreign currency found in these two former capitals were immediately transferred to Berlin. The possession by Austria and Czechoslovakia of large stocks of both of these valuables hastened Germany's decision to occupy their territories by military force. The booty in Vienna amounted to 416 million shillings or $78,000,000, three times the currency reserve of the Reichsbank at that time. The raid on the Prague National Bank was a little disappointing because a large percentage of the Czechoslovakian reserves was deposited abroad, principally in London, and, to a smaller extent, in New York. Official stocks amounted to $81,000,000, or over four times the Reichsbank reserves.[1]

In addition, all private holdings of gold, foreign currency and other types of foreign property had to be handed over to the Reich. According to private estimates, this booty in Austria was more than double the amount of gold and foreign currency found in the vaults of the Austrian National Bank (about 1,000,000,000 shillings, or $188,000,000). The private holdings in former Czechoslovakia[2] were even greater. Large quantities of materials, machines, foodstuffs and so on were "requisitioned" and sent to the Reich.

> Germany is extracting a maximum amount of plunder from these conquered lands [Bohemia and Moravia]. The equipment of a superb army, food reserves calculated to supply the whole Czechoslovak Republic for eighteen months, and a small but welcome sum in foreign exchange are but a fraction of the real gains. To this must be added the skill of hundreds of thousands of workers, and the property and industries of Jews which are being bought with paper money seized last October with the Sudeten territories.[3]

Dr. Eduard Benes, former president of the Czechoslovakian Republic, supplemented this picture of the fate of Bohemia and of Moravia.

> I hear that preparations are now made to transport important objects of culture and art [to the Reich]. Factories are being ruined and industry crippled as machinery is carried away for war purposes. . . . Safety deposit boxes and safes may be opened only in the presence of the Gestapo.[4]

Foreign property rights likewise were abolished in fact, if not in law. This was true not only of foreign loans granted to the preceding governments, but also of private foreign holdings. French stockholders in the Vienna Laenderbank, which controlled a great many industrial enterprises in Austria and southeastern Europe, were forced to sell out for almost nothing. Numerous industrial enterprises owned by "non-Aryans" were expropriated without compensation and handed over a new State-owned concern, called the Hermann Wilhelm Gustloff Stiftung.[5] The greater part of Austria's large-scale industry has been concentrated in this trust and in another large State trust, the Hermann Goering Reich Iron Works.

Fascist conquest has still another aim, more permanent in character—the acquisition of monopolies. The strict control which the fascist State imposes on production and sales of raw materials, as well as on exports and imports, is used to compel the "protectorate" to sell its agricultural products and raw materials to the "mother country" at artificially low prices, while prices for industrial goods imported from the "mother country" are maintained at artificially high levels. The German cartels and syndicates which control the market within Germany keep internal prices much higher than prices abroad. These national monopolies are now able to extend their "internal market" by including the conquered areas which are under the political control of the Nazi State.

Thus, by the use of military force, the fascist State gains new monopolies or extends the power of the existing monopolies without developing new productive forces.

Austria, for example, was a highly developed industrial country before it became a province of the "Greater Reich." Formerly Austria imported 24 per cent of its food supply (in Germany prior to the annexation the figure was 19 per cent). The most important food imports were wheat, 43.2 per cent; rye, 28.4 per cent, and corn, 66.6 per cent.[6] Coal and iron were imported in large quantities from Poland, Czechoslovakia, and to a smaller extent from Germany. Austrian importers had formed a syndicate in order to obtain cheap coal. This syndicate was, of course, independent of the German coal syndicates, since it could obtain coal from sources other than Germany. After the occupation of Austria, trustees who were Nazis connected with the German coal syndicates replaced the former directors of the Austrian coal syndicate. Now Austrian manufacturers must pay a higher price for coal than formerly and must accept the domination of the Reich's coal concerns. The bulk of the profits of the Austrian coal syndicate is under control of the Nazi party.

In Austria, as in the other newly acquired countries, only those industries are flourishing which supplement German industry. Specifically this means armament factories, which are important from the strategic point of view as industrial strongholds for German militarism.

Austria's contribution to Goering's Four-Year Plan consists mainly in supplying ore, timber, hydroelectric power and labor to Germany and, to a smaller extent, machinery and materials for armament factories. Aside from these resources, however, Austria has relatively few raw materials and is largely dependent on supplies from abroad, which can no longer be obtained in sufficient quantities. To a certain extent, Austria will participate in ersatz production. For example, cell wool will be produced from Austrian wood to replace cotton and wool, previously imported from America and Britain. Apart from considerable construction work for fortifications, only a few factories in Austria are being constructed or enlarged. And even these are devoted to the armament industry or to ersatz production, as, for instance, the iron and steel works now being erected at Linz. New roads are being built for strategic reasons. But this much advertised construction work means little or nothing when compared with the decline which has taken place in other important branches of Austrian industry. Formerly most Austrian factories produced for the world market in competition with German industry. Today Austria's iron ore or iron is being used for armaments. Previously Austria had a flourishing trade with Czechoslovakia. Now this market is dominated by central German and Saxon industrialists. Only an enlargement of the Reich to the shores of the Black Sea and through Turkey to Asia might give Austria's export trade an opportunity to revive under the hegemony of the Reich. But this imperialistic dream of the future offers no remedy for the distressed conditions of today.

Through the absorption of Czechoslovakia, Germany's heavy industries further strengthened their monopolist position. Formerly their largest competitor in central and southeastern Europe was the Witkowitzer Iron Works owned by Czech industrialists. As a matter of fact, these industrialists had thought that by making concessions they could co-operate with the Nazi Government. Their attempt to do so was doomed to failure. Not a vestige of their former independence remains. German iron and steel magnates no longer need reckon with the strong Czechoslovakian competitors who had many geographical advantages in central and south-eastern Europe. The Ruhr industrialists have simply extended their domestic market and swallowed up their former competitors.

It is no longer possible for the fascist State to build up its own monopolies on the basis of hitherto undeveloped resources. Therefore Abyssinia has been a burden rather than an asset to Italian imperialism. There are no raw material resources or industries already developed, hence there is nothing to requisition. Superior military strength made possible the conquest of Abyssinia, but the Italian military victory did not, and will not, lead to economic wealth. In order to make the victory profitable, vast amounts of capital would have to be invested. A tremendous amount of technical equipment would be necessary to open up the unexplored wealth of the conquered country. But Italy itself is suffering from a scarcity of these very materials and technical means which are necessary to the development of productive forces in colonial lands. Therefore, Abyssinia has for Mussolini a strategic rather than an economic value—not counting the increase in prestige.

Nazi imperialism was more fortunate than Italian imperialism. The Third Reich was in a position to conquer countries which had achieved a relatively high degree of development. These countries had accumulated considerable wealth—at least in comparison with Abyssinia—and their raw material resources are more easily accessible.

In a very illuminating study,[7] Freda Utley has shown the manner in which Japanese imperialism is exploiting newly conquered countries. Trade monopolies were established and as much economic wealth of native citizens acquired as could be obtained without developing any new productive forces, except those which supported Japanese industry and militarism. "Something for nothing" is a dominant principle in the methods of imperialist expansion adopted by all "have not" powers.

There are certain peculiarities of imperialist expansion in Europe which distinguish it from the Japanese conquest in China. Germany, for instance, is surrounded by countries where the natural resources have already been developed and where modern industries are in existence. Japan is not. It is true that industrialization of southeastern and eastern Europe is less advanced than in Germany, yet in these areas, especially in former Czechoslovakia, modern industries already existed. Czechoslovakia manufactured articles from raw materials which are rare in Germany and exported finished products largely in competition with German manufacturers. Czechoslovakia and Austria possessed highly developed modern industries which distributed manufactured goods to all parts of the world. German monopolistic control of southeastern European markets was impossible as long as the rival industries remained independent. Establishment of a "protectorate" over the semi-industrialized countries of central Europe by the Nazi Reich, therefore, entailed the throttling of existing industrial productive forces in the interest of Germany's monopolies. This policy involved the expropriation, even to the point of ruin, of the propertied classes of the new colony. Because of this, the Nazi Reich was unable to find any social stratum among the native population through which it could exercise an effective but indirect control over the country. Direct military intervention and constant police supervision became necessary.

In some instances, it is true, attempts were made to form governments which would be the tools of the Nazi Reich. Such a government, for instance, was the last Czechoslovakian government prior to the march of the German army into Prague. Another example was the "autonomous" Slovakian government which agreed to remove all "ideological" obstacles to an understanding with the Nazi Reich, and to adopt certain Nazi principles, such as anti-Jewish "racial laws." The Slovakian government stood ready to grant preferential treatment to German businessmen and to export surplus foodstuffs and raw materials to Germany in exchange for industrial goods. There are always groups within such groups which are ready and willing to sacrifice the wealth and the interests of others in order to clear away the obstacle to co-operation with the imperialist power. But this was not sufficient. Complete direct domination was necessary. As long as a subjugated country keeps some degree of political independence, its Government, no matter how dictatorial or subservient to the interests of German imperialism, must consider the requirements of domestic business and agrarian interests. Even the farmers were concerned in the maintenance of domestic industry, because the downfall of the latter would mean the ruin of the internal market for agricultural products and a rise in the prices of the industrial goods which the farmers need.

Statistics on production reveal that there was a definite trend toward an industrial growth in those semiagrarian or agrarian countries which were trying to preserve their independence.

In nearly all countries industrial production has increased since 1932, exceeding in many cases the 1929 level. The increase has been much more rapid in agrarian or semi-agrarian countries than in industrial countries. The agrarian producers in southeastern Europe consume only a few industrial products; their standard of living was, and is, exceedingly low. The greater growth of industrial production in agrarian countries was due, in the final analysis, to governmental action. The governments tried to strengthen national forces of resistance by promoting and subsidizing industries of military importance.

In 1937, industrial production in southeastern Europe was 112.6 per cent above the 1928 level. In the rest of Europe the increase was only 37.1 per cent.[8] This unequal development continued during 1938. In commenting on this situation, the German Institute for Business Research stated:

"Southeastern European countries are gradually beginning to build up their own capital goods industries. . . . This development, which is primarily due to military considerations, has also led to a considerable expansion of heavy industry in Yugoslavia, Rumania and Greece. It is to be assumed that these tendencies will become stronger in the next few years." [9]

Increased domestic production replaced imported articles, thus hurting foreign industries which formerly supplied the agrarian countries with finished products. This development had not yet gone far enough to revolutionize the economic structure of these countries, which still remained backward by comparison with Germany. Yet it prevented German industrial monopolies from gaining absolute control of the markets and dictating prices. It also aided in solving the problem of outlets for domestic raw materials; they could now be utilized within the boundaries of each country.

The Sudetenland and the remainder of Czechoslovakia possessed large industries which produced finished goods not merely for domestic consumption but also for the world market. Not only did they supply southeastern Europe with textiles, machinery, etc., but they also carried on considerable export trade with England and the United States. In order to supply this extensive export trade, Czechoslovakia imported large quantities of raw materials. Nearly a quarter of the population of the Sudetenland was engaged in the production of textiles, many of which were shipped abroad. There were many other industries producing for export in competition with German industry.

Following the Anschluss, industrial life in the Sudetenland decayed, but "flax cultivation and sheep breeding are once more beginning to increase." [10]

An English author recently commented on industrial conditions in Czechoslovakia as follows:

"The cotton industry, which is the most important branch of Czechoslovak industries, has a capacity far in excess of the home demand, so that it is particularly dependent on exports. . . . A large proportion of the wool used is imported from British sources.

"After the cotton and wool industries come flax spinning, linen manufacture, the jute industry and the silk industry. . . . The Czechoslovak jute industry buys its raw materials very largely from India and has a great export to the United States.

". . . Comparatively little of the pig-iron produced in Czechoslovakia is exported, about 83 per cent of it being used in the country for the manufacture of steel and malleable iron.

"The iron manufacturing industries, on the other hand, produce very largely for export. Thus the enameled ware industry exports some four-fifths of its production and the agricultural machines and implements are produced mainly for export. A great many of these go to the Soviet Union." [11]

Before the dismemberment of Czechoslovakia, Czech industries had a distinct competitive advantage because of Czechoslovakia's favorable commercial treaties with England and the United States and because of its geographical position in southeastern Europe. These advantages have now been lost. Czech industries can no longer compete with the better-equipped German factories, especially when the latter have a greater supply of raw materials at their disposal.

The deterioration of industries has progressed much further in Czechoslovakia proper than in Austria and the Sudetenland. Czechoslovakian industries were larger and they have not been given the few privileges granted "Aryan" manufacturers in the Sudetenland and Austria. The ruin of these industries was initiated by the application of "racial principles" shortly before Prague was occupied and Czechoslovakia proclaimed a "protectorate" of the Third Reich.

Prior to the end of Czechoslovakia, Jewish manufacturers who had fled from the Sudetenland with their machines and with some capital tried in vain to transfer their plants and capital to Slovakia. Early in 1939, a member of the Slovakian government received a deputation of Jewish capitalists. He encouraged them to settle in Slovakia with the object of transforming it into a new manufacturing center producing for the Balkan market. The Slovakian government promised to respect the property rights of the manufacturers. The erection of a soap factory in Tyrnau was decided upon and was to be financed by Jewish capital, but with State representatives as members of the management. These plans for developing Slovakian industries would have hurt the German monopolistic position in the Balkans. Consequently the Nazi magazine *Der Wirtschaftsdienst,* which is closely connected with German export interests, described the intended development of Slovakian industries as creating "a serious and dangerous situation. . . .[12] This warning foreshadowed the military occupation of Czechoslovakia.

A clear indication of future Nazi plans for the economic development of her "protectorates" can be gleaned from a consideration of the negotiations between the German and Rumanian governments in March, 1939. As an essential condition for future cooperation, the Nazi government openly demanded the suppression of all domestic industries which were competitive with German industries, hoping thus to obtain an absolute monopoly for the Nazi industrialists. This demand was considered necessary because in recent years the Rumanian government, desirous of decreasing its dependence on foreign countries, especially in the armament field, had systematically encouraged the development of its own domestic industry. According to the plans of the Nazi government, only those industries should be developed which would help to open up Rumania's raw material resources and to increase its agricultural production to supplement Germany's economy.

Foreign capital has financed most of the industry in semiagrarian countries. Consequently, the Nazi policy of ruining industries they regard as "undesirable competitors" is tied up with their propaganda for a "National-Socialist" regime and for "racial principles" which will destroy the property rights of "alien elements."

This open attack on the sanctity of private property is used even outside of Europe as a propaganda weapon against the "have" powers. Britain and the United States have important investments in certain South American countries with large raw material resources, where governments are in debt to them. As governments which guarantee the sanctity of private property—for foreign investors—they are dictatorships whose power depends on military force rather than on popular consent. In these countries fascist agitators find it easy to gain ground by advocating rebellion of debtors against creditors. Nazi propagandists approach such countries with the slogans: "no payment of foreign debts," and "against exploitation by foreign [Jewish] capital."

In commenting on the changes which have taken place in Rumanian industry, a German periodical declared:

"Many overseas countries are economically dependent on foreign capital . . . or they are countries producing raw materials. Foreign capital was conceded a superior position since it undertook to develop such resources. In every case one can observe a distinctive one-sidedness in economic relationships. All these countries are able to export huge quantities of domestic goods, but the capacity to export is much greater than their capacity to import. This is due to the fact that only a minor part of the income from exports remains with the producing countries. A more or less large part of this income is taken by the leading corporations and remains with the mother countries of these corporations. . . . This disproportion between the capacity to export and to import is especially great in Africa. All African colonies must do statute labor for foreign capital since the colony receives too little for its exported products." [13]

Nazi imperialists cannot make large loans to States whose raw materials and foodstuffs they need, but as a substitute they can offer assistance in expropriating the capital invested by the "have" powers. Such propaganda spread by Nazi agents is very persuasive and has obtained response in some parts of South America. Of course, the Nazis do not intend to make large-scale investments of their own in the Western Hemisphere, if only because of strategic considerations. In case of war, connections with South America would be severed. Therefore, whatever limited capital Germany is able to export will be directed into areas which can be controlled by German militarism in the event of another world war.

In countries, however, which have become Nazi "protectorates," the sanctity of private property is preserved in a one-sided way, disappointing to native businessmen and foreign capitalists. At the time of the occupation of the Sudetenland, most Sudeten manufacturers were heavily indebted to banks which were largely under Czech and Jewish management and in which both British and French capital participated. Before the

Anschluss the Nazis promised that no debts need be paid to Jewish or foreign capitalists. "Interest slavery" would cease under National Socialism. This part of the program has been fulfilled—in so far as Czech, Jewish or foreign capitalists are concerned. Most of their capital has been expropriated; they are paid neither interest nor amortization. Foreign creditors can look forward to receiving only a tiny fraction of the credits they have advanced.

When the Sudetenland was occupied, its "Aryan" manufacturers welcomed the Nazi commissars who took over the banks in their districts, but they wondered how they would obtain further credits urgently needed for new investments. At that time, Herr Henlein, Sudetenland Fuehrer, solved the problem of what to do with the banks and their credit facilities.

He often promised his Sudeten German Party comrades that the Third Reich would cancel banking debts. This was privately said and never published. We can therefore only quote him from confidential reports of some of his Party friends.

"There are no difficulties," Herr Henlein used to say. "Sudeten German industrialists who do not want to pay their debts to Czech banks need not bother to do so. And they need have no fear about obtaining further credits. We shall open a new regional bank for the Sudetenland. We have all the accumulated capital of the country at our disposal. The Czech and Jewish banks will have to hand over their stocks and bonds at a price we shall decide upon. We will fix the value of these assets and pay for them with State debentures while the new banks will be under our control."

The Reichsbank was informed that certain counter-measures would be taken if the Nazis expropriated British and French investments in the newly occupied areas. Schacht hastened to warn the Nazi leaders of possible serious consequences if Herr Henlein were allowed to follow the policy of expropriation of foreign capital investments. British and French capitalists could not be treated like the Jews. A compromise was reached. In June, 1939, the British and the Reich Governments agreed that the Sudetenland should fall within the scope of the Anglo-German debt payments. The German Government successfully insisted that the date of September 29, 1939 (Munich Conference) be set as determining the ownership of debts so that nothing must be paid for credits which were transferred to British creditors after that date.

The Nazis used the threat of complete expropriation and boycott, however, in order to intimidate foreign banks and foreign investors. The threat was at least partially successful. Foreign investors were willing to surrender a large part of their investments and regarded themselves as lucky to have salvaged anything. But the regional banks became mere branches of the Berlin big banks.

The Deutsche Bank acquired 23 branches of the Bohemian Union Bank, the Dresdner Bank, the branches of the Czech Escompte Bank; the Allgemeine Deutsche Kredit-Anstalt, the branches of the Anglo-Czech Bank (subsidiary of the Laenderbank) and of the Czech Industrie Bank.

In the future, the money paid in by Sudeten manufacturers will flow to Berlin and not remain in the Sudetenland. New capital will not be invested in areas where competitive industries are undesirable.

A few big German trusts "bought" those Sudeten factories which were likely to have a prosperous future in connection with the armament boom. The I. G. Farbenindustrie "purchased" the stock of the Bruexer Bergbaugesellschaft and of the Nordboehmische Bergbaugesellschaft (in which Lord Runciman has an interest). The I. G. Farbenindustrie intends to construct a factory near Bruenn for the production of synthetic gasoline from coal. Mannesmann, a German concern well known in the armament business, acquired several mines from Witkowitz, the Czech iron firm.

Businessmen in the newly conquered areas who at first welcomed Nazi rule because of dissatisfaction with former conditions were disillusioned almost overnight. In addition to full interest payments on their debts—their debts have not been diminished, only the nationality of the creditors has changed—they now pay higher taxes and higher prices for raw materials—mostly ersatz. Worst of all, they have lost their export markets without receiving any compensation in the domestic market, because, on the whole, they produced consumption goods, not armaments. Small and medium-sized enterprises have deteriorated to a much greater extent than similar enterprises in the Reich proper. A few big trusts have become predominant in industrial life. They own the new armament factories in the Sudeten area and they exploit the raw material resources of the region for the benefit of the Reich's economy.

Apart from strategically important armament factories, industries in the newly acquired territories must operate at minimum capacity so that all raw material resources may be exploited fully in the interest of the "mother country." Czech manufacturers in Bohemia and Moravia try in vain to obtain from their new rulers sufficient supplies of those raw materials which are scarce in Germany. Only a fraction of the allotments granted the Germans is accorded the Czech manufacturers. Allotments for scarce raw materials granted to Czech manufacturers amounted to only 15 per cent of the allotments for German manufacturers.[14] The imperialist "mother country" tries to satisfy its deficiencies at the expense of the new colony. Since there is not enough raw material to go around, the colony's productive forces are permitted to deteriorate.

The handicaps under which the industries of the Reich are laboring are being felt with even greater intensity in the newly conquered countries. State interference in business and private life assumes greater proportions in the vassal states than in the "mother country" itself.

The greater the exploitation and economic devastation in the vassal states, the more necessary does it become to build a strong military machine under centralized authoritarian leadership. Party leaders have hailed this growth of the State machine because it gives them more power. Within the Reich proper they have tried and probably will continue trying to increase their authority and popularity by new conquests. From the territory thus acquired, the leaders have been able to recover at least a fraction of their huge expenditures by levying tribute on the "colonies." They can also slightly extend the narrow base of the privileged "friends of the State bureaucracy" at the expense of the new vassal States.

But the number of the underprivileged grows much more rapidly than the number of the privileged. The further this development proceeds, the more absolute is the power needed for the maintenance of the regime.

*Chapter XV*

# *PLANNING FOR WAR*

"Not the military experts, but the Party leaders, decided the tempo of militarization and rearmament."

MANY businessmen had nurtured the hope that the Army could be relied upon to prevent tyrannical abuse of power and that it would restore the traditional basis of bourgeois society—the sanctity of private property. This—when Hitler came to power—was the viewpoint of the political leader of the German conservative nationalists, Alfred Hugenberg, as well as of Dr. Hjalmar Schacht.

There naturally existed, and to a certain extent still exists, an important distinction between the Army and the Party. The Army was primarily an instrument for external war. German generals were patriots fond of their profession, who thought in terms of "serving the fatherland" and wanted to make practical use of the military power at their command for this purpose only. They were reluctant to apply their power to maintain order within Germany itself. They wanted to stand "above the parties" because they did not want to share responsibility for unpopular measures of the Government or of the Reichstag. They wanted Hitler and the Party to assure internal order so that they, the Army leaders, might better prepare the whole nation for external war. But fascist party leaders cannot be satisfied with playing a subsidiary role. Their controlling position cannot be maintained if they are reduced to the role of commanders of the police force. The leader of a totalitarian State cannot allow the Army to stand apart from the Party. The Party leaders must make it clear to the Army that the existence of the Army itself is dependent on the preservation of the Party regime, for a situation might well arise where the internal war front is even more important than the external war front. The Army must openly demonstrate its readiness to protect the regime—internally and externally. Army and Party troops—the S.S., S.A. and Gestapo—are sections of one Greater Army, both wearing the insignia of the Party and owing unconditional allegiance to the Party leader.

The widespread hope that the Army would restrain the dictatorship of the Party was an illusion. Two absolute powers cannot coexist in one totalitarian State. But there has been no complete victory either of the Party over the Army or of the Army over the Party; the armed forces of the Party—the S.S., S.A. and Gestapo—and the Army still exist as separate organizations. Hitler, the Party Leader, is in control of the Army. The commanders of the S.S. and S.A.—mere Party formations—do not control the Army, although the Gestapo keeps a close watch over the leaders of the Army. No Army man is allowed to be a member of the Party, while the Party's military forces—the S.S., S.A., Gestapo and the ordinary police—are kept apart from the command of the Army. There still exists, however, a division of labor between the Army and the armed forces of the Party, with the major functions of the latter being the preservation of internal order, while the main function of the Army is the preparation of the country for wars against foreign powers.

There is no "conservative" army officer who did not welcome the open flouting of the Versailles Treaty and the strengthening of German militarism. But many military experts regarded with skepticism not only the armament policies of the Nazi regime, but also its return to the prewar style of army, based on general conscription.

A retired army officer, Major Soldau, former editor of the official army organ, *Deutsche Wehr,* wrote in 1933:

"I am strictly opposed to conscription. . . . A return to conscription means a step backward to the old system as contrasted with the new system represented by the army of today; it means disregarding the essential lessons of the World War and implies fatal ignorance of the political developments since the end of the war." [1]

Many leading army officers are extremely dissatisfied with Hitler's armament policies as well as with his foreign policies, yet they do not see any chance of acting contrary to his wishes without such a breakdown of the system as would bury the whole structure of German militarism.

It is a common mistake to count the military strength of a State in terms of the number of planes ready to fly, the number of guns available at the moment a war starts, or the number of soldiers who can be put in uniform at a moment's notice. Counting these factors only, Hitler's armament policies have been exceedingly successful. There is no other country in the world—except the Soviet Union—with as large an army and as great an air fleet as Nazi Germany. But increase in armaments does not in itself mean a corresponding growth of military strength. It might be the decisive factor if there were a chance of winning a final victory in the first battle, a battle which would crush the adversary before he had a chance to mobilize his forces. Such a quick victory, however, would be possible only against a small country or against a big country in no way prepared for war. Under any other circumstances, a war cannot possibly be decided in a single battle. Other factors then become more decisive than the number of planes, guns and soldiers ready to fight on the day the next war is declared; these factors are the capacity for the production of all kinds of war materials in huge quantities and the production of sufficient consumption goods to prevent starvation. Particularly in a long war are these factors vital to the maintenance of morale.

Furthermore, the horrors of modern warfare make it more necessary than ever before that the soldiers and the people be firmly convinced that the war is unavoidable. From this point of view, the fascist philosophy does not promote the required war morale. The fascist philosophy, expressed by Mussolini himself, declares war to be something which is in itself desirable, regardless of the fact that complete destruction might be the final outcome of that war.

"All doctrines which postulate peace at all costs are incompatible with Fascism. Equally foreign to the spirit of Fascism—even if accepted as useful in meeting a special political situation—are all international or League superstructures which, as history shows, crumble to the ground whenever the heart of nations is deeply stirred by sentimental, idealistic or practical considerations. Fascism carries this anti-pacifist attitude into the life of the individual. 'I don't care a damn'—the proud motto of the fighting squad—is not only an act of philosophical stoicism; it . . . is evidence of a fighting spirit which accepts all risks." [2]

Hitler's armament policies seem to follow the fatal example of the plans of the leading war strategist of the Kaiser's army, von Schlieffen, who relied on a few "great decisive strokes" to insure an immediate and decisive victory.

"We learned that what Your Excellency aspired to was not partial successes, but great decisive blows. Your Excellency does not want a war which would be prolonged indefinitely until the power of one country is exhausted by the power of the other. You want great decisive strokes, and your goal was the destruction of the adversary. All forces should be directed toward that supreme goal, and the will which led you was the will for victory." [3]

Recent war experience and the development of war technique contradict the possibility of an army's winning a quick victory against an adversary who can defend himself with the same means and tactics as those used by the aggressor.

"It is probable that a European war will start as a war of position. . . . This means a considerable weakening of the war strategy and war policies of the German State as a result of its geographical situation and its raw material dependence." [4]

Nobody can foresee how long a new European war will last. The hope that one short decisive battle might decide the whole war prevailed among German pre-War militarists who thought in terms of the Franco-Prussian War of 1870. German post-War strategists abandoned the hope of a quick and easy victory against another big power. This implied a change in the traditional conception of war preparations. It is no longer sufficient to have a few large armament plants and to store enough materials to satisfy the demands of a short war. A steady supply of raw materials and foodstuffs is as important as the existence of armament and gun factories.

Enough has been written about the probable character of the next large-scale war. Practical experience has shown that such a war would be "totalitarian" because the whole nation, all the economic forces of the country, would have to be mobilized for it. Such a vast mass of material and human beings will be needed that a country unable quickly to mobilize all its material and human forces for the purpose of war would be doomed to fail.

It seems as if a totalitarian State should be the ideal political regime for the preparation of totalitarian war, since it should be able to secure complete preparation of the entire social system for war. The fascist war preparations, however, have defeated their own ends. They have created tremendous armies and vast masses of war materials, but simultaneously there has been such strain on the whole economy, such an exhaustion of economic reserves, such a decline of the "morale of the people"—a factor as important as reserves of raw materials, guns or planes—as to make the State unable to stand the strain of a real totalitarian war for any length of time. It is even doubtful whether the most recent increases of army strength and of the number of planes, guns and the big naval program have not weakened rather than strengthened the military system, and whether further increases will not have similar adverse effects.

The real strength of the military system of a totalitarian regime has not yet been seriously tested. Therefore whatever may be claimed for it is open to doubt. There are, however, certain fundamental facts which modern militarism has to take into account. In the long run there is scarcely a single branch of industry that can be spared during a totalitarian war. One industry might be more important than another, and some industries might be superfluous if the war lasted only a few weeks or months. But a totalitarian war makes claims upon the entire economic structure. One missing link might bring the war machine to a standstill. Production of uniforms must continue during a war because the soldiers cannot march and fight in worn-out rags. Butter is no less important than guns—Goering to the contrary notwithstanding—for without butter the physical strength of the soldier breaks down and he will lack the fighting spirit and morale which will be more necessary than ever in the war of the future.

"In a totalitarian war, every State reaches its optimum of war power only by a balance between land, air and sea forces in accordance with the availability of supplies. . . . Decisions of the commander which result in an exhaustion of the available reserves before having achieved the purpose of the war have a decisive effect. . . ." [5]

The Nazi leaders have disregarded this aspect of armament. They have built up a large army and air fleet, but there has been no corresponding growth in the other parts of the economic system necessary for maintaining and supplying such a huge army and air fleet.

The armament policies of fascism, and especially of Hitler in Germany, have strengthened the military forces and certain branches of war production on so large a scale that the foreign world has wondered how such huge armament expenses could be undertaken without a financial breakdown. It did not see the impoverishment of the economy as a whole, nor the shrinkage of the economic reserves which are so essential for a totalitarian war. This latter factor is not so readily discernible as the impressive growth of the army and the air fleet.

Tremendous fortifications were erected in western and eastern Germany; new investments in ersatz production industries signalized the growth of economic preparations for war. But simultaneously Germany's dependence on foreign raw materials has grown because raw material reserves have had to be used up without sufficient replacement, and because industries which do not directly produce munitions, but which are also essential for totalitarian warfare, have decayed.

The Army leaders were alarmed over the complete lack of gold and foreign currency reserves, for they appreciated the absolute necessity of Germany's importing huge quantities of foreign materials in wartime in order to keep the war machine running and to avoid starvation of the people. An influential representative of the Army leadership wrote as an answer to declarations of Party leaders that a totalitarian State does not need gold:

"One cannot expect in another war that neutral, or even friendly, countries will send supplies which . . . cannot be paid for in gold, foreign currency or essential goods. Therefore, it may happen that gold will become the most important war material. From the point of view of war economy . . . limitation of the measures of self-sufficiency might become necessary." [6]

Last but not least—the morale of the people has suffered under the economic strain and under the militarization of the country in peacetime. The will to defend the Nazi fatherland has not grown with the increase in numbers of planes and guns and soldiers. All reports which indicate the trend of war morale in Germany—and the same applies to Italy—confirm the fact that it has declined, and that the increase in armaments has been achieved at the expense of the whole economic system, which has been made subservient to militarization and to the parasitic existence of the Party and State administration.

As a warning against the illusions raised by the self-sufficiency policy of the Nazi government, the organ of the Army Staff pointed to pre-War experiences:

"Full foodstuff independence was impossible before the war. We should have had to pay for such an attempt with heavy losses to our industrial world position. . . . Peace economy should be burdened as little as possible by economic preparations for war. The principal aim must be the formation of wealth, the creation of reserves. . . . Foodstuff independence in peacetime is no guarantee of foodstuff independence in wartime. . . . World economy has not undermined our safety, but it was one of the most important factors of our ability to resist during the World War." [7]

Nazi militarism might be compared to the athlete who overtrains one part of his body for some special purpose, disregarding the training of other parts. He might boast of the tremendous size of a few specially trained muscles and yet be unable to stand the strain of an effort involving his entire body.

The Nazi State has a tremendous air fleet. It is equipped with well-organized factories for mass production of planes. But other essential parts of the economy are weaker than at the beginning of the big armament program.

Armaments are by their very nature unproductive; at best, they are not used at all and become obsolete. In case of war, there will be a suddenly increased production and consumption of armaments. Capacity to increase this kind of production will be a decisive factor in military strength. Such production can be greatly expanded only if huge economic reserves exist. The greater the economic wealth of the nation, the more can be wasted—used up—in wartime. If, however, there is such a strain on the economy in peacetime that the necessary reserves needed for carrying on a totalitarian war cannot be built up, then the war preparations are jeopardized. This is a circumstance peculiar to the economic structure of the totalitarian states.

"Germany is far behind her capabilities, not because her working population works too little, but because so large a proportion is engaged in unproductive work, and in piling up overhead charges; because so large a proportion of her resources remains dormant or is misdirected without due reference to calculations of ultimate advantage; because her present economic situation is so little adapted to developing her real but latent powers." [8]

This picture resembles the development of German economy during the World War. A study of the economic trends in that period shows a close similarity to the economic development of Germany under the Nazi regime.

"Germany is spending about two billion marks a month on the war. About one-sixth of the national capital will thus have been spent by the end of the year. Whence do all these billions come? The shells are shot off, the guns are worn out, motors are used until they become old iron, the soldiers' uniforms are worn into rags, and so forth. We work exclusively for the war, and a great part of the cost of war is covered by this work. For the rest we are living on capital. The first and chief cause is the fact that we are using up our stocks—the copper reserves in the home (urns, kitchen utensils, etc.) . . . as well as the accumulated raw materials in the warehouses. Another cause, which also means a drawing on capital, consists in the fact that plants are worn out without immediate repairs being made. In peacetime the industrialist regularly writes off big sums for the depreciation of buildings, machinery and other assets, and then acquires new machinery to replace the old in order to avoid being faced in the end by the fact that his whole factory has been worn out. Such sums are, of course, still being written off the balance sheets; but the industrialist generally abstains from making the actual replacement purchase, either because he cannot obtain the necessary goods or because, in view of the fundamental changes in markets and prices, he wishes to wait and see what methods of production he will be able to use in the future. As private individuals, people save money in order to invest it in war loans, but in the economic sense, for the requirements of war, we are saving materials and labor which in peacetime would otherwise have been used in order to make good wear and tear. We are living on capital in order to finance the immediate needs of wartime economy." [9]

This is exactly what is happening in Germany today, although the country is not yet involved in another world war. The nation's savings are used for unproductive expenditure to the detriment of consumption and investment for truly productive purposes.

These huge armament expenditures represent only one aspect of the inroads of the totalitarian State on the economic life of the country. There is still another aspect of State interference. Unforeseen economic difficulties are encountered which necessitate sudden changes in economic plans and state policies in order to satisfy the most urgent needs of the moment.

Yet the authoritarian State always pretends to act in accordance with a grandiose plan, in execution of a "program." The character of the authoritarian State, however, makes it necessary to prevent its actions from appearing as the result of unforeseen developments or subject to the force of circumstances or emergency situations.

The rulers of a totalitarian State boast that their interference with the economic processes eliminates the effects of the business cycle. The State itself "manipulates economic laws."

"We intend to manipulate economic laws ourselves in place of private interests and of Jews. . . . The Germans are no longer dependent on the restrictions and artificial speculation in a glutted market. The Germans are no longer the proletarians of world economy, but workers for Germany." [10]

Even though State policies are officially independent

of the business cycle, the authoritarian rulers, like all others, must take into consideration basic economic facts. Whether or not they are willing to admit it, they must make concessions to economic conditions. The totalitarian State must always pretend that its Fuehrer or Duce cannot be mistaken, that he foresaw what would happen, that his power cannot be impaired by economic difficulties. Yet it would be virtually impossible to find a plan or scheme which substantiates these pretensions.

"Out of import restrictions there arose the system of State administration of raw materials with its system of purchasing and processing permits, and prohibitions against investment and use of raw materials; and out of the State control of raw materials there arose in turn the control of production, of investments and of consumption and the exact regimentation of the volume of labor to be employed for given purposes. The development of the twenty-eight control offices is particularly significant, for this machinery which at present is responsible for the direction of every economic process is a definite emergency measure. This also explains its complicated nature and its obscurities. It would be different if a planned economy of this kind had been deliberately aimed at. The freedom of business is restricted to such a degree that a paralysis of the economic forces is to be feared in the long run." [11]

When we search for a predominant plan in the Nazi economy, we see that apparently all individual activities are directed toward military preparation. It seems that the State is co-ordinating all State acts and private activities according to a single consideration: does it help to strengthen us from the military point of view?

Economic restrictions are officially justified by the

claim of military necessity. In reality, the rearmament plan which the Army Staff worked out, important as it is, is not the sole guiding principle of the fascist State. Fascist State policies are largely designed to strengthen and to preserve the autocratic power of the Party leaders. Consequently, armament policies are largely influenced by the narrow interests of the fascist bureaucracy. This explains why the fascist regimes disregarded the plans and recommendations of their best military experts, compelling them to adapt or change their military plans according to the policies and interests of the authoritarian dictators.

German military experts never desired the peacetime autocratic rule of an unpopular bureaucracy. They did not approve of the State's suppression of private initiative in economic life.

"As to industry, we should not forget that the Fuehrer has said: 'The new State will not be and does not want to be an entrepreneur. Planned economy must be rejected from the point of view of rearmament. . . . We insist upon free initiative and full responsibility of the businessman in accordance with the general policy of the State.' "[12]

German military leaders wanted to prepare and equip the entire industrial machinery and to mobilize the whole people for war. They recognized the futility of having an inflated State-owned or State-subsidized industry for the production of airplanes or machine guns if other important branches of industry were to be allowed to deteriorate. The "conservative" Army leaders did not wish the State to abolish private enterprise in armament manufacture. They were afraid that such a measure would interfere with the balanced development of all industries necessary for a wartime economy and would thus hinder rather than aid the country's preparation for a totalitarian war.

"State ownership of armaments industries . . . might be justified for Italy. It does not suit Germany. We want to mobilize the full strength of the highly developed German economy. The more peacetime industries can be put on a war footing, the more efficient will be the German war economy.

"We do not want to abolish the private initiative of the German businessman."[13]

The Army officers approved of a policy which would "direct" the private initiative of the entrepreneurs in such a way as to make their business conform to the interests of militarism. The German Army leadership rejected plans for a "corporate state" with "guilds" or corporations in control of production and prices. They supported Schacht's endeavor to strengthen or reconsolidate the system of privately owned banks and industries.

The Party leaders, however, welcomed the necessity of extending the centralized administration because it put them in charge of a more powerful State bureaucracy. They needed quick successes in foreign policy in order to consolidate their autocratic power and to justify their suppression of individual rights and liberties. They thought that the difficulties arising from an intensification of the economic strain would enable them to extend their power in the direction of State capitalism. Not the military experts, but the Party leaders, decided the tempo of militarization and rearmament. They enforced a peacetime extension of the Army and of the air fleet which was out of proportion to the strength of the economic basis on which the Army and the air fleet had to rely.

Hitler's foreign policy was greatly influenced by the internal condition of the Nazi party. The Party leaders undermined the position of defiant nationalist generals by a more rigid militarization than the militarists themselves had advocated. Their foreign policy created situations which made it necessary to prepare for another world war against the West, the East, or both. The creator of the German Reichswehr, von Seeckt, was fearful of another war in which German militarism might be cut off from foreign resources and might be completely isolated. He preferred to follow the policy of Bismarck rather than that of the Kaiser, trying to neutralize Russia in case of a conflict with the Western powers. Hitler's aggressive foreign policy, however, compelled German militarism to change the militarization program; to prepare for another conflict in which Germany would be cut off from supplies from overseas as well as from Russia.

The more unstable the economic system becomes, the greater is the necessity for a repressive leadership and State bureaucracy. It has to whip up the militancy of its Party members, and raise the prestige of the Leader. It orders Party actions, the economic effects of which cannot be foreseen by businessmen.

## *Chapter XVI*

# *BUREAUCRACY IN CONTROL*

"They do no work which adds goods or social services to the market. Their job is to hold their job. The rest of the community finds itself serving as the hardworking host upon which the bureaucratic clique is feeding and fattening."

THE capitalist in Germany is confused. The fascist State has, it is true, saved many private concerns from bankruptcy. Under the totalitarian regime, business has been freed from trade-unionism and strikes, and has therefore been able to depress wages and lengthen working hours at will while huge investments in armaments have resulted in prosperity for many enterprises. Nevertheless, most German businessmen insist that they have lost more under Nazism than have the workers.

The subservience of businessmen to the Party, the devious dealings and precarious existence which they suffer at the hands of the State, the complete loss of that independence which characterizes capitalist ventures in a non-totalitarian economy have proved a special disappointment to those who helped to finance the Nazi party before it came to power. It was their hope that the Nazi party would serve as their tool. Especially was this the belief of the important industrialists who had feared the loss of their monopolies, and of the big agrarians who could not survive the crisis without fresh State subsidies. Both eagerly sought political power in order to safeguard their positions—not merely against social revolutionary forces, but also against business competitors who attacked their monopolist privileges. They invested huge amounts of money in the Nazis. They did this, or had to do it, on too large a scale. For the power they helped create all too soon became the master of its creators—"authoritarian," independent of their will and regulation. Co-operation of the businessmen, big and small, with the State and Party bureaucracy is being enforced by those who now have political power, while those who command mere money power are forced to "co-operate" with the new government at the risk of their very existence. This co-operation entails generous spending and the greasing of official palms, but it does not in any way increase the businessman's chance of regaining economic independence and freedom.

When Germany's leading bankers and financiers met at the National Congress of their group association (Banken und Versicherungsanstalten) on October 21, 1938, they were addressed as follows by the Government's spokesman, Secretary of State Rudolf Brinkmann, who after Schacht's removal was to become Vice-President of the Reichsbank:

"Schenkendorff [a German poet at the time of Germany's 'War of Delivery' from Napoleon's rule] sang in 1813, a heroic period, his song 'Freiheit, die ich meine . . .' [My idea of freedom . . .] and I see you, grimly smiling, making comparisons and especially asking me where that freedom of business and of business activity is, of which I have spoken and which I so love . . ."[1]

The bureaucracy of the Nazi State is a special phenomenon. It is like a huge and growing incubus living off the body politic and becoming more parasitic as it increases in size and numbers. Secretary of State Brinkmann has said:

"To be sure, the new State has had to establish an alarming number of economic administrative boards, and, certainly, many a decision which is made by the foreign exchange control boards, by the examination boards, by the supervisory boards, by the economic groups, by the finance authorities is bureaucratic, that is, it is born more of excessive desire for order and love for the letter of the law than of knowledge and understanding of actual business life. However, bureaucracy exists not only in the governmental division of our economic life. In large concerns many bureaucratic decisions are to be observed. . . . Cartels also are not always free from bureaucracy. . . ." [2]

The bureaucracy of the totalitarian State is much more bureaucratic and top-heavy than was the bureaucracy of private cartels, concerns and trusts in pre-Hitler Germany. Yet these corporations had already violated the laws of free competition under liberal capitalism and had, therefore, paved the way for further suppression of the rights of the independent entrepreneur.

This development did not originate in the minds of a few men who were especially unscrupulous. It was a development which grew out of a certain stage of the competitive struggle. Curious as it may seem, large concerns, trusts and cartels had abolished free competition in the name of free competition, and in the name of the rights of the independent entrepreneur who was typical of an earlier stage of liberal capitalism. Paradoxically, those entrepreneurs who did not attain a monopolistic position and who had to compete with each other in the open market, often, under the Weimar regime, asked State help or interference against "free," that is, ruinous competition. Such a policy leads to a state of affairs where the State becomes a superpower, restricting and reducing the rights of all businessmen, granting privileges to a few concerns and trusts which are closely connected with the State bureaucracy and with the armament business and transforming private monopolies into State-protected monopolies.

The State dictates to the individual businessman how he must act in order that his activities may best serve the "national interest."

A word must be said here about the character of the "common" or "national" interest.

The government of a totalitarian State might claim that only the strong arm of the State can prevent the individual businessman from looking after his private interests at the expense of society. The possibility of such a clash between individual and "common" interests certainly exists. A stubborn defender of a liberal economy—free competition—might deny the possibility of such a clash if there were such a thing as a "pure" competitive economy. But only if individual and social interests were identical would there be no need for laws and rules to regulate property rights and business life.

The term "common" or "national" interest is an abstraction, a conception which exists as a result of certain common interests or peculiarities of a stratum of citizens whose welfare is conceived of, under a totalitarian regime, as synonymous with the welfare of the State. These citizens, however, have private or individual interests which they may try to satisfy at the expense of members of their own class or group. Such acts would very often threaten the social group while enriching the individual.

This is particularly obvious in emergency situations—famine, earthquakes, war—when the reckless pursuit of private interests might endanger the whole social system. The State must then step in to discipline the individual miscreant "in the common interest," that is, in defense of the whole social system.

Industrialists who are members of cartels or syndicates may be confronted by such clashes between individual and common or group interests. There are always firms which try to obtain special privileges for themselves at the expense of the whole group or "group community." The clash between such private and group interests becomes dangerous when market conditions turn critical. Then common interests make it more necessary that a cartel or syndicate restrict individual business activities effectively. Under just such critical conditions, however, it becomes more tempting for independent enterprises to strengthen their position, their share in production and sales, at the expense of the other group members. The same holds true for the whole of society as long as it is based on a competitive economy. For competition implies the right of every individual to advance his own private interests as much as possible. The clash, however, between these individual or private interests and the social or group interests may be lessened by laws, decrees, and government measures, which restrict and diminish the individual rights.

The establishment of central authorities which control and restrict private business activities is a necessary consequence of this need for regulation. The growth of the central authorities promotes the formation of a powerful administration which becomes so strong that those who are in control of it easily become a quasi-independent power. Such a development is inevitable in a totalitarian State with a one-party dictatorship where the Party bureaucracy penetrates all government offices and grows to gigantic dimensions.

The new State bureaucracy compels the businessman to conform to restrictions and rules which conflict with the essential functions and rights of an independent capitalist. State officials may violate the sanctity of private property. This even becomes their duty if the businessman fails to conform to suggestions or orders of the State bureaucracy or shows insufficient devotion to the Party or to the leader.

The businessman is still "free" and "independent"—"free" in that he has no pension rights, "independent" in that he may risk losing his capital and economic status.

As a rule, a fascist government does not free the private businessman from the risk of losing his capital or from the burden of managerial activities. It does forbid him to increase or reduce production merely according to his private interests. The State orders private capital to produce and does not itself function as a producer. Insofar as the State owns enterprises which participate in production, this can be regarded as an exception rather than as the general rule.

The fascist State does not merely grant the private entrepreneur the right to produce for the market, but insists on production as a duty which must be fulfilled even though there be no profit. The businessman cannot close down his factory or shop because he finds it unprofitable. To do this requires a special permit issued by the authorities.

According to Dr. Brinkmann, the fascist State has "proclaimed the right to work and ownership of private property" as rights of the citizen. But "private property" in turn imposes the obligation to make good the "right to work." This claim is not advanced because the State is sentimental about workers who lose their jobs, but because any considerable decline in employment would endanger the existence of the inflated State bureaucracy and the progress of rearmament.

The totalitarian State bureaucracy cannot tolerate another industrial crisis, leading to a serious decline in production, without risking a serious crisis for the whole regime. In Italy as well as in Germany the totalitarian State is the biggest consumer. Its demands exceed 50 per cent of the total production. A decline of production by only one-third would mean that the State would take 75 per cent of the total production, leaving only 25 per cent for the private citizens who are neither State-employed nor receive a State income. This would entail such an increase in direct and indirect taxation as to render private business completely unprofitable. The State bureaucracy would have to resort to further measures of coercion in order to maintain the industrial and social system. Under such conditions, the State itself might be compelled to operate industrial enterprises and thereby abolish the system of private enterprise. But this would immediately lead to a further growth of unproductive bureaucracy and an enlarged administrative apparatus, without inspiring workers or managements to increased production. The stimulus which still remains for workers and management to increase production would be absent. In its place would be even more naked force and fear. Voluntary co-operation could be achieved only if those who are engaged in production would receive higher incomes and more personal liberty.

The Nazi government has expressly threatened the private entrepreneur with increased State coercion and reduction of personal rights and liberties unless he fulfills adequately the "duty to produce" according to the State's demands. The threat is implicit in the following "pep talk" of a high Nazi leader to German businessmen:

"Acknowledge frankly, without any reservations, your obligation to produce, and subscribe completely to the principle of unfalsified competition on a performance basis. If you do not do this, the strong State in which you share will no longer be in a position to allow business the wide field of free activity it now enjoys." [3]

Like schoolboys, Nazi Germany's big bankers and industrialists had to listen to and applaud the State Secretary of the Ministry of Economics—formerly a Reichsbank employee of minor importance—who raised his finger warningly to Germany's biggest private entrepreneurs and threatened: "Either you do what we tell you and satisfy our demands, or we shall take away the 'freedom' still left you!" Dr. Schacht emphasized frequently the conception that the State restricted private business activities only as an emergency and temporary measure. He clung to the idea, which has become old-fashioned under a totalitarian regime and is officially regarded as a heritage of "reactionary conservatives," that the State should serve the interests of private business and protect its property rights. The Party leaders, on the contrary, insisted that the main function of private business is to serve the interests of the State—the individual exists for the State, not the State for the individual.

The Nazi regime maintains that private property is a basic principle of society, but in practice it controls and regulates the use of such property. This was not what the capitalist who favored the Nazi party during the 1931-32 depression had wanted. He merely wanted the State to find a way out for him. He felt he could no longer survive under the old competitive conditions. On one hand, his reserves were shrinking; on the other, he was the target of the labor movement. But the Fuehrer whom he then acclaimed as his savior has become the leader of an authoritarian State and Party bureaucracy. This bureaucracy regulates and controls the struggle for survival of private enterprise. Formerly the competitive struggle of business interests decided who would bear the inevitable capital losses during a crisis. Today it is the State bureaucracy which dictates who is to be eliminated from business. A private enterprise can survive only to the extent to which it has closer and better relations with the State bureaucracy than its competitors.

The greater the economic difficulties, the more the individual businessman fears that he will be sacrificed by the authoritarian regime "in the interest of the State."

Therefore the dictatorship of the State bureaucracy becomes increasingly a dictatorship over the capitalist entrepreneurs, the small as well as the big businessmen, the shopkeepers as well as the great corporations.

Such conditions strengthen the independent power

of the State bureaucracy so that it can become—*and to a certain extent already has become*—a dictatorship which defends its own selfish interests at the expense of all classes, not excepting the private capitalists.

The selfish interests of the State bureaucracy are of an economic as well as of a political nature. When Dr. Schacht was still President of the Reichsbank and a powerful figure in Nazi Germany, he suggested curtailing the State bureaucracy and the expenses of the administration so as to reduce the weight of taxation, thereby helping the businessman. Dr. Schacht was told by the Party leaders that the maintenance of the Party and the bureaucratic administrative machine came ahead of the interests of the business community, which is allowed to exist only in order to pay its tribute to the State.

This tribute which private citizens have to pay to the totalitarian State might be bearable during prosperity when private business is making large profits and can earn an adequate income even in the face of increased taxation. However, when no such prosperity exists and depression wipes out private profits, then the weight of increased taxation and the financial demands of the State bureaucracy mean an increase in overhead for private enterprise, intensifying and lengthening the depression.

The totalitarian State cannot give heed to such contingencies. It cannot adapt its budget to the business cycle. It might perhaps cut unemployment relief, but the expenses for the maintenance of the State bureaucracy itself, as well as for armaments, cannot be reduced at will.

As the State takes on new and wider functions, it breeds an army of officeholders to take care of them.

The entrepreneur finds that almost daily new State committees are created to pre-empt the functions of private business. Committees for Accounting, Supervisory Boards, Raw Material Purchase and Distribution Offices, Organizations for Preparation of War Production in Peace Industries, Labor Front Secretariats, Investment Control Boards—these and countless other State committees are manned by Nazi officials who are independent of private business and responsible to no one but the Fuehrer. And under each Nazi leader there are scores of subleaders.

The authoritarian State breeds irresponsibility on the part of this ever-growing and legally privileged group. Their position is secure—unless they are purged by their own friends, often as a result of rivalries—whereas the general economy is insecure. They do no work which adds goods or social services to the market. Their job is: to hold their job. The rest of the community finds itself serving as the hardworking host upon which the bureaucratic clique is feeding and fattening.

This does not yet prove that the ruling Party or the totalitarian regime has purposely betrayed its former sponsors. Increased State interference and the restriction of rights imposed even on big industrialists might be taken to show that the State has been compelling the individual businessman or industrialist to sacrifice materially and personally for the larger State or social group interests. But the fact is that the fascist State bureaucracy has steadily gained strength as the internal economy has weakened, and it now operates as a sprawling parasitic agency, identifying its own narrow bureaucratic interests with the general interests of society.

The Nazi party has warned the private entrepreneur

that he must completely subordinate his private interests to the "public weal." "The principle of primacy of public weal means also that the possibility of following personal interest ends where personal interest clashes with justified interests of others and thus threatens to plunge the whole system into conflict. These limits are pointed out to the individual, in some cases by business ethics and in some cases by State order." [4]

This development has fundamentally changed the social position of the businessman. He no longer belongs to the top stratum of society even if he is a big businessman. His social position is beneath that of the leading members of the State bureaucracy or of the Army. This is reflected in his steady fear of the State bureaucracy. He is no longer a law-abiding citizen who sticks to the letter of the law because he believes the law is good and court decisions usually just. He fears the power of the State bureaucrats and he knows all too well their contempt for the ideas which he has cherished. He no longer believes that the sacredness of private property will be respected, for he has experienced too often the arbitrary curtailment of property rights. He knows too intimately that State bureaucrats use their absolute power to enrich themselves at the expense of other less powerful citizens. There may be less likelihood of losing his capital through "ruinous competition," but this has been more than offset by new business risks. Previously, when he failed in a competitive struggle, he inclined to blame himself for his failure, but not the system. If he fails under the totalitarian State, he blames the system—and his inability to win the favor of an influential State bureaucrat.

Under such a system two categories of businessmen

can be distinguished: those who are willing to take risks and those who are not. Not that the former seek new fields of investment or new possibilities of production. They devote their energies to circumventing bureaucratic decisions and to cunning violations of the law. They do not lose the respect of their competitors; on the contrary, they are regarded almost as heroes who risk their existence and their lives in the struggle against the State bureaucracy.

They may reduce their risks by paying an insurance premium—bribing State bureaucrats and paying higher contributions to the Party treasury.

Those who do not wish to take chances spend their energy worrying lest they violate some decree or law, and behave timorously toward any State bureaucrat.

A big German manufacturer was asked by the author: "How has the spirit of the businessman changed under the Nazi regime?"

The laconic answer was:

"The German businessman *riecht nach Angstschweiss* (sweats with fear). He does not know whether he has broken some law, whether and when he will be caught. He wakes up in the morning dreaming of an investigation by some State bureaucrat who has discovered some irregularity of which he, the businessman, knew or did not know. He enters his office fearing that he will find the announcement of a new decree which curbs his business, or that the condition of State finances will lead to some new measure of expropriation. When the office door opens he expects a tax official who will investigate his business affairs for many years back until he finds some 'irregularity.' You may think this anxiety unreasonable. But unfortunately I cannot help fearing that

I will experience tomorrow what is happening to others today."

Fascism has deprived the businessman of his self-confidence and feeling of economic security, even if he still is a well-to-do capitalist. The totalitarian regime has annihilated the most important conservative force of capitalism, the belief that private property ought to be a sacred right of every citizen and that the private property of every citizen ought to be protected. Respect for private property has penetrated the spirit of the people in all capitalist countries. It is the strongest bulwark of capitalism. Fascism has succeeded in destroying this conservative force—without having created a new and better social principle. For it still relies on private property and on private production. People still have to work for money and have to live on money incomes. Possession of capital still provides income. But this income is largely at the mercy of State bureaucrats and Party officials.

*Chapter XVII*

# A WORLD OF ABSURDITIES

"The fascist dictatorship grows stronger—internally and externally—the more it increases the dangers against which it pretends to protect the businessman."

In Nazi Germany there is no field of business activity in which the State does not interfere. In more or less detailed form it prescribes how the businessman may use capital which is still presumably his private property. And because of this, the German businessman has become a fatalist; he does not believe that the new rules will work out well, yet he knows that he cannot alter the course of events. He has been made the tool of a gigantic machine which he cannot direct. He looks at the rest of the capitalist world, hoping for help in winning back from the State his lost rights and freedom. But wherever he turns there are trends and changes of a similar, though milder, character, indicating that the totalitarian regime in Germany cannot be attributed to the madness of one man or to the self-interest of one ruling party; that it represents in caricature some of the fundamental phenomena in modern capitalism, which lead to more and more State interference and consequent usurpation of the businessman's rights and privileges.

State Secretary Brinkmann summarized the lost rights of the German businessman as follows:

"You will call attention to the fact that the freedom

of disposition of the entrepreneur in the sphere of commodity purchases is chained down by the system of supervisory boards and other regulations, that the utilization of labor is subject to various restrictions, that the wage ceiling and prohibition of price increases [*Preis-Stop*] force a price level which in a liberal economy would be impossible, that money intended for consumption is forcibly shifted to capital investment and the entrepreneur sees himself forced under State interference to make capital investments which he would never have made if he had been left to his own doing, that money capital is enfeebled by the law for the Compulsory Investment of Surplus Dividends[1] [*Anleihestock*] and is forced by the prohibition of private issues to offer itself at a cheap rate for purposes in which it is but little interested.

"And you will argue further that in the shadow of this governmental procedure, which you call economy of coercion, there is occurring under the eyes of the same state the very thing it wishes to prevent, namely, choking up of individual initiative by administrative activity, a burdening, perhaps even an overburdening, of the economic apparatus with dead costs; the impairment of a standard of living to be derived from a certain nominal income, due to rising taxes and monopoly prices; a still further expansion of the already great concerns, and death or dormancy among the small and medium-sized businesses." [2]

This frankness on the part of the former State Secretary is evidence that he is speaking of something which is the common experience and knowledge of any businessman in Germany.

That it is also the common experience of businessmen internationally, the Nazi leaders never fail to stress. They impress the German businessman with the international character of his own experiences and thus deprive him of any hope that the "good old days" will return. They increase his fatalistic point of view, directing his gaze to the rest of the world, so that he may see, once and for all, that he has no alternative, that he must accept the totalitarian State as the new form of society, as his destiny and inescapable future.

It is worth while to quote the German government's spokesman again:

"It may be that other countries use different methods, and, indeed, in some cases in the Anglo-Saxon countries a word from a leading man often suffices for direction of business, while in Germany we still need law and regulation. We call a spade a spade and openly admit that in the National-Socialist State the primacy of general policy prevails. The parliamentary states come to practically the same result, but the governments there allow themselves to be empowered to undertake measures which are no longer in accordance with the principles of individualism and liberalism but which are in accordance with the principle of planned economy. But the interventions are, at least in substance, as similar to ours as one egg is to another. Or was it no great intervention of the state in business, when first England, then the United States, then France and finally about fifty countries devalued their currencies? . . . Great Britain, in order to counteract the credit withdrawals in 1931 and, by maintaining stable wages and prices, to revive domestic business activity through exports; the United States in order to force a decrease in domestic indebtedness and by a rise in prices to let loose the forces of revival; France in order to close the gap between domestic and foreign prices. We were not the founders of trade quotas for the purpose of isolation, nor were we the inventors of clearing agreements with their destructive result on commodity trade. Furthermore, was it not management of business when England went over to a protective tariff and signed the Ottawa Agreements, and were not the international production restrictions for tin, rubber, copper and other materials, as well as the formation of an association of the English coal mines and of the Manchester cotton spinners, a regulation of markets? Prohibition of private issues on the capital market was known in England and the United States before it was known in Germany, under reference to the national obligation of business, and forced interest reductions, before we ever carried out conversions. No matter where you look you will see: State economic leadership attempting by the granting of State orders, especially by utilization of armament programs, to maintain the level of business activity, attempting to make up for the inability or lack of desire of private business to make capital investments, attempting to finance these orders by tax revenues. You will see export management, export subsidies, the hindering of economically undesirable imports, and exertion of influence on the price level in one form or another right down to, and including, our prohibition of price increases. You see, not we alone have State economic leadership and restriction of freedom in business life, even though the form, name and degree in other countries may differ from ours." [3]

The representative of the German State bureaucracy makes it appear that State interference has increased less in Germany than abroad. This obvious misrepresentation of facts is a product of his effort to make palatable the very unpopular measures taken in Germany. Many businessmen in Germany would like to flee to a free country with their capital, to some part of the world where money power is still unrestricted and has an independent existence. But any attempt to do so is very risky. The new penal code in Germany provides the death penalty for any person caught trying to take money out of the country.

What position in society does the businessman have when he lives under a totalitarian regime from which he cannot escape? Many businessmen in Germany would answer this question with an anecdote which is very popular among them. It tells of two peasants who did not understand the difference between Bolshevism and National Socialism. One of them asked the other his opinion on the matter. The answer was:

"Under Bolshevism all your cows will be taken away from you because you are a kulak. Under National Socialism you are allowed to keep the cows; but the State takes all the milk, and you have the expense and labor of feeding them."

In order that a capitalist may exercise his proper function, it is essential that he use his capital freely for his own personal advantage. But this principle is no longer valid in Germany. The State bureaucracy "directs" the use of capital "in the interests of the State." The attitude of the businessman toward his loss of freedom, and what he thinks about the State's diversion of capital to its own uses, is well illustrated by the story of the owner of a Westphalian machine-tool plant. In describing his experiences to a friend, this industrialist declared:

"I have a million marks to invest. If I could use this money as I please, I would buy gold. This I would put in a safe deposit vault where not even the Reichsbank president could touch it. The gold would earn no interest. I would lose possible profits. But I would be free of the constant fear of losing my capital. I would not have to worry about having to invest it where I can never be sure of its worth from day to day. But I cannot buy gold with my million marks. I must invest it as soon as possible, since if I leave it in my bank account too long, it may be confiscated by the tax controller, the Party may demand a large contribution, or the Party secretary may inform me that I am to be honored as the founder of a new enterprise for the unprofitable production of some ersatz product. Before I receive some such suggestion, I must make up my mind about the possibilities of investment. Two years ago I might have decided to buy a new house for my family, or to erect an apartment building. I would not have cared particularly whether there were tenants or not, inasmuch as I would at least have had some real property that could not be wiped out by inflation, and that would be at my free disposal. But today this is out of the question without a special permit from the State. The only way out seems to be to invest the money in extending my own plant."

A few weeks later the manufacturer again met his friend and reported to him:

"New decrees forbid installation of machinery made of iron and steel, whenever ersatz materials can be used. I cannot get any new machinery for the next fifteen months. However, the State has taken care of my worries. I was 'asked' to build a huge refuge where valuables could be safely stored and workers accommodated during air raids. It will cost nearly 150,000 marks. Then our manufacturers' association worked out several new machines for using ersatz materials. Replacement of my obsolete machines cost me 500,000 marks. Then the tax controller discovered I had liquid assets and found a 'mistake' in a tax return I made some years ago; I had to pay a fine of 350,000 marks. So I am relieved of the worry of how to invest my million marks."

Nevertheless the State refuses to become the owner of industrial or distribution enterprises; it prefers to leave the difficulties of production to the private entrepreneur. But markets with price movements dependent mainly on the business cycle have been supplanted by markets dependent on State policies and on the whims of the commissars who carry them out. The markets as such, however, still exist. Private enterprises do not buy or sell goods as agents of the State; they still act on private calculation. The system thus is a strange mixture of State interference and planning combined with private management—an economic system which is neither competitive capitalism, nor the planned economy of state socialism nor state capitalism. It is so bewildering in its complexity that the capitalist no longer knows whether he is a capitalist or whether he has become a mere agent of the State.

The new system has, as its representative, a powerful bureaucracy which is not particularly interested in the defense of any system—except insofar as it contributes to the bureaucracy's own absolute power. Capitalist enterprises are desirable and tolerated as long as their existence is compatible with and useful to the State bureaucracy.

This raises the question of the position in society of the State bureaucracy. Is it a dictatorship standing above and against all social classes? A comparison with the State which emerged from the Russian Revolution is relevant.

The fate of the proletarian revolution in Russia has aroused extensive discussion among socialists. Is the Soviet system a dictatorship *of* the workers or *over* the workers? This question cannot be answered categorically one way or the other. Even the early Soviets, which were democratically elected, had, on occasion, to suppress the individual rights and liberties of the workers who elected them. In emergency situations the individual worker had to be restricted for the sake of the common interest. Such a dictatorship is a dictatorship *of* as well as *over* the working class. But when the State bureaucracy degenerates and fosters certain interests of its own at the expense of the common interests of the citizens, then it becomes a dictatorship *over and against* the general class interest.

Similar questions might be raised in discussing the character of the fascist dictatorship. The fascist parties, which were originally largely financed and sponsored by influential capitalist groups, have also established dictatorships *over* and even *against* capitalist enterprise. However, it would probably be more accurate to describe the dictatorship of the fascist party as a dictatorship *for and against* capitalist enterprise.

Although defending a system of private property, the fascist State bureaucracy and all those whose existence is dependent on the absolute power of the totalitarian

State must act in defense of their own interests even if this hurts the interests of all classes in society.

Many German capitalists who demonstratively show their devotion to the Fuehrer, secretly believe that fascism or National Socialism is "almost the same" or "just the same" as Bolshevism. Under both regimes the State bureaucracy is independent of any democratic institution; it is under the sole command of an authoritarian leadership.

In both countries the economic system is difficult to define because of its complexity. This is particularly true of fascism. Here the capitalists may feel that they are mere agents of a State which is building up a new anti-capitalist society. But it is easy to prove that fascism relies on capitalist economy. Capitalist owners or managers—so-called "leaders"—still try to enrich themselves by obtaining as much profit as possible. State regulations restrict their activities and they may disagree with State policies. Yet the fact that this clash of interests between the State and the capitalist still occurs is in itself proof that private property and the search for profit have not ceased to exist under fascism. Balance-sheets may reveal that dividends have increased, yet the amounts paid in taxes considerably exceed these profits. There is much planning, leading to more State interference in private enterprise, yet there is no national plan which abolishes private enterprise as such, except in the event of a wartime economy.

The present economic system under fascism or National Socialism escapes definition in a single term, such as "capitalist" or "socialist." Two mutually contradictory systems exist side by side—the genesis of a planned economy and unplanned private enterprise.

Capitalism still exists, because private enterprise still owns as private property most of the means of production and distribution. But the State has already introduced measures typical of state socialism, such as national investment boards, state control of prices, banking, and foreign trade, general regimentation of business activities. These measures have not, however, been introduced on the basis of any new principle, but in order to maintain and increase the absolute power of the State.

The progress which state capitalism has made in fascist countries has created economic phenomena similar to those in Soviet Russia. In both cases the Five- and Four-Year Plans diverted capital funds into the army's budget and into armament industries. At the end of the first Five-Year Plan in the U.S.S.R., just as at the end of the first Four-Year Plan in Nazi Germany, the one-sided development of the armament industries led to a distressing shortage of consumption goods. For similar reasons both countries experienced a serious railway crisis; too little capital had been spent for repairs and extension.

Under both systems an inflationary increase of State credits and currency circulation took place, but the immediate effect of this process was not a general rise in prices; a number of State-regulated prices remained "stable" while other prices rose considerably and the quality of most goods declined. The peasants felt that they were being exploited and that the prices they received for agricultural products no longer made their production worthwhile. Consequently, they answered with "sabotage" of production for the market, while at the same time the State tried to compel the peasants to fulfill "their duty" and feed the towns. A new type of agrarian crisis had occurred, quite different from such crises under a competitive economy. The German peasants were not yet threatened with starvation, but they lost interest in producing for a State-regulated market.

This was also a feature of the agricultural crisis in the U.S.S.R. during the first Five-Year Plan, when the peasants received almost nothing in return for the grain they were forced to deliver to the State. In 1932-33, it was realized that some inducement must be given to the peasants. So they were allowed to sell in the free market any produce they might have left after delivering their quotas to the State. For a time two price systems existed side by side: a free market where shortage of foodstuffs led to excessively high prices, and the State shops where all workers and employees could buy their bread rations and a very few other necessities.

During this period there existed in addition "closed distributors" (shops where only those who have a special permit may buy) ranging from those for the highest functionaries where many articles could be bought at low prices, to those for the skilled workers where rations of meat and butter and a few other consumption goods were provided. In 1935 most of the "closed distributors" were abolished, bread prices were increased but bread ceased to be rationed, and all goods were sold freely to all citizens at prices lower than the previous free market prices, but much higher than the prices charged by the "closed distributors." This change meant, in effect, that bread was no longer sold at artificially low prices in the towns, and that the income of the peasantry was increased—mainly at the expense of the workers. However, the major profit from the increased price of bread was retained by the State.

This is equally true of Nazi Germany where the State is playing a similar role. The Reich Nutrition Estate—a huge bureaucratic State organization—has completely replaced private grain dealers and has established a strict control over sales of most foodstuffs. State agencies buy grain at artificially low prices while the price for flour has been increased. The higher profit of the "distributor" State is largely spent by the administration for the huge costs of its bureaucratic machine. In Germany the Government has somewhat disguised the increased profit which it takes from producers and consumers by lowering the quality of the bread supplied. In addition, the Party bureaucracy endeavors to foster an artificial antagonism between town and country by telling the workers that the peasants are responsible for the poor supplies. When workers visit the villages they are astonished to find how little the peasants are, in fact, receiving, and both feel oppressed.

In Germany the peasants have not been "collectivized" and they therefore feel the more keenly the loss of their right and freedom to sell their products as they please. But a loosening of State control and a return to private marketing of agricultural products could be inaugurated only if the Government agreed to an increase of prices for these products.

Will the Nazi government have to make a change in its price policy similar to the new agrarian policy in the U.S.S.R.? This would mean granting higher prices to the agrarian producers, thereby encouraging them to supply the market. The inauguration of such a price policy does not depend merely on the Government's will. When the second Five-Year Plan in Russia and the second Four-Year Plan in Nazi Germany were under discussion, a greater rate of increase in consumption goods was promised, but this promise was rendered largely inoperative by a further increase in armament production caused by the international armaments race. Consequently the second Five- and Four-Year Plans differed less from the first plans than originally intended. There are other features of State bureaucratic control of economic life which can be observed in both Soviet Russia and Nazi Germany.

Although there is no such clash between the State and the capitalists in the Soviet Union as in Nazi Germany, industrial managers in the Soviet Union also have experienced difficulties as a result of the tremendous growth of State bureaucracy, which compelled them to act on their own initiative, independent of, and even against, the decisions of that bureaucracy.

It seems to be a general characteristic of too extensive a State bureaucratic regulation of economic life that "middlemen" should appear who correct and change the "plan" and supplement the bureaucratic regimentation by private initiative. This also happened in Soviet Russia at the end of the first Five-Year Plan. There, only State enterprises existed; all directors of factories were mere State functionaries; bureaucratic decisions accorded with the "plan" but often not with real life.[4]

Further confusion was introduced by so-called "socialist competition," which led to one factory competing against another for raw materials in the effort to "overfulfill" its quota.

The economic system of this period in Soviet Russia represented a clash between theory and practice in all spheres. For example, according to the general plan, a factory was to be supplied with a certain quantity of raw materials and credits and was expected to fulfill a set production schedule. On paper, there was an effective control of the financial affairs of a State trust or factory, and each allotment of materials was calculated in advance at prices fixed by the State. Costs of production likewise had been calculated in advance. A credit plan had been fixed based on cost of raw materials, labor, new machinery, etc. The task of the director was to meet his production quota, or even to exceed it. But in practice the director had to try to fulfill this plan against odds which had been neither foreseen nor calculated. Most factories were unable to obtain on time the raw materials they were supposed to receive, and the quantities and qualities differed from the original specifications. Complaints were dealt with bureaucratically. A stoppage of production in one industrial plant led to the interruption of production in other dependent plants.

The director of a plant was often in an extremely difficult position. If he kept to the official rules and made his complaints in the prescribed way, the chances were that he would fail to get the raw materials he needed. He might also be short of food for the workers. Responsible for failure to fulfill the plan and unable to resign, he was compelled to develop sufficient "private initiative" to overcome the difficulties created by bureaucratic decisions and ineptitudes. It would seem that in such a state of regulated economy "private initiative" on the part of industrial leaders would cease, inasmuch as everything was planned and regulated by the State. In reality, however, the whole economic life would have come to a standstill had not the directors of industrial plants and trusts developed initiative in violation and circumvention of bureaucratic decisions and official rules. To carry on their business it was absolutely vital that they obtain materials with or without plan or provisions. A typical experience was reported to the author by a Communist who worked as the technical director of a new industrial combine in Caucasia. He was responsible for completing the construction of a new factory before the beginning of winter. But his building materials did not arrive in time despite dozens of complaints. Work had to stop. Workers received wages but did no work. The whole budget fixed by the Planning Commission was overthrown by the tremendous rise of unproductive costs. And worse than that, if the new plant could not be finished before winter set in, the half-finished work would be destroyed by the weather.

Finally he started out on his own to discover whether building materials might be found in his district. In a neighboring town he located building materials of the kind he needed. They had been stored many months for construction work planned for the coming year. He demanded that they be given to him in exchange for the materials he would receive too late for his needs. But it was impossible to obtain the necessary official permits for such an exchange. His work was delayed more and more. Finally he acted on his own initiative, but in agreement with the local Party secretary. The trucks which were at his disposal transported the building materials from the neighboring town to his work location without any official permit. The authorities of the other town tried to mobilize the G.P.U. against him. The case was serious—according to official rules. But the local G.P.U. chief, an experienced Communist, approved the director's action.

In many other cases factory managers, who needed materials they could not obtain but had to have for their work, tried to save the situation by private barter. The director of a plant which produced shoes would arrange with the director of another plant which produced tools for an exchange of shoes for tools. This was done as a private arrangement without an authoritative permit and in violation of the plans and official rules. But it often had the approval of the local Party authorities and even of the local G.P.U., because sticking to the letter of the laws or decrees would have caused a disastrous decline in production and waste of materials. The danger, however, was that the G.P.U. might later use this against the manager and have him "purged."

Private barter deals and illegal purchases of raw materials reached such a point by the end of the first Five-Year Plan that regular "middlemen" began to operate. They had an expert knowledge of what different factories produced and what they needed, so that they could arrange or facilitate barter deals. The G.P.U. must have known of the existence of such "middlemen" but tolerated them because they helped to overcome anarchy of production within the planned economy. The role of these "middlemen" is similar to the role of "contact men" under fascism. The fascist "contact man" works for private firms and for bribes. The "middlemen" in Soviet Russia arranged exchanges of industrial products from one State plant to another, receiving an illegal commission for this service. Nevertheless, by violating the Plan they facilitated its fulfillment.

The industrial manager in fascist Germany or Italy is not merely interested in production as an end in itself. He is also interested in profits. His income (or dividends to the shareholders) is not fixed by the State, although the size of it depends largely on his relationship with the State bureaucracy. As a manager he is under pressure from two sides—from the State and from the private owners or shareholders. They may both be in harmony, but more often they disagree and a compromise is arranged, leading to the many economic absurdities described in previous chapters.

The fascist State bureaucracy appears as a supercapitalist power, which takes a heavy toll from all private enterprises, treating them as subsidiaries of one big State trust, from which the supreme leadership requisitions the greater part of the aggregate profit. But the leaders of the subsidiaries, the private capitalists, are bound to the trust—or the system—unless they wish to lose what the State has left them.

The U.S.S.R. does not have a capitalist class tied to the regime by privileges which are of a nature different from those a State bureaucrat can obtain from society. Yet a very interesting social phenomenon can be observed both in the U.S.S.R. and in Nazi Germany—an authoritarian Party dictatorship which is strong because it can suppress antagonistic forces from the right as well as from the left.

Many capitalists may fear and despise the State bureaucrats, yet they are afraid of losing everything with the downfall of the regime. The fascist regime rests on two pillars: the absolute power of the State and the power of private property holders whose property rights are protected by and are dependent on the State.

This is not the first time in history that an absolute dictatorship has become independent of all social classes and yet has retained the support of those who fear the worst from a change in the regime. Napoleon was able to gain and hold the support of the peasantry because they were afraid of losing their new property rights under whatever regime might follow. If the Vendée had won, the feudal landlords might have been restored to power and the peasants might have been forced to return the land they had taken. On the other hand, the left-wing Jacobins had too little respect for private property rights to gain the support of the peasants. Consequently Napoleon appeared to the peasants as the best protector of their new property rights. But his imperialist policy was so expensive for the people in France and cost so many lives that in the end even the peasants became dissatisfied.

Because the Nazis are under some compulsion to make palatable the decrees which make them feared and despised, they have attempted to connect totalitarian philosophy with the respectable and historic policy of mercantilism. Nazi economists often picture fascism as the beginning of a new age of mercantilism—neo-mercantilism—under the inspiring guidance of the fascist totalitarian State.

The comparison of the economic policies of a totalitarian regime with the mercantilist state is not entirely out of place. There are, indeed, some striking parallels: The State exercises the function of deciding which industries should be developed and which should be suppressed; it regiments foreign trade and all economic life in order to become self-sufficient and militarily strong. Military strength is identified with economic self-sufficiency. The philosophy of mercantilism agrees in many respects with the philosophy of the totalitarian regime—"The State is everything—the individual nothing." (Mussolini.) Yet in spite of many mercantilist trends there is no real return to the mercantilism of the seventeenth century.

Mercantilism was the prevailing policy at a time when bourgeois society was just emerging from feudalism; when commodity production was superseding individual production by the feudal family or village unit.

The world situation is quite different today. This discussion would take us too far afield, but there is one interesting historical parallel worth noting. Just as the Prussian king in the eighteenth century, in an effort to strengthen the State which still defended the privileges of the formerly independent feudal class, found it necessary to introduce and encourage new methods of production appropriate to the coming social order, so the Nazi leaders must use methods of social planning which are appropriate to socialism, in order to buttress the shaky State power which is dedicated to the preservation of a private property economy.

The fascist totalitarian State of today is essentially a capitalist society with private enterprise and private property as the foundation of its economy. Yet it already applies methods and policies typical of another society. In an effort to defend the old, decaying system, it introduces measures which may be part of a future system, but which do not create a new society. At the same time the fascist State weakens and undermines the forces on which the old capitalist system relied. It has expropriated and ruined the greater part of the middle class—

to which, incidentally, most of the Jews in Germany belonged.

The ruin of the middle class has strengthened the position of a few great concerns and trusts; the standard of living of large sections of the middle classes has declined to such an extent that their income is often below that of the working class. Middle-class businessmen have witnessed a rise of the *nouveaux riches,* whose wealth has not been accumulated as a result of efficient business methods or general prosperity but through the application of the absolute power of the State bureaucracy. Respect for private property has vanished, because property morale has been destroyed. The new justification for the ownership of private property is absolute power.

Regimented and led by a power over which he has no control, the businessman under a totalitarian regime is compelled to carry on. He has lost faith in the old competitive system, although he cannot help thinking with fatalistic nostalgia of the "good old days." He finds it impossible to believe that they will ever return, yet he thinks of them wistfully in a vain attempt to forget his anxieties for the future. For the economic policy pursued by the fascist dictators deepens social antagonisms, weakens the capitalist system and increases the danger of a proletarian revolution with which the dictators blackmail other imperialist powers. The fascist dictators endeavor to strengthen their authoritarian position by making themselves indispensable to those who fear the loss of their privileges and property rights. The narrower the stratum of those whose business interests are still protected by the regime, the more these businessmen become dependent on the absolute power of the State as represented by the fascist bureaucracy. The fascist dictatorship grows stronger—internally and externally—the more it increases the dangers against which it pretends to protect the businessman.

In the name of militarism business is treated with contempt, but even purely military interests suffer, because first and foremost the system serves the absolute power of an authoritarian bureaucracy. New privileged business interests and supermilitarization have a disastrous effect on the system of private business as such because they increase the absolute power of the state bureaucracy rather than make the whole nation strong. A member of the German General Staff expressed the strongest possible criticism of fascist militarization as follows:

"If indirect costs are increased more and more by economic preparations for war, and if a war economy is carried on in peacetime, domestic investments will depreciate and in the end the nation will not succeed in its national defense plan. The effects and difficulties of war will be better endured by the people if they are well fed and dressed and trained, if the reserves are great and industry well equipped." [5]

General Thomas, Chief of the Economic Council of the War Department, also expressed his anxiety over the probable final result of fascist militarization:

"Experience has shown us the close relationship between military and economic leadership in war. Men like Alexander the Great and Hannibal, in spite of their great strategic talents, had to give way on account of economic facts. . . . And whether we quote Frederick the Great's attempts to strengthen Prussia economically for war or the collapse of Napoleon's world power on account of its inadequate economic foundation, we always find proof of the close interdependence of economic and military leadership in history. In particular, we see the consequences if military leaders err in estimating the economic forces of their own country or of the enemy's." [6]

But the conservative leaders who appraise the strength and inner force of a system in the traditional way do not recognize the dynamic strength of a totalitarian dictatorship. They do not recognize that explosive forces have been created which may be used as weapons against hostile powers.

The position of the fascist dictators might be compared to that of Schweik, the "good soldier" in a tale by Hajek, the Czech writer.

Looking for a place where he could defy his superiors, Schweik entered a gunpowder magazine. Seating himself on a keg of gunpowder, he pulled out his pipe and contentedly began to smoke. But he did not remain undisturbed for long. The sergeant appeared. Excitedly he began to berate Schweik and threaten to punish him, but the sight of a few sparks from Schweik's pipe halted his tirade. Schweik smiled innocently at the sergeant and puffed again on the pipe. The sergeant trembled and changed his tone. In the friendliest manner he tried to hint that Schweik would really feel much better in the fresh air. Wouldn't Schweik take a walk with him? But Schweik declared that he was quite contented to sit on the keg of gunpowder smoking his pipe. Schweik could continue to defy his sergeant not because he was inherently strong, but because of his position on the keg of gunpowder. The sergeant represented a gigantic military machine which Schweik could never have hoped to overpower. But Schweik could destroy the whole barracks, the sergeant and all superior officers with a single spark from hi‿ pipe.

The fascist dictator is in the same position as Schweik. The preponderant weight of force, both internally and externally, is against him, but he, like Schweik, with lighted pipe in hand, is seated on a keg of gunpowder. The conservative forces which helped the fascist dictator to power thought they would be able to control him, but now they do not dare to make use of their power against him. They know that nothing of the old system would remain if the structure he has built were to fall.

# *REFERENCE NOTES*

## *Chapter II*

[1] *Jahrbuch des Oeffentlichen Rechtes der Gegenwart,* ed. by Otto Koellreuther (1935), p. 267.

[2] *Zeitschrift der Akademie fuer Deutsches Recht,* July 1, 1938, p. 513.

[3] Fritz Nonnenbruch, *Die Dynamische Wirtschaft* (Munich, Centralverlag der N.S.D.A.P., 1936), p. 114.

[4] *Ibid.,* p. 119.

[5] Schacht's speech at the School for Reichsbank Officials, May, 1936.

[6] May 21, 1936.

[7] *Frankfurter Zeitung,* January 28, 1937.

[8] *Ibid.,* January 28, 1937.

[9] Bernard Koehler, Chief of the Party Department of Economic Policy, in his speech on "Economic Leadership and Economic Government," 1934.

## *Chapter III*

[1] Decision of the Supreme District Court (*Oberlandesgericht*) in Hamburg, June 17, 1936, published in *Kartellrundschau,* January, 1938, p. 29.

## *Chapter IV*

[1] *Frankfurter Zeitung,* April 2, 1939.

[2] *Ibid.,* April 12, 1939.

[3] *Ibid.,* April 9, 1939.

[4] Published as a pamphlet, *Export steigerung durch Einschaltung in die Industrialisierung der Welt* (Kiel, 1938).

## *Chapter V*

[1] *Koelnische Zeitung,* December 22, 1938.

[2] The contractor has to use his share of iron and steel for building work already contracted for.

## *Chapter VI*

[1] *Deutsche Handelsrundschau,* organ of the Edeka (Association of Co-operatives), August 2, 1939.

[2] *Ibid.*

[3] U. S. Department of Commerce, *Economic Review of Foreign Countries,* 1937, p. 20 ff.

[4] Theo Loehr, in *Die Deutsche Polizei,* January 10, 1939.

[5] *Der Deutsche Volkswirt,* September 2, 1938, pp. 2375-2376.

[6] Reichs-Kredit-Gesellschaft, *Germany's Economic Situation at the Turn of 1938-1939,* pp. 50-51.

[7] *Deutsche Arbeitskorrespondenz,* October, 1936.

## *Chapter VII*

[1] *Der Vierjahresplan,* July, 1938, p. 407.

[2] *Deutsche Handelsrundschau,* July 15, 1938.

[3] *Die Bank,* January 4, 1939, p. 2.

## *Chapter VIII*

[1] Walter E. Kinkel, *Unternehmer und Betriebsfuehrer in der gewerblichen Wirtschaft* (Munich and Berlin, 1938), p. 58.

[2] *Ibid.,* p. 72.

[3] *Deutsche Wirtschaftszeitung,* January 19, 1939.

[4] Fritz Nonnenbruch, *Die Dynamische Wirtschaft,* p. 144.

## *Chapter IX*

[1] Reichs-Kredit Gesellschaft, *Germany's Economic Situation at the Turn of 1938-1939,* pp. 26-27.

[2] *Ibid.,* p. 13.

[3] Translated from the German text of the annual report of the Friedrich Krupp A.G. for its fiscal year 1937-1938, dated March, 1939.

[4] *Die Deutsche Volkswirtschaft,* September 1, 1938.

[5] The Ford Motor Company (General Sales Department) wrote to the author on September 8, 1938:

"Some of the questions you ask in your letter . . . call for answers which obviously it is impossible to give since they would be predicated on certain economic conditions of which there is no present assurance. Replies to others would be based largely upon personal opinions, which the writer is not in a position to express. . . . Upon the return of Mr. W. J. Cameron your letter will be referred to him for any further comments he may have to offer."

No further comments were received.

[6] *Frankfurter Zeitung,* November 13, 1938.

[7] *Nachrichtenblatt der Reichsbahn,* September 3, 1938.

[8] *Der Deutsche Volkswirt,* November 18, 1939, pp. 284-285.

[9] German Institute for Business Research, *Weekly Report,* May 23, 1939, p. 92.

[10] *Ibid.,* June 19, 1939, pp. 65-66.

## *Chapter X*

[1] *The Banker* (London), February, 1937, pp. 110-111.

[2] Rudolf Brinkmann, *"Rechtliche Grundlagen der Kapitallenung,"* in *Zeitschrift der Akademie fuer Deutsches Recht,* January 1, 1939, p. 4.

[3] Former Secretary of State, Dr. Karl Schwarzkopf, Managing Director of the Landeskreditbank, Kassel, in a speech at a meeting of the Reichsgruppe Banken (Reich Banking Group), Hamburg, June 29, 1936. Published as a pamphlet

by the financial weekly, *Die Bank,* under the title *Quellen und Lage des Kapitalmarktes* (Berlin, 1936), pp. 13-14.

[4] The corresponding figure for the U. S. A. is about 50 per cent, according to a private estimate.

[5] From a survey made by *Das Bankarchiv,* organ of the German Bankers' Association, September 1, 1938, p. 38.

[6] *Die Bank,* November 2, 1938, p. 47.

[7] The author is obligated not to reveal the source of information.

[8] German Institute for Business Research, Berlin, *Weekly Report,* March 9, 1938, Supplement.

[9] *Neue Zuericher Zeitung,* November 8, 1938.

[10] Figures about "money in circulation" compiled and published by the German Institute for Business Research. See statistical surveys in *Weekly Report.*

[11] "Germany, The Results of Four Years National Socialism," *The Banker* (London), February, 1937, pp. 115, 118.

## *Chapter XI*

[1] An exception has been made for foreign holders of blocked marks if the deposits are the proceeds from the sale of stocks and are immediately spent for the purchase of other stocks.

[2] Rudolf Brinkmann, *"Rechtliche Grundlagen der Kapitallenkung," Zeitschrift der Akademie fuer Deutsches Recht,* January 1, 1939, p. 4.

[3] "There are three classes of members, the sworn brokers, the free brokers, and other members. . . .

"The majority of the Stock Exchange members are in the third class. They are not subject to particular restrictions and might more properly be called 'visitors.' They are mainly bankers or representatives of banks. Many of them rarely appear at the Exchange but have their orders executed by the brokers."

*The Security Markets, Findings and Recommendations of a Special Staff of the Twentieth Century Fund,* edited by Alfred L. Bernheim (New York, 1935), pp. 543, 544.

[4] *Ministerialblatt,* September, 1938, quoted in *Die Bank,* September 7, 1938, p. 1169.

[5] *Die Bank,* September 7, 1938, p. 1169.

[6] *Frankfurter Zeitung,* December 25, 1937.

[7] United States Department of Commerce, *Economic Review of Foreign Commerce of the United States,* 1937, p. 20.

[8] *Big Business, Its Growth and Its Place,* Twentieth Century Fund (New York, 1937), p. 5.

[9] According to *Wirtschaft und Statistik,* published by Statistisches Reichsamt, Berlin.

[10] Quoted from a forthcoming article by Dr. F. T. Schmidt, "A Note on the Concentration of Joint-Stock Companies in Italy," to appear in the *American Economic Review,* 1939. The figures refer to "non-financial corporations." Dr. Schmidt made the following comment: "Financial companies—banks, insurance firms, etc.—have been excluded from the present estimate so as to minimize duplication in respect to assets."

[11] *Der Zeitspiegel,* Berlin, July, 1937.

[12] *Zeitschrift fuer Aktiengesellschaften und Gesellschaften mit beschraenkter Haftung,* Leipzig, February-March, 1938, p. 44.

[13] See the revealing study by Dr. Guenter Keiser, Berlin, *"Der Juengste Konzentrationsprocess"* ("The Newest Process of Concentration"), in *Die Wirtschaftskurve,* Frankfurt, No. II, 1939, pp. 136 ff.

## *Chapter XII*

[1] Dr. C. M. A. Stine, "Chemistry and You," *The Du Pont Magazine,* June, 1937, p. 22.

[2] According to figures of the Statistische Reichsamt.

[3] Germany's Statistisches Reichsamt, *Statistisches Jahrbuch fuer das Deutsche Reich,* various volumes.

[4] "The term rayon properly applies to all types of synthetic fibers whose basic raw material is cellulose. . . . At present spruce, Western hemlock, and cotton linters are the most economical sources of cellulose suitable for making rayon, though it is possible to obtain chemically satisfactory cellulose from many other different plants and trees."

*Report on Development and Use of Rayon and Other Synthetic Fibers,* prepared by the committee appointed by the United States Secretary of Agriculture, October, 1938, p. 2.

[5] *Ibid.*

[6] German Institute for Business Research, *Weekly Report,* November 18, 1938, p. 94.

[7] *Report on Development and Use of Rayon and Other Synthetic Fibers,* prepared by the committee appointed by the U. S. Secretary of Agriculture, October, 1938, p. 7.

[8] German Institute for Business Research, *Weekly Report,* November 18, 1938, pp. 95-96.

[9] Saechsische Zellwolle A.G., Plauen; Sueddeutsche Zellwolle A.G., Kulmbach; Schlesische Zellwolle A.G., Hirschberg; Thueringische Zellwolle A.G., Schwarza.

[10] See Fr. Sarow, *"Zellwolle,"* in *Die Wirtschaftskurve,* Frankfurt, a. M., No. II, 1938, pp. 263 ff.

[11] Estimate. See *Weekly Report* of the German Institute for Business Research, June 2, 1939, p. 59.

[12] Computed from figures of consumption in *Die Wirtschaftskurve,* 1938, No. 3, p. 265.

[13] July 1, 1938.

[14] *Deutsches Amt fuer Roh- und Werkstoffe.*

[15] German Institute for Business Research, *Weekly Report,* November 18, 1938, p. 94.

[16] Institut fuer Konjunkturforschung, *Halbjahresbericht,* 1938-1939.

[17] *Ibid.,* 1937, No. 1, p. 34.

[18] Dr. Rudolf Regul in the *Vierteljahreshefte zur Wirtschaftsforschung,* 1938-1939, No. I, p. 83.

[19] H. Steinberger, in *Deutsche Wehr,* January, 1936, p. 3, and Fr. F. Friedensberg in *Der Deutsche Volkswirt,* April 16, 1937, p. 1405, and *Der Deutsche Volkswirt,* April 23, 1937, p. 1453.

[20] *Die Braune Wirtschaftspost,* August 1, 1938.

[21] The first Buna factory in Schopkau, near Leipzig, started operating in 1937. A second factory is to be finished in 1939 or 1940. The output in 1937 was 20,000-25,000 tons, or about 25 per cent of crude rubber imports.

[22] Dr. R. Eicke (director of the Reichsbank), *Warum Aussenhandel* (4th edition, Berlin, 1938), p. 64.

[23] *Die Braune Wirtschaftspost,* September 9, 1937.

[24] *New York Herald Tribune,* July 4, 1939.

## *Chapter XIII*

[1] At the present time barter transactions and trading with Aski marks are forbidden except where individual transactions exceed 50,000 marks. In addition to this, a circular issued by the Reich Foreign Exchange Board on February 23, 1937, restricted the list of countries with which even these transactions were permitted; barter deals could henceforth be effected only with South and Central America, Australia, and New Zealand. The prevailing tendency is to liquidate all *private* barter transactions.

[2] The United States Government introduced "Countervailing Duties on Imports from Germany" in March, 1939.

[3] *The Economist* (London), November 5, 1938, pp. 262-263.

[4] *Neue Zuericher Zeitung,* December 1, 1938.

[5] Quoted in a letter of the U. S. Attorney General Frank Murphy to the U. S. Secretary of the Treasury, of March 18, 1939.

[6] Figures quoted in a lecture given by Dr. Wilhelm Tannenberg, German Embassy Council, at the Graduate School of the Fordham University on April 23, 1939. See *German-American Commerce Bulletin,* published by the Board of Trade for German-American Commerce, New York, May 1939, p. 3.

[7] Quoted from an address delivered at the Latin American Conference, March 11, 1939.

[8] *Der Deutsche Volkswirt,* July 1, 1938, p. 1940.

[9] Reichs-Kredit-Gesellschaft (Berlin), *Germany's Economic Situation at the Turn of 1938-1939,* p. 117.

[10] *Zeitschrift der Akademie fuer Deutsche Recht,* January 1, 1939, p. 21.

[11] *Deutsche Wirtschaftszeitung,* 1937, No. 5, p. 152.

[12] British holders of German bonds, for instance, received 4 per cent funding bonds; no arrangements were made, however, for payment of dividends and rents. Dutch holders of German bonds get 3½ per cent interest in guilders, four-fifths of house and other rents; dividends up to .5 per cent are paid in foreign exchange, the balance being paid in "Holland marks" or 4 per cent funding bonds. Swiss holders of German bonds were conceded 4½ per cent interest in Swiss francs and the balance in 4 per cent funding bonds; rents, dividends, etc., up to 4½ per cent in Swiss francs, the balance in 4 per cent funding bonds.

[13] M. Sering, *Deutsche Agrarpolitik* (Leipzig, 1934), p. 651.

[14] Institut fuer Konjunkturforschung, *Vierteljahreshefte zur Wirtschaftsforschung,* 1938-1939, No. 3, p. 305.

[15] Figures from *Der Vierjahresplan.*

[16] Institut fuer Konjunkturforschung, *Vierteljahreshefte zur Witschaftsforschung,* 1938-1939, No. III, p. 31.

[17] The following figures indicate structural changes of the world market since the victory of fascism in Germany.

*Germany's Foreign Trade with Different Groups of Countries*
(In percentage of total exports (E) and imports (I)

| | *Payment Agreement Countries* | | | | | | *Clearing Agreement Countries* | |
|---|---|---|---|---|---|---|---|---|
| | *With Free Exchange Surplus for Reichsbank* | | *Import: Export = 1 : 1* | | *Special Agreement* | | *With Countries Having No Exchange Control* | |
| | *I.* | *E.* | *I.* | *E.* | *I.* | *E.* | *I.* | *E.* |
| 1932 | .. | .. | .. | .. | .. | .. | 34.4 | 50.0 |
| 1938 | 13.3 | 15.6 | 1.7 | 1.3 | 3.6 | 2.0 | 21.1 | 26.9 |

| | *Clearing Agreements with Countries Having Exchange Control* | | *Aski Mark Countries* | | | | | |
|---|---|---|---|---|---|---|---|---|
| | | | *With Countries Having Exchange Control* | | *With Other Countries* | | *Cash Countries (No Special Agreement)* | |
| | *I.* | *E.* | *I.* | *E.* | *I.* | *E.* | *I.* | *E.* |
| 1932 | 15.9 | 20.0 | .. | .. | .. | .. | .. | .. |
| 1938 | 37.9 | 38.2 | .8 | .7 | 5.6 | 5.5 | 16.0 | 9.8 |

German Institute for Business Research, *Weekly Report,* May 23, 1939, p. 4.

[18] State Secretary Dr. Reinhard in a special issue of the magazine *Weltwirtschaft,* 1938.

[19] Reichs-Kredit-Gesellschaft, *Germany's Economic Situation at the Turn of 1938-1939,* p. 109.

## *Chapter XIV*

[1] Czech gold deposits kept in the name of the Bank of International Settlements—about $30,000,000 worth—were handed over to the Reichsbank by the Bank of England.

[2] Private Czech deposits in London amounted to about $12,000,000 and were retained according to a decision of the British Parliament.

[3] *The New York Times,* June 4, 1939.

[4] *Ibid.,* June 3, 1939.

[5] Hermann Wilhelm Gustloff is the name of a Nazi agent who was shot in Switzerland by a Yugoslav student.

[6] *Die Wirtschaftskurve,* Frankfurt, a. M., No. II, 1939, p. 191.

[7] Freda Utley, *Japan's Feet of Clay,* New York, 1937.

[8] German Institute for Business Research, *Weekly Report,* May 4, 1938, p. 34.

[9] *Ibid.,* p. 35.

[10] *Ibid.,* October 7, 1938, p. 1342.

[11] Edgar P. Young, *Czecho-Slovakia* (London, 1938), pp. 78-80.

[12] *Der Wirtschaftsdienst,* January 13, 1939, p. 46.

[13] *Der Wirtschaftsdienst,* February 10, 1939, p. 180.

[14] Spring, 1939.

## *Chapter XV*

[1] Quoted by Major K. Hess in his book *Miliz* (Hamburg, 1933), p. 34.

[2] Mussolini, *Fascism, Doctrine and Institutions* (Rome, 1935), p. 19.

[3] From a speech of Bolke to Von Schlieffen, on the latter's retirement from the German Army Staff in 1905, in W. Foerster, *Aus der Gedankenwelt des Deutschen Generalstabes* (Berlin, 1931), p. 15.

[4] Captain P. Ruprecht (retired), "*Totaler Krieg, Strategie und Wehrpolitik,*" in *Militaerwissenschaftliche Rundschau* (1937), p. 458.

[5] *Ibid.*

[6] *Der Deutsche Volkswirt,* 1938.

[7] Dr. Gumpert, "*Weltkrieg und Weltwirtschaft,*" in *Das Militaerwochenblatt,* December 27, 1937.

[8] A. Parker, "The Economic Outlook of Germany," *Lloyds Bank Monthly Review,* July, 1937, p. 392.

[9] *Frankfurter Zeitung,* August, 1916, reprinted in the issue of August 13, 1936.

[10] Bernhard Koehler, chief of the Commission for Eco-

nomic Policies of the N.S.D.A.P., in a speech at the Party Congress in Nuernberg, 1936.

[11] *Frankfurter Zeitung*, July 11, 1937.

[12] Col. Otto Thomas at a meeting of the Association for World Economy, Kiel, February, 1937.

[13] *Der Deutsche Volkswirt*, April 9, 1936.

## *Chapter XVI*

[1] German Institute for Business Research, *Weekly Report*, November 2, 1938, p. 7.

[2] German Institute for Business Research, *Weekly Report*, November 2, 1938, p. 4.

[3] *Ibid.*, p. 6.

[4] *Ibid.*, p. 5.

## *Chapter XVII*

[1] This tax was abolished in May, 1939.

[2] Dr. Rudolf Brinkmann, Secretary of State, in an address delivered to the National Congress of the group, "*Banken und Versicherungen*," in Düsseldorf on Ocober 21, 1938. See *Weekly Report* of the German Institute for Business Research, November 2, 1938, p. 7.

[3] German Institute for Business Research, *Weekly Report*, November 2, 1938, pp. 8-9.

[4] The author was able to study factory conditions and industrial management during several trips to different parts of the U.S.S.R., where he had the opportunity of interviewing government officials, technical experts, and workers.

[5] Colonel Warlimont (member of the German General Staff), "*Volk und Wehrwirtschaft*," in *Volk und Wehrkraft: Jahrbuch der Deutschen Gesellschaft fuer Wehrpolitik und Wehrwissenschaft* (1937), pp. 37-38.

[6] Colonel Otto Thomas, "*Kriegfuehrung und Wehrwirtschaft in Der Geschichte*" in *Wehrwirtschaft*, No. 3, 1937.

Colonel Thomas was later promoted to the rank of general.

# GLOSSARY

*Amt fuer Deutsche Roh- und Werkstoffe*—Office for German Raw and Work Materials; one of the bureaus of the Ministry of Economics, in control of production and distribution of raw materials produced in Germany.

*Arbeitsfront*—Labor Front; State-administered organization of employers and employees.

*Aski Mark*—Aski is an abbreviation for "Auslaender-Sonderkonto fuer Inlands-Zahlungen," meaning "Foreigners Special Account for Internal Payments." The term is used to designate marks received from exports to Germany which the foreign seller must spend in Germany, at a specified rate of exchange, in payment for purchases made there.

*Aufsichtsrat*—Supervisory Board; controlling body of a corporation, elected by the stockholders' meeting. It has no counterpart in American or British corporations, but its function is similar to that of the Board of Directors.

*Betriebsfuehrer*—Factory Leader or manager, who is responsible to the State for labor relations and production and whose orders must be followed by the employees of the firm (see "Gefolgschaft").

*Erbhofbauer*—Owner of a hereditary farm that cannot be mortgaged and will always be inherited by the oldest son, excluding all other children.

*Dego-Mark*—Dego marks are issued by the German Gold Discount Bank and offered to foreign travelers to Germany at a discount (about 50 per cent). According to the Standstill Agreement, foreign currency derived from the sale of Dego mark is shared by the Gold Discount Bank and foreign creditors.

*Deutsche Golddiscont-Bank*—German Gold-Discount Bank, a subsidiary banking institute of the Reichsbank, used for financial transactions which the Reichsbank cannot or does not want to execute.

*Gefolgschaft*—"Followers," employees who under Nazi rule have to "follow" orders of the boss (see Betriebsfuehrer).

*Gesellschaftsgesetz*—Corporation Law, to ensure the "independent" authority and initiative on the part of the managing directors in corporations.

*Gestapo*—Abbreviation for *Geheime Staats-Polizei,* Secret State Police.

*Gruppe*—Group, new Nazi term for a trade which is organized by the Government. This term largely corresponds to the Fascist term "Corporation" in Italy.

*Kommissar*—Commissar, a term applied by the Nazi Government to State-appointed "Leaders" in industry and trade.

*Kommission fuer Wirtschaftspolitik*—Commission for Economic Policy, economic advisory and research department of the N.S.D.A.P.

*Kraft Durch Freude*—"Strength Through Joy," subsidiary of the Labor Front, organizing recreation for employees, especially cheap trips during vacation.

*Kriegswirtschaftsrat*—War Economic Council, subdivision of the General Staff, supervising and directing national preparations for a wartime economy; supreme authority in economic affairs during wartime.

*Marktvereinigung*—Marketing Board, administration in control of production, sales and prices of various articles.

*Neuer Plan*—New Plan, Schacht's decree of September 21, 1934 (put in force on September 24, 1934), establishing a system of control boards for imports of all categories of goods.

*Preisstop-Verordnung*—Price Stop Decree of November 26, 1936, prohibiting any price increase of commodities and services above the level of October 18, 1936.

*Protektorat*—Protectorate, a foreign country or colony under control of an imperialist "mother country." "Protectorates" of the Reich: Bohemia and Moravia.

*Reichsautobahn*—Reich Auto Highway, 5,000 kilometers of strategically important automobile roads (only in part completed), financed by the Government.

*Reichsdevisenamt*—Reich Foreign Exchange Board, issuing certificates to business firms and individuals entitling them to purchase a certain amount of foreign exchange or to fulfill a financial obligation abroad.

*Reichsgetreideamt*—Reich Grain Board, which alone is entitled to import grain and which is in control of grain prices in Germany.

*Reichsnaehrstand*—Reich Nutrition Estate, State organization of all agrarian producers, manufacturers of, and traders in, agrarian foodstuffs, in control of production and prices of most foodstuffs.

*Reichsstand des Deutschen Handwerks*—Reich Estate of German Handicrafts, State administered organization of all artisan groups, with a State appointed leadership. The independent artisan guilds were dissolved in 1934.

*Reichsstatthalter*—Special Appointee of the Reich Government, functioning instead of the constitutional president of a state or of a Protectorate.

*Reichswirtschaftskammer*—Reich Economic Chamber, central organization of German industry, commerce, handicraft, banking and insurance firms, under Government control according to the law of February 27, 1934, and the decree of July 7, 1936.

*Selbsthilfe-Aktion Deutscher Industrie*—Self-Help Action of German Industry, fund raised by a special tax on all German manufacturers, spent for subsidizing exports. This fund is also subsidized by the Government.

*Sperr-Mark*—"Blocked mark," a mark "blocked" in Germany because it may be spent only for certain specific payments inside Germany.

*Stand*—Estate, a social class or caste, meaning, under the Nazis, any professional organization.

*Stillhalte-Abkommen*—Standstill Agreement between the Reichsbank and representatives of foreign creditors about repayment of German short-term credits or recommercialization of foreign credits.

*Treuhaender der Arbeit*—Labor Trustees, Government appointed, for the supervision of relations between labor and industry in specific districts, authorized to regulate labor conditions.

*Ueberwachungsausschuss*—Supervisory Board, executive of a State Administration for the control and distribution of scarce raw materials.

*Verrechnungsmark*—Clearance mark, derived from clearance agreements between the German and foreign governments. Exports to Germany from a country which has a clearance agreement create clearance mark deposits which are used by the corresponding Government for payments of imports from Germany at a fixed rate of exchange.

*Vertrauensrat*—Council of Trusted Men, employees appointed by the manager (factory leader) in agreement with the Nazi Party Cell. The official function of the Council is to assist the factory leader in the creation of a "Work Community" (Labor Code of January 20, 1934).

*Vierjahresplan*—Four-Year Plan, at first announced at the Congress of the N.S.D.A.P. in September, 1936, is to make Germany independent of imported raw materials within a period of four years. A plan of new investments and protective measures for new industries worked out by a special commission at the Ministry of Economics, under the leadership of Goering (Special Appointee for the Execution of the Four-Year Plan).

*Wehrwirtschaft*—Defense Economy, an economy preparing for war.

*Wehrwirtschaftsfuehrer*—Leader of Defense Economy, Army

officer especially trained in industrial management under a wartime economy, supervising industries, concerns and trusts of special importance for armaments.

*Werkschar*—Work Guard, organization of especially "reliable" workers militarily trained and willing to safeguard the works in emergency situations during strikes and civil war. The Work Guard has lost in importance because of the scarcity of "reliable" workers.

*Winterhilfe*—Winter Help, State organization for the support of those who are "in need," financed by "voluntary contributions" (often compulsory) of employers and employees.

*Wirtschaftskammer*—Chamber of Business, regional compulsory organization of all firms and businessmen—previously Chamber of Industry and Commerce.

# INDEX